Journeys on a Football Carpet

An inside look at Qatar's football story
and its transformation
into the 2022 FIFA World Cup™ host

MATTHIAS KRUG

Hamad Bin Khalifa University Press
P O Box 5825
Doha, Qatar

www.hbkupress.com

Text Copyright © Matthias Krug, 2019
All rights reserved.

No part of this publication may be reproduced or transmitted in any form or by any means, electronic or mechanical, including photocopying, recording, or any information storage or retrieval system, without prior permission in writing from the publishers.

No responsibility for loss caused to any individual or organization acting on or refraining from action as a result of the material in this publication can be accepted by HBKU Press or the author.

ISBN: 9789927137716

Printed in Doha-Qatar

Qatar National Library Cataloging-in-Publication (CIP)

Krug, Matthias, author.

Journeys on a Football Carpet: An inside look at Qatar's football story and its transformation into the 2022 FIFA World Cup host / Matthias Krug. - Doha : Hamad Bin Khalifa University Press, 2019.

Pages ; cm

ISBN 978-992-713-771-6

1. Soccer -- Qatar -- History -- 21th century. 2. World Cup (Soccer) -- (2022: Qatar). 3. FIFA. I. Title.

GV943.Q38. K78 2019
796.334--dc23   201927417682

Contents

FOREWORD
   By Xavi Hernandez,
   2010 FIFA World Cup™ winner with Spain
   and FC Barcelona legend 9

INTRODUCTION
   A football miracle takes shape 13

1958. AL RAYYAN, QATAR
   The boy with the socks ball 17

1972. IN THE (DIVIDED) HEART OF GERMANY
   The ballerina in the minefield 29

1973. DOHA STADIUM
   The Greatest comes to town 37

1981. AUSTRALIA
   The Qatari striker who surprised the English 43

1982. KHALIFA INTERNATIONAL STADIUM
   The athletes from Aladdin's lamp 51

1984. HAMAD HOSPITAL
   The Olympics, baby 55

1989. SINGAPORE
Miracle men wear maroon 63

1992. BARCELONA
Mubarak Mustafa's golden header 75

1992. DOHA
The falcon that swooped from the mountains 85

1992. KHALIFA INTERNATIONAL STADIUM
Evaristo's legacy 89

1994. KHALIFA TENNIS COMPLEX
Boris Becker and his sweaty towels 93

1995. AL AHLI STADIUM
The stars of the future arrive in Doha 103

2003. THE GULF TIMES BUILDING
Finding Romario 115

2004. FROM DOHA TO NOTTINGHAM
Football animals 125

2006. DOHA ASIAN GAMES
The sheikh who rode to the top of the stadium 143

2007. QATAR OLYMPIC COMMITTEE TOWER
Mr Front Page 155

2008. WOMEN'S SPORTS COMMITTEE BUILDING
The girls who bent it like Beckham 167

2010. ZURICH
'And the host nation for 2022 is…' 179

2013. NEW DOHA
 The football revolutionaries 191

2013. RIO DE JANEIRO
 The man with the magic touch 203

2014. AL GHARAFA SPORTS CLUB
 The Nepalese defender who lifted the Cup 211

SPRING 2014. THE NEWSROOM
 A chat with the World Cup-winning captain 221

2015. DOHA, SPORTS CAPITAL OF THE WORLD
 The football nomad 227

SUMMER OF 2015. AL SADD STADIUM
 Xavi's survival instinct 239

2016. RAS ABU ABOUD
 The Qataris shaping the most futuristic World Cup ever 247

2017. LUSAIL STADIUM
 The man who wrote about Mandela 259

2017. KHALIFA INTERNATIONAL STADIUM
 The man who can make it snow in the summer 271

JUNE 2018. MOSCOW
 A World Cup love story 285

EPILOGUE: FEBRUARY 2019. DOHA
 The young Qatar team that brought home the Asian Cup ... 293

*To my father, my mother and my family.
To Luisa, Kimi and Lisa, with love.
To my country, to those who dare to dream big.*

FOREWORD

By Xavi Hernandez, 2010 FIFA World Cup™ winner with Spain and FC Barcelona legend

When I arrived in Qatar in the summer of 2015 to sign for Al Sadd Sports Club, it was an entirely new experience after seventeen years at FC Barcelona. We had just lifted the UEFA Champions League trophy in Berlin a few weeks previously to complete a historic second treble, and I knew that the time was right to leave the club of my life and embark on a completely new adventure.

Although I had spoken to great footballers such as Pep Guardiola and Raul Gonzalez who had played in Doha before me – and told me many good things about the country – I did not know exactly what to expect. On a warm summer day in June, my family and I left The Torch hotel in Doha to go to my first press conference for my new club.

As I stood outside, across from Khalifa International Stadium, a tall German introduced himself and spoke to me in Spanish. He asked what it was like for me being unveiled at a club, because I'd never had to do a presentation before. I had one on a much smaller scale when I was 11 years old, when I came to Barcelona, but never anything like this. The way I was received in Qatar was marvellous. I am very grateful to Al Sadd, to the children who welcomed me on that day, and to the fanatical football fans in this country who have received me so passionately.

Of course, I miss some things about Barcelona: my former teammates, the training sessions starting with the 'rondo', the happiness we shared in the dressing room. But I can say that it has been one of the best decisions of my life to come to Qatar. It is a fantastic country which has welcomed me and my family warmly, and it is a great project working here with Aspire Academy and the 2022 FIFA World Cup™.

This country has surprised me positively in many ways. I can only speak marvels of Qatar, which has placed a big focus on sports. For me, it is a great place to be and to develop further in the long term, with everyone's sights set on 2022. With Al Sadd I had the opportunity to continue winning trophies, including the memorable Amir Cup at the opening of the first stadium completed for the 2022 World Cup (as described in this book). I also began my coaching journey here, with the Qatar youth teams and at Aspire Academy.

There are good young teams being developed in Qatar, with talented players. Many players currently in the under-23 and under-19 teams could be very important when the country takes to the pitch in 2022, and there are some very important coaches at Aspire and in the Qatar Football Association. During my years in Doha I began helping to coach the under-23 team, and I enjoyed it greatly. The organisation for the World Cup is going well, and in terms of football development we are able to work with these players, so the foundation is there to have a great tournament.

Qatar right now is one of the sporting capitals of the world. They invest a lot in sport, and they have a genuine passion and vision which you can feel in every conversation, from fans to football decision-makers. It is not just football: every week you have top competitions here in athletics, chess, rugby, swimming and many other disciplines, all of them organised with great efficiency. Qatar wants to be known as a world capital of sport, and that is laudable in itself.

I believe that to understand a world-changing sporting development you need to go back to its origins and the philosophy which drives it forward. At Barcelona, those historic years where we lifted so many titles and played beautiful football can be traced back to the philosophy of Johan Cruyff and the values of La Masia, which were instilled in us from our earliest football days. Without these, as a small player lacking a strong physical presence in midfield, I would not have had the opportunity to do everything that we were able to achieve with Barcelona and Spain.

Similarly, as a small nation Qatar understood that it needed a vision and a philosophy which would allow it to become known around the world. This book is essential reading for an understanding of why Qatar has chosen to make sport, and football in particular, such an integral part of its national DNA. It relates the colourful and fascinating football history of Qatar in a very personal way, including anecdotes from Pep Guardiola's and my own time here in Doha.

That tall German surprised me that day by saying he had been born and raised in Qatar, and that his father and family had first arrived in Doha in 1982. He has written a book here that is as important as it is inspirational: the story of a small country that dreamed big, and surprised the sporting world – one pass at a time.

Xavi Hernandez

INTRODUCTION
A football miracle takes shape

We all love a good football miracle. The classic story of a team that no one expected to do well challenging for ultimate glory. The surprise small team from Leicester that goes all the way and wins the Premier League title in England. Or the home nation, in the first World Cup in Asia, driven on by feverishly chanting South Korean supporters to embark on a remarkable run to the semi-finals. Why do we love these underdog stories, these football miracles? Perhaps because they fuel the inner belief we all have that anything is possible if you believe in it and work hard enough to make it happen. If you dare to dream.

This book is about a small country that dared to dream big on the football pitch. It traces the story from the earliest days of the sport in Qatar, when the lines of the pitch were marked out in the sand with oil, and when youngsters used makeshift balls made out of socks, defying their parents in order to play the game they loved. It has been an untold story until now, because no one has looked at Qatar's football history in a sustained way before; and it is one which I have put together with the care and passion of someone born on this small peninsula that juts out confidently into the Arabian Gulf.

On 2 December 2010, Qatar wrote sporting history by becoming the first Arab and Middle Eastern country to be granted the right to host the FIFA World Cup™. That day I wrote an article for the BBC entitled 'A World Cup miracle'. Qatar had beaten tough competition from the United States, Japan, South Korea and Australia to have its name drawn out of the white winner's envelope. As my article that day noted: 'In many ways, the decision to award the 2022 World Cup to Qatar is a sporting miracle. The people of Qatar – and by extension those of the Middle East – have finally been given a chance to show their true potential. It promises to be a brave new world for the beautiful game.'

After the initial ecstatic celebrations in Doha and across this football-mad region, the critics quickly set to work. Many were from the countries whose bids had not been successful on that cold December day in Zurich. For them, this could not possibly be right – something must have gone wrong, they argued, if tiny Qatar had won the right to host the biggest football tournament in the world. In truth, not many people knew much about this unlikely new host nation. Some didn't even know how to pronounce its name. Many claimed that it had no football history – so why was it even trying to host a tournament on this scale?

I have set out to dismantle that myth of a lack of football history, by telling for the first time the story of Qatar's rich sporting and football history. A colourful, fascinating history, which is told in a personal way alongside the story of my father, who arrived in Doha in 1982 as one of Qatar's first foreign sports coaches, when the country was still only dreaming of what it wanted to achieve one day. It includes the story of the first yellow card of the great Pele's career, at Doha Stadium, the first grass pitch stadium in the entire Gulf region. There are also the giant-killing exploits of Evaristo de Macedo's young Qatar team, which stunned the world by reaching the final of the World Youth Championship in Australia in 1981, beating Brazil and England along the way. And the moment a brave horseman carrying a blazing torch rode to the top of the country's most iconic stadium, signalling Qatar's entry into the world of hosting major sporting events.

As this book clearly sets out, Qatar does have a vibrant football and sports history, and one of which the people of this country are immensely and deeply proud. Throughout Qatar's sporting journey, recounted in these pages with valuable insights from those who helped to shape it, including Qatari legends like Mubarak Mustafa and Badr Bilal, leading FIFA World Cup Qatar 2022™ officials like Hassan Al Thawadi and Nasser Al Khater, and World Cup-winning legends such as Xavi Hernandez and Philipp Lahm, a common theme becomes apparent. Qatar has consistently used sport as a vehicle for positive change, both when the fiercest criticism came its way and also long beforehand. The country with the football team wearing maroon always had faith in its sporting vision: that if you dream big and work hard, miracles can happen.

This is a book about a sporting underdog that took a big chance. More than anything, Qatar wanted to place itself on the world map by forging a new national identity, associated with the round ball which the world so loves. It did so by grasping a timely opportunity to make a difference for this conflict-riddled part of the world. As Her Highness Sheikha Moza bint Nasser, the First Lady of Qatar, said during the Qatari presentation in Zurich: 'When? When do you think is the right time for the World Cup to come to the Middle East? And do you recognise how important this is to our region and to our world?... The time has come, the time is now.'

The time truly is now for the first World Cup in the Middle East, because people in this part of the world crave the impetus and the positive social development opportunities the tournament brings with it. As Alberto Testa and Mahfoud Amara write: 'The desire of Muslim communities to be part of the global sporting experience is real.'[1]

This book takes a real inside look at Qatar's incredible sporting transformation, from the earliest days of the 'koora' being kicked around in the country to the futuristic plans and preparations for the FIFA World Cup Qatar 2022™. It attempts to do so in a way that is

---

1 Sport in Islam and in Muslim Communities, edited by Alberto Testa and Mahfoud Amara (2015).

sincere and honest, addressing the challenges and main areas of criticism, and how the country has dealt with them. It also examines the opportunities that give this World Cup greater potential than any previous major event to leave a lasting legacy and change lives for the better.

Sporting miracles don't happen very often, which is what makes them so special. But when they do, you will only completely understand them by going back to their origins, to find out how they really came about. Qatar's World Cup miracle did not start in 2010, or even two years earlier when I was the first to break the news of Qatar's intention to bid for the tournament. The Maroon Miracle began to take shape many decades earlier.

History, it seems to me, after years of study, is a complex and yet essential equation which could be described more simply as something like $(T + P)$ x H. That is, Time plus Place, with an important multiplying factor of the Humans who make the decisions which turn it into actual history.

So much for the formula. Thereafter the decisive factor in the equation is L – what you learn from it all.

1958. AL RAYYAN, QATAR
The boy with the socks ball

In the late 1950s, a young Qatari boy called Khattab Omar Al Daffa started playing football. The first time he kicked a ball, he just wanted to have a go at this exotic-looking game, and then suddenly he couldn't get enough of it. At the age of seven, Khattab began playing football with friends in his neighbourhood of Doha, Al Rayyan, before going to school. The balls they used were a far cry from the leather confection which Pele so elegantly mastered and then propelled into the back of the net in the 1958 FIFA World Cup™ final.

'We kids in our village started playing for fun before going to school,' Al Daffa remembered fondly. 'We played without shoes, and with a ball made out of old cloths or socks knotted together and formed into a makeshift ball.'

This makeshift version of 'al-koora' (the ball) was also being kicked passionately around in other Arab countries, and known colloquially as 'koora sharab' (socks ball). It was a form of street football played by youngsters across the region in whatever open areas they could find.

As Pele enthralled the world, Al Daffa started dreaming of scoring spectacular goals for his country himself. The man who would go on to make his name as an early football star in Qatar (and later become a government minister) said he saw this phase as the veritable birth of football as a sport of the masses in Qatar. It was hard going, though, to begin with.

'No adults played the game in those days, and nobody supported it. Football was more a form of entertainment for small children. But in school we had teachers from Egypt and Palestine who helped us and encouraged us to play the game.'

In both those countries football had already taken hold in the popular fabric of society. Egypt qualified for the 1934 World Cup in Italy only to lose 4-2 to Hungary in a first-round match in Naples, but 'Egypt's early participation in the 1934 World Cup served as a great boost to the emerging national pastime'.[1] In those days the tournament was still played in a knockout format right from the first stage. Clearly, a football tradition and passion had begun which would enthral the entire Arab world. The same was evident in Palestine, where the Palestine Football Association had been founded as early as 1928. The Palestinian team failed to qualify for the 1934 World Cup, but football was equally gaining popularity there. Teachers from those countries were now passing on their football passion to Qatari students like the wide-eyed Khattab.

A second generation of Arab football players was taking shape in Egypt and Palestine. In both countries, the British occupation was not exactly popular; in fact, the opposite may safely be said. Much has been written to suggest that football was becoming a form of indirect resistance to occupation. Beating a team of occupiers, or having football teams of an equivalent standard to the British ones, was a metaphorical victory for those Arab teams.

While this was one form of national pride, soon the game took on its own Arab dimensions and nuances. Football vocabulary like 'koora sharab' began to emerge and mix into the Arabic language, producing linguistic gems like 'goan' (goalkeeper), 'backat' (defenders), 'farawda' (forwards) and 'blenty' (penalty).[2]

---

1 The Linguistics of Football, edited by Eva Lavric (2008), p. 90.
2 Ibid.

So what was the decisive factor in the game catching on in Qatar in such spectacular fashion during Al Daffa's childhood? A journey further back in time and history offers some insights.

Initially, the world played football without Qatar. The game of football likely originated in Han dynasty China (206 BCE-221 CE), and was given formal rules in the late 19th century in the northern English town of Sheffield, but it simply did not pass through the small peninsula jutting into the Arabian Gulf. The small fishing and pearling community, with traces of civilisation dating back to 8,000 BCE, had traditional sports like falconry, saluki hunting and camel racing to entertain its roaming people.

These activities are still well-conserved traditions to this day, and will make for an entirely new experience for visiting World Cup fans. The charming Souq Waqif, a bustling and colourful hub of restaurants, coffee shops and narrow bazaars, offers everything from silver tea-kettles to rainbow-coloured handbags, delightfully scented spices and traditional golden Arabian swords, to falconry shops where tourists can have their picture taken with a falcon sitting on their arm. Friendly falcon handlers will explain the subtleties of colour, shape and species which can make these birds extremely expensive companions, costing anywhere up to a million Qatari riyals. Here, in surroundings which allow a thousand and one discoveries and bargains to be made in just a single afternoon, you can learn about the various types of falcons used for hunting animals sometimes the size of deer, including the 'al-hurr' falcon, meaning 'the free one'.

Camel and saluki racing will make equally fascinating pastimes for visiting fans, who will have seen nothing quite like them in their lifetime as football supporters. According to research, dogs of the saluki breed were the traditional hunting companions of the earliest inhabitants of the region. These slender, immensely fast dogs can be traced back to 7,000-5,000 BCE. Early stone inscriptions depict the young King Tutankhamun hunting with his pair of royal salukis. Salukis were then taken by traders from the fertile soils of Mesopotamia throughout the Middle East, where they became the beloved hounds of the nomadic Bedouin tribes of the region.

These 'traditional sports', though, all required a trained animal, which acted as an external accessory during the favoured pastime. In football, the only equipment needed is a round ball. Is it reasonable to suppose, then, that a round ball simply kicked with the feet would have had little initial popularity in such surroundings? In 1913, as Europe hurtled toward the deadly conflict which would escalate into World War I, Sheikh Abdullah bin Jassim Al Thani became the ruler of Qatar. Qatari writings about this time[1] recall that the only early signs of sport in those days were physical exercises to prepare for battles against invaders – no sign of football yet.

On 3 November 1916, Britain signed a treaty with Sheikh Abdullah bringing Qatar under the protection of the British Empire from all aggression by sea. But was Qatar a colony in the same sense as India or Algeria? As Allen Fromherz writes in his history of the country, 'Qatar was never really colonised, especially not in a way remotely similar to the colonisation of states such as Algeria or the Congo'.[2] The British policy of supporting the Arab Revolt against the Ottoman Empire during World War I – under the influence of the famous 'Lawrence of Arabia' depicted in the 1962 movie of the same name – also needs to be considered in this complex mosaic of pre-independence Qatar. Qatari tribal leaders had struggled to shake off the expansive Ottoman Empire, which reached as far as the gates of Vienna at one point. But now that vast empire was beginning to crumble. Some of its last bastions remained in the Arab region, where the British also had numerous colonies and interests. The German Kaiser had declared himself a friend of all Muslims

---

1   Retrieved from the 'Culture of Sports in Qatar' section of the QOC website (olympic.qa).
2   Qatar: A Modern History, by Allen J. Fromherz (2012), p. 6.

and was willing to support an uprising in the British colonies with arms and money.

But Lawrence of Arabia had outmanoeuvred the Germans. His government had promised the Arab leaders independence, although it also made a number of infamous promises to other countries, including France, which would complicate the future of the entire region. Guerrilla-style warfare against Ottoman rulers in the Arabian Gulf began. When it was over, the Ottomans had finally withdrawn their troops. But instead of granting Arab independence, the British simply went back on their word. In such circumstances, with large empires vying for strategic power, modern sports had difficulty developing in the early part of the twentieth century. Political survival was of the utmost importance, and all the more so for a small state like Qatar. The origins of Qatar's 21st-century policy of sports as a means of nation-building may be found in this delicate balancing act of survival in a geopolitically vital region. So a pragmatic approach was taken.

The British Empire had swallowed up parts of Persia (modern-day Iran) – just a short way across the waters of the Arabian Gulf from Qatar – for its massive oil production, which the colonialists were able to profit from. On 17 May 1935, Sheikh Abdullah signed the first Qatari oil concession agreement with the Anglo-Persian Oil Company. Three years later, drilling began of a first well in Qatar. The British were ever-present at this stage in the country's development, and brought along expertise for the development of oil production. But they were still a colonial power in a country which, like all the others in the region, obviously wanted independence.

So was it a case of natural scepticism towards a sport that came from a vastly different cultural context? For some fifty years the 'beautiful game' had begun to move the masses in large parts of the world without a ball ever being kicked in Doha. The arrival of football in Spain, the 2010 FIFA World Cup™ winners, can be placed around 1889, when the club Recreativo de Huelva was formed in

Andalusia. More than half a century would pass before the ball first started rolling in an organised way in Qatar. This relatively late start makes the country's rapid sporting transformation all the more remarkable.

Conditions were not right for that development to flourish just yet. World War II had an extremely negative impact on Qatar. In 1940, the entire population of the country was down to just 16,000,[1] and a period of dire austerity began. Oil production was suspended, and the British Political Resident provided a pessimistic glimpse into daily life in Doha, calling it 'little more than a miserable fishing village'.[2] An aerial shot of Doha in the Qatari archives from the late 1930s shows only a cluster of small buildings near the waterfront.

So where can the origins of football in Qatar be found? In the year 1948, oil companies brought their foreign staff and games with them. As such they also brought along the round ball, or 'koora' as it was called in Arabic. At first, football was played only by oil company workers. Then Qataris occasionally joined in matches. Finally, the sport began to spread to Qatari residential areas, or 'furjan'. In 1950 Al Najah, Qatar's first football club, was formed. Some uncertainty reigns about the exact name of the first club. Others relate it as being Itihad Al Arab, an immediate precursor of Al Najah which was established in Dukhan. What is certain is that Al Najah morphed into modern-day Al Ahli, the club where Josep Guardiola, the legendary Catalan midfielder, spent two seasons before becoming the most successful coach in FC Barcelona history. By 1980 eleven more clubs would follow, and by 2015 the Qatari league had a full fourteen teams.

Football was evidently first played in Dukhan, near Qatar's west coast. Some oral accounts recall that early football field boundaries were marked out with crude oil. A placard still hangs in Dukhan to this day commemorating the first discovery of oil in Qatar. Archive

---

1 Qatar: A Modern History, by Allen J. Fromherz (2012).
2 Ibid.

pictures show 'Rig number 1', a solitary construction out in the desert with nothing else in view. Dukhan is indeed still a sleepy little town, where no World Cup matches will be held. I recall from early childhood memories that my family would drive there sometimes on a Friday. A one-hour drive through desert landscapes with occasional hilly relief (Qatar is a very flat country, the highest point being Qurayn Abu al-Bawl, at 105 metres) took us to the Dukhan Club, a leisure and sports club with a swimming pool and beach access. A good two decades later I'd be driving my wife along the same stretch of Qatari desert landscape as we headed to the Cuban Hospital in Dukhan for regular check-ups during her second pregnancy.

Home advantage proved useful for the football team from Dukhan. Little did I know that very near to the place where I used to drift on the waves on those Fridays, the first-ever football tournament in Qatar had taken place. Dukhan won the final and became the first champions of Qatar around the time that West Germany first won the World Cup, in 1954. Is this the origin of Western claims that Qatar has 'no football tradition' to speak of in 'a game which, by most historical accounts, had a tendency to spread like wildfire', according to football historian Phil Ball? By the time the first club was created in Qatar, both Italy and Uruguay had already won the World Cup twice. It will be 2050 before the first Qatari club, Al Ahli, can hold a celebratory centenary match, as Barcelona did in 1999 and Real Madrid in 2002.

On 1 September 1952, a new oil agreement was signed between Qatar's ruler and the Iraq Petroleum Company (later Qatar Petroleum Company); under the terms of the agreement Qatar acquired 50 per cent of the profits from oil exports. It was a first momentous step toward nationalisation of the vast oil and gas discoveries which half a century later would make Qatar the per capita richest nation in the world.

It was around this time that the Qatari youngster Khattab Al Daffa began playing football. At first he faced great resistance from his family, but Al Daffa's father gradually began to change his mind about football. Khattab continued improving his considerable football skills and soon began playing for Qatar's first-ever national team. In 1966, the year England won the World Cup final at home against West Germany (with the famous extra-time goal which of course, from a German perspective, never crossed the line), Khattab first pulled on the maroon uniform of Qatar to play for his country.

'Later, having been so against my football passion early on, my father and grandfather went to matches where I played, and I think they were proud to see me playing,' he recalled. 'I played in the national team from 1966 to 1970. In 1969 I was voted Player of the Year in Qatar.'

Just a year before Pele repeated his World Cup magic in the 1970 edition in Mexico, as part of one of the greatest teams in history, Qatar had found its first football star. Khattab Al Daffa had taken the Qatari league by storm. Predictably, though, there were no astronomical transfer fees in Qatar's early football days, and of course no global media attention. Until 1962, players were unrestricted and could move easily between clubs. A player simply had to provide a resignation letter and 10 Indian rupees, the currency in Qatar at the time.

The fiercely loyal Khattab had no intention of moving from his home team, though. He was intent on winning more trophies with Al Rayyan. In those early days, as Khattab played for the 'Lions', there were no global superstars playing in Qatar, and matches were still arranged orally or by writing a letter to a rival team. A formal league had yet to be established. And it was not always financially advantageous to arrange a match – the club that asked for the tie usually also brought along the trophy for which the teams would vie.

All that soon changed. The country's football association began to provide the trophies. In 1960 the Qatar Football Association (QFA) was founded, and in 1972 it became an affiliated member of FIFA. The country's first official league tournament was launched in the

1963-64 season – the same year the German Bundesliga was officially launched. Matches were played at Doha Stadium, and Al Daffa remembers proudly that all the players in those days were locals.

'Spectators only came to Doha Stadium in those days to see special players from their village. In those days no foreign players were playing in our league.'

The number of spectators was still seemingly modest, and so was the number of teams involved. In the 1972-73 season, the number of teams was reduced from eleven to just six: Al Ahli, Al Rayyan, Al Sadd, Al Arabi, Al Istiqlal (currently named Qatar Sports Club) and Al Wakrah. Al Daffa's team was founded in 1967 after a merger between the old Rayyan team and Nusoor Club. Some forty years later Real Madrid's Champions League-winning captain Fernando Hierro would pull on the official team colours of red and black to represent 'Al Raheeb' ('the Fierce'), another nickname for Al Rayyan, which has one of the largest and most loyal groups of supporters in Qatar.

On 3 September 1971, Qatar became an independent state, thereby separating itself from what remained of the British Empire. In effusive language, which contrasts nicely with England's direct 'long ball' style of football, the British Political Resident in Bahrain wrote to the Ruler of Qatar to confirm the discussions which had already taken place about the imminent separation.

'I avail myself of this opportunity to renew to Your Highness the assurances of my highest consideration,' the last line of the letter reads. Three weeks later, the hoisting of the maroon-and-white Qatari flag in a ceremony at the UN building in New York made Qatar member number 130 of the United Nations.

Modern-day Qatar had been born.

Perhaps it was the distinctly local feel which made football a sport of the masses in Qatar, given that, as David Goldblatt writes in his extensive world history of the game, 'the geographical reach and cultural cachet of Britain and British sports did not guarantee their adoption in general, let alone that it would be football that would catch on'.[1]

Most of all, just as in countries everywhere around the world, football spread like wildfire due to the incredible passion for the game. Each country added its own distinct touch and flavour to a game that had the same rules everywhere it was played. In Qatar the traditional men's white robes, or 'thobes', were part of the early football experience for youngsters playing the game.

'No uniforms were available in those early days,' Al Daffa explained, 'so we tied our thobes around our waists and just began playing. We played on any small area of land where not too many stones were lying around. We had no lines, and no grass, and the goals were made out of wooden sticks without any net. First we played with 'koora sharab', then later on we had some plastic balls into which we put air by blowing.'

The ball made of socks was something anyone could string together, and it caught on quickly across the country and the region. As Brazil defended their World Cup crown in historic manner by winning the 1962 edition in Chile, Qatar too celebrated a momentous occasion, as Al Daffa remembered: 'The first grass pitch stadium was opened in 1962, near the National Museum. It was called Doha Stadium, and it was the first grass pitch not only in Qatar but in all the Gulf countries. That was something really special for us.'

Despite the shiny new turf, though, it was not always easy going for football-crazy youngsters like Khattab. Resistance to the new pastime often came from the most unexpected of places – within their own families.

'In the beginning my father was not happy,' Al Daffa said with a fond smile. 'I had to hide that I was going to play football. One day he got very angry and went to the father of my friend. There he told

---

1   The Ball is Round: A Global History of Soccer, by David Goldblatt, p. 901.

him that he should not allow his son to pick me up for football any more.'

Coincidentally, at exactly the same time as Al Daffa was getting his makeshift football education in Doha, my father first took up sports in the former East Germany. The young man who would later become a German shot put and discus champion faced the same objections from his family: stop wasting your time and energy, and help out on the farm instead. So the ambitious youngster slipped out of his house secretly to practice sports, at times receiving beatings from his father as a result.

Al Daffa did not heed his father's warnings either. He had a dream and would not give up on it so easily. He continued playing football, this new and exciting game which none of the family elders seemed to support. Not yet, anyhow. Very soon, Al Daffa would become one of the country's first football heroes. A young nation was eager to begin writing its own football history.

1972. IN THE (DIVIDED) HEART OF GERMANY
The ballerina in the minefield

This story about Qatar continues, rather surprisingly, in the middle of a minefield in Germany. Right in the heart of a country divided by the Cold War. You probably couldn't find a more central spot even if you were trying with one of those pointy compass things from the geography class at school which the naughty kids jab into each other, provoking howls of pain.

The man in the brown leather jacket is tall and has fashionably (for the time) long, brown hair down to his shoulders. Those shoulders are as broad as a barn door, above bulging arm muscles refined through endless hours of training. He stands at this moment in time delicately poised like a ballerina frozen in mid-air. This is, quite literally, an explosive situation. This journey started with a dream, a simple dream of freedom. The ballerina in the minefield wants to escape Communist East Germany and reach freedom and democracy in West Germany. Even though the dream is now visible, only a few long steps away behind the second wall, it seems more impossible than ever.

This book is also about seemingly impossible dreams, and how to realise them if you have a good enough plan.

Joachim Werner Krug was an athlete of enormous build, as they all tend to be in his discipline – the shot put, or as they call it in Germany 'Kugelstossen', where you hurl a metal ball as far as you can. He had decided that day to escape the oppressive Communist sports factory which had moulded him, even if it cost him his life. He told me the details of his great escape one warm night in one of the fantastically elaborate gardens he and Mom always cultivated together in our back yard in Qatar, as if to create a small oasis of their own in the desert. A white cactus flower bloomed behind him as he spoke.

Attempting to escape East Germany was an extremely risky undertaking, which cost an estimated one thousand people their lives. Everything spoke against his chances of making it to the other side. The odds were heavily stacked against him. No one ever made it, so you shouldn't even think about it, the state-controlled media regularly pointed out in their discouraging propaganda messages. But he wanted to get away anyway. His mind was made up, perhaps more than anything *because* they forbade him from crossing that border. But there were other, smaller, things as well that fed into the larger mosaic of his new-found desire to get out. He had never been able to taste bananas as a youngster. They never reached East Germany. Did freedom mean being able to eat bananas if you wanted to? Many years later in Qatar, when we kids were winning every tennis tournament we entered, Dad would always ensure we stocked up on bananas.

'They give you energy during the match, and Boris Becker always eats them on changeovers,' he would say. Apparently they also fuelled dreams of escape.

He reached for his banana-less sports bag and walked out of a door he would never again enter. If he was being watched, it would seem the most natural thing in the world for the 20-year-old athlete to be closing that door behind him at that time on that afternoon. If they were watching him, the Stasi (the feared East German secret service) wouldn't necessarily know that there was no afternoon training session that day. The coach had decided to give them the afternoon off. What anyone who *was* watching him closely might have observed was that his sports bag was much heavier than usual;

instead of his normal sporting equipment it had a different load that day.

The escape had already been planned and played through a thousand and one times in his mind, and now he was weary of visualising it and just wanted to get it over with. Either way, whether he ended up dead or alive, he was going to give it a try. Before he left, though, and without revealing that they would probably never see each other again, he said goodbye to his good friend Siggy.

'Pst, Siggy,' Joachim said, crouching down and shaking his friend softly in his bed as he took an afternoon nap.

'What? Where are you going with that sports bag?' Siggy asked.

Joachim looked around and then lowered his voice even further. 'I'm going to visit my family. Back home, in Thuringia.'

'What, when?' Siggy asked. 'You never told me about this.'

'Leaving now. I'll catch you later.'

'OK,' Siggy said, and that was the last the two room-mates and good friends saw of each other for over three decades.

Joachim made the journey back home in thoughtful mood, unsure whether his friends or family would ever see him alive again. He had read stories about people trying to escape. They were usually riddled by machine-gun fire, or torn to pieces in the minefields, or caught out by the sniffer dogs and brought back in shame to serve a lengthy prison sentence in the East.

That night, under cover of darkness, Joachim set out alone to the place he had scouted while watching cows for his family as a youngster, in Bad Salzungen. The small town he comes from lies right at the heart of Germany, and is also near where the border ran between East and West Germany during the Cold War.

He arrived at the location he had chosen for the escape somewhat out of breath. It wasn't the trek to the spot which had caused this, for he was used to far more demanding training routines, but rather the gravity of what he was about to attempt. He took two deep breaths, as he usually did before important throws in competitions, with the

'DDR' of East Germany emblazoned on the front of his sports shirt. All that would be left behind now, one way or the other. He was switching sides. The cold night showed up his breath in thick plumes in front of his face. Then he set down the sports bag full of stones he had slung over his strong shoulders, and began to implement his plan.

The town of Bad Salzungen is situated on the River Werra, and unfortunately I only know this because of the popular search engine I used to check the location. In the pictures it looks like a truly beautiful, classically German place, with castles and woods and pointy cathedrals and things. The 'Wartburg', a castle idyllically perched on a hill surrounded by rolling woodland, is something I remember Dad talking about regularly during our youth. We never went to visit there, partly because of the divide between East and West, and partly because Mom had some bad culinary and life experiences with her in-laws when she visited them there, and never hesitated to tell us about them in great detail over the subsequent years in Doha. As a result we never actually visited our father's birthplace.

So the story of the escape from East Germany was shrouded in even more mystery for us four kids, because it was not a place we could easily conjure up in our minds. We were growing up with a dad who was a muscleman with a bone-crushing handshake, who lifted more weights in his daily workouts than everyone else at the gym combined, and who now and then mentioned snippets of the tale of his escape: 'jumped over two walls', 'avoided German shepherd sniffer dogs', 'hopped through a field of landmines', 'ignored bloodied hands after jumping over barbed wire', 'dodged machine-gun fire' and more. We turned our father into a Superman from Bad Salzungen as a result, because by the smallest of margins he might not have been there at all. His personal kryptonite was smoking, that deadly habit which we could never get him to stop, no matter how many times my siblings Tomi and Anna conspired to throw his cartons of cigarettes into the rubbish.

He took another long drag from his cigarette as we sat in the garden with the blooming white cactus flower that day he told me the details of how he escaped.

The setup at the border between East and West Germany was tightly controlled by the East Germans, who did not want their citizens escaping to the West at any cost. So they spared no cost themselves, and built two walls of different sizes. They popped industrial-standard barbed wire on top. Tossed in a minefield for good measure. Upgraded all this with trip wires which set off a flare to alert the guards. And topped everything off with machine-gunning watchtowers and patrolling sniffer dogs which were supposed to mop up anything the monstrous infrastructure around them had not killed already. The mere sound of it kept most people in their living rooms at night. Some tried anyhow, by whatever devices they could think of, even building their own flying machines or hiding in car boots at checkpoints to try and make the short journey across. Very few people escaped. But Joachim thought he had a plan.

He was an exceptional athlete, and now, after looking around for a few moments more to make sure no man or dog was around and no one had followed him, he slung the bag over his shoulder and took off. He climbed up the first of the two walls. The barbed wire shredded his hands at the top, but the adrenaline pumping through his veins meant that he felt no pain and only a numb sense of the shredding as he lowered himself carefully down on the other side. Next, he unslung his small sports bag and with bleeding, somewhat jittery, hands took out the stones he had placed inside. He looked around once more, but nothing was moving and no spotlight was nearby. With deft, expert motions which he knew so well from the sport in which he held a junior world record, he threw the heavy stones ahead of him to create a makeshift pathway. He was planning to hop over the minefield from stone to stone.

A few stones landed close to him, others further away, though without any deafening explosion, which could have given him away but would at least have left him in one piece rather than blowing him to bits. He now started hopping through the minefield. The most important thing here was balance, a crucial element in the discus throw that he had also mastered. Each hop seemed to last an eternity, but he took his time. A few dogs barked in the distance. Was someone else escaping over there? Had they found the poor guy or girl? He took his habitual two deep breaths and focused on the target ahead. The next wall was getting closer. He controlled his breathing and attempted another hop.

No explosion. Again he hopped, and again he hoped. No explosion. With each hop he steadied himself with arms stretched out to either side, as if he were flying. Each jump was one jump closer to freedom. He hopped one last time and breathed a sigh of relief as he reached a wooded area that he would have to run through. It was there that he accidentally tripped the wire which set off the flare.

Should he keep running towards freedom or turn back? Surely, with the guards alerted, it was best now to turn back? His instincts were overruled by the overwhelming desire to escape, and he decided to run forward. On the other side of the wall a few hours later they told him this had probably saved his life. Although the instinctive reaction was to turn back, by that stage there was no way to avoid arrest, or worse.

Joachim sprinted through the trees to the bottom of the second fence. A spotlight swung across the wall nearby from one of the watchtowers, so he pressed himself up against the fence and did not move at all. He wanted to shout out loud, as he always did after a winning effort in the shot put, in relief at getting through the landmines and all the way to the last wall, but that would alert the guards and might start up the machine-gunners. The spotlight moved on, and he abandoned the sports bag at the foot of the fence, an empty souvenir of his escape attempt which might offer some hope to others trying to leave in future.

Then he started climbing up the second wall. It was slightly smaller than the first, and he managed to reach the top in a few seconds, making as little noise as he could. His torn hands were by now a completely secondary issue, as he grabbed hold of the barbed wire with gritty determination. Freedom awaited him below. He dropped down into it with a feeling of elation, hurrying into the forest on the other side to avoid detection, and then heading to the nearest town in search of something to eat. He was a sportsman after all, and needed to replenish his muscles, even if his hands were completely shredded and bleeding. He had just managed the greatest escape of his life, and he was still alive. It was definitely time for a bloody cigarette. After all, if a minefield hadn't killed you, what harm would a lousy cigarette do?

From there Joachim was brought to a refugee centre, where people who had escaped from different points along the Eastern European borders were first registered and assigned new places to live by means of a quota system. Ironically, he was assigned to live in the western part of Berlin, a city completely encircled by East Germany. The train ride through East Germany to reach Berlin was a daunting one.

'My goodness, I thought, they're putting me on a train to go right back where I came from. These guys are trying to send me back,' he later told me with a laugh. He made it to Berlin safely, but clearly, being so close to the place he had just escaped from was not something he would feel happy about in the long run.

So he applied for a place at university, and headed into the heart of West Germany. He ended up in Cologne, where he studied at the Sports University and competed for the nearby Bayer Leverkusen sports club in athletics competitions. There was not a lot of money on offer, but he loved his sport. To make some extra money, he coached the university athletics team. One of the students there was a certain young Antje Engelhardt.

My mother did discus throw in the athletics club, and according to Dad she had a lot of talent. They were young and fell in love as young people do: instantly, and with no immediate idea what the future might hold. A short time later they found themselves living, as young couples do, in a tiny apartment of their own. Theirs was on Aachener Strasse, a long road leading right into the centre of Cologne. Money was always hard to come by, as it tends to be for students. They tried different things. Once Joachim posed in a play as a golden statue. Wearing only swimming briefs, he was spray-painted gold all over his body and then had to stand still for the duration of the play, posing as a Greek god. It was not sustainable, though, being a Greek god. Especially when your first baby arrived. My mother gave birth to Anna on 31 March 1981.

A year earlier, the West had boycotted the Olympic Games in Moscow because of the Soviet invasion of Afghanistan. Sports and politics had clashed, robbing my father of his dream of competing in the Olympics. When he was approached by a delegation of head-hunters in early 1982, he saw an opportunity to support his young family by going into coaching. He knew next to nothing about the exotic little country where they said they needed good athletics coaches: Qatar.

His dream of freedom had come true, but that was really only the starting point. He had risked everything because he had a plan and a strong belief in his seemingly superhuman powers. That slightly insane belief – that the impossible was possible, if only you had a good enough plan and a strong enough conviction that you could achieve it – would serve him well where he was going, where they too were starting to formulate a sporting dream. In a way his journey had really only just begun when he finished hopping through the minefield like a giant German ballerina.

1973. DOHA STADIUM
The Greatest comes to town

Just a decade after it had opened, Doha Stadium decked itself out in its finest colours and prepared for the honour of receiving the greatest football player in the world. Pele was at this time the unrivalled global superstar, having won his third FIFA World Cup™ in Mexico in 1970 with a team many still regard as among the best five teams ever to have played the beautiful game. For a country like Qatar, which had only two years earlier declared its independence from the British Empire, this was quite a statement of intent. Pele was coming to Doha with his fabled Santos team in 1973.

The young nation had already shown its pioneering sporting spirit two years earlier, when Muhammad Ali had visited Doha in 1971 to fight an exhibition bout at Doha Stadium.

Qatar Boxing Federation (QBF) President Yousuf Ali Al Kazim later looked back on this special occasion from his childhood, when the legendary boxer visited, in an interview with a local newspaper. 'I remember with nostalgic feelings the first visit of "The Greatest" to Qatar in 1971. It was a visit that still lingers in my memory. Though I was very young at that time, I can still remember how Doha Stadium was filled to capacity. Everyone wanted to catch a glimpse of this man whose famous exploits inside and outside the ring had captivated the world.'

While the match in Qatar was little more than an exhibition bout, it had a profound impact on the young and developing sporting nation. 'Ali was on a tour of the Arab world in the build-up to his fight against

Joe Frazier, and he was well received everywhere he went. During his visit to Doha, an exhibition match was held in his honour under the auspices of Sheikh Jassim bin Hamad Al Thani, the then Minister of Education and Chairman of the Youth Board. Ali came into the ring after a brief introduction and wowed the crowd with his fancy footwork and his endearing charm. At the end, to the admiration of everyone present, he gave a short speech in which he said he'd never known he had such a fan following in this part of the world. That bout was like a seed that led to further development of boxing in the country.'

A similar seed was about to be planted for the development of football in Qatar. Two years after Ali's much-celebrated visit, reigning World Cup winner Pele arrived at the same venue to play a friendly with Santos against Al Ahli of Qatar, the country's first football club. The crowds turned up in equally large numbers to see what these global sporting stars were all about.

One day in October 2015, I went out to have a look at the historic stadium with which so much of Qatar's early sporting history seemed to be linked. It was early in the afternoon and still quite warm outside. In the car next to me as we drove up the small road from the Museum of Islamic Art sat the head of a veritable football colossus: the chairman of the oldest club in the world, Richard Tims of Sheffield FC in England. We had agreed to do an interview, and I told him it might be fitting to conduct it at Doha Stadium, the first stadium and first grass pitch in Qatar and the entire Gulf region. Except that when we arrived there was no one there to let us in.

We didn't give up, but knocked on a door to the janitor's office, which smelt like a hospital ward with its disinfected hallways. There was a board with a whole lot of keys dangling from it, some of which must have been used to unlock the gates the day Pele came to play and Muhammad Ali came to fight. But in the end we didn't need to 'borrow' any of those historic keys – the doors to the stands were open, and we were able to walk straight in.

It was from these very stands that the people of Qatar had watched Pele play way back in 1973, as his world-renowned Santos side defeated Qatar's Al Ahli 3-0 against a background of local drums beating. The black-and-white photos of the day clearly show that the venue was sold out, though the stands rose no higher than a few metres from the ground at the time. I cannot imagine that the venue held more than 10,000 spectators. But everyone that day wanted to catch a glimpse of Pele, the player who had mesmerised the world once more as his magical Brazil side claimed the 1970 World Cup three years earlier.

'That day I was a young boy watching wide-eyed from the stands,' remembered football legend Obaid Juma, drawing on one of his many cigarettes, when I interviewed him years later. 'We watched the Al Ahli team lose to the great Pele's Santos side, and he was a true wonder to watch.'

In Qatar, the widely respected Obaid Juma used to provide his insights on football matches for the Al Kass TV show *Al Majlis*. This is a hugely popular show where football experts sit on the floor in a traditional, colourful Arab sitting room on red and green patterned cushions, talking about football for hours on end. Massive bowls of fruit adorn the floor in front of them, while in the background carved wooden panels give the whole occasion an unforgettable flavour. Even Lionel Messi has made an appearance on this show, which forms part of Qatari football folklore.

Obaid, who played for the country's first national team in the 1970s, blew cigarette smoke my way as he talked dreamily of the day he saw the great Brazilian striker dribble the ball across the first grass pitch in Qatar. Then something surprising happened.

'The stands were packed full, with not a single seat left to be had, because everyone wanted to catch a glimpse of the world's best player. He was of course magnificent. But one thing happened to him in Qatar that had happened nowhere else. Perhaps it was just the referee trying to make a name for himself, but whatever the reason, it was during that match that Pele got the first yellow card of his career,' Obaid said with a laugh.

Obaid played in the third Gulf Cup, the first to take place in Qatar. Like any other legend, in any country in the world, he thought that everything was better in the good old days. Anyone who says Qatar has no football history has not done their research, and they have certainly not talked to Obaid Juma and had him blow the wistful smoke of his nostalgia in their face. He could remember the days when the kit-man of the Qatar national team used to collect the maroon shirts after every game to have them washed and dried, because there was not enough money to keep buying new ones. He also recalled the one game Qatar played in canary yellow, as if they really were the 'Brazilians of the Gulf', as they were nicknamed, because that was their second kit and the opposing team's shirt was too similar. That day with the yellow shirts reminded Obaid of the visit of Brazil's most famous son, Pele, and his world-beating Santos side. If you really won his trust, Obaid might tell you the story of the time the pitch at Khalifa Stadium was spray-painted green because the grass had not grown lush enough in time for a game, and any player who fell on the ground that day got a green smudge as a souvenir to take home with him.

We wouldn't know these fascinating details if we didn't talk to people like Obaid. To deny a country's football history is to revert to colonial-style thinking: all that matters is what my country has done and will do for football, and I will not take the time to learn about yours. It is only by understanding its football history that you can understand the country you see today. And to understand the football history of the countries in this region, you need to understand the importance of the Gulf Cup.

'It is almost more important than the World Cup for the people of our region,' Omani academic Dr Omar Babood told me on the sidelines of a football history conference in Manchester at the National Football Museum in 2013. 'If you want to see the passion we have for football, go and watch matches of the Gulf Cup. Then come back and tell me that we don't love football.'

That day in October 2015, I had a fond look around the stadium which had seen the very first sporting steps of the country I called home. It was not the decaying relic of former times I had expected. Doha Stadium is still in fantastic shape, regularly hosting community football matches, with the charmingly small stands in perfect order. We walked onto the pitch, and the English club chairman had beads of sweat on his forehead as he said: 'Qatar is the new pioneer of world football.'

It was an interesting line, but perhaps more interesting was how life had thrown the two of us together in that place. A German born in Qatar, and an Englishman from the birthplace of modern football who was desperately trying to get the world's oldest football club some much-deserved recognition. We had both ended up in the small stadium, just a minute's drive from Doha's cubistic Museum of Islamic Art, where football had first begun to take off in Qatar and where, it was claimed, Pele got the only yellow card of his career.

The pioneering Doha Stadium's days in the football spotlight were coming to a fond end. With the passion for football ever increasing in the country, Qatar decided to build a new national stadium in time for the 1976 Gulf Cup, to which it had been awarded hosting rights. The newly constructed Khalifa Stadium was situated at the other end of town, and was massive in comparison to the homely Doha Stadium. By 1976 the country was ready to take the next step in a remarkably rapid sporting transformation. It was starting to acquire a liking for hosting sporting stars and events. Now it just needed a new home in which to do so.

The opening of Khalifa Stadium that year marked a new era in Qatari sports. Where the Gulf Cup was played that year was more important than who won the hugely popular tournament. With Iraq playing in the event for the first time, a young Mansour Muftah made his debut for Qatar; he scored four goals in six matches as the home team finished in third position, behind Kuwait and Iraq.

'Muftah' means 'key' in Arabic, and the skilful striker would be a key component of Qatar's rapid football development in the coming decades. The 21-year-old was an exciting prospect in the young Qatari team, and would become the all-time leading scorer for his nation over the next fifteen years or so. In eighty-six appearances for the national team, known as Al Ennabi ('the Maroons', in reference to the colour of the country's flag), Muftah scored fifty-three goals – an astonishing strike rate. Even more impressive was his record in over two decades playing for Al Rayyan Club, where he notched 317 goals in 324 appearances – almost a goal per game.

The stadium where he scored in the Gulf Cup that year would become a key part of a dream that was beginning to form in the minds of the hosts. If they believed in it and worked hard enough at their plan, Qatar could use sport to put itself on the world map. It was as a result of the Qataris putting this plan into action that the giant German shot put champion hopped on a plane to Doha and decided to try his luck.

1981. AUSTRALIA
The Qatari striker who surprised the English

Just ten years after Qatar's independence in 1971, the country's football players were the pride of the new nation. The young Qataris had qualified for the 1981 FIFA World Youth Championship in Australia. This was a momentous achievement in itself, and heralded the country's arrival on the international football scene. Al Ennabi, the Maroon team, made the long journey halfway round the world from Qatar with the intention of not just participating but actually winning some football games.

In order to do so, they had brought on board a coach with a winning mentality. Evaristo de Macedo was born in Rio de Janeiro in 1933. The President of the Qatar Football Association (QFA) at the time said he thought the Qatari style of play and temperament was most similar to the magnificent Brazilian samba style which had culminated in Brazil's third World Cup crown in 1970. This was indeed a confident statement, but also one which showed just how ambitious this young nation was in the sporting arena. Some forty years later, Qatar would replicate this approach of bringing in coaches from the winning World Cup nation, as an armada of Spanish coaches began arriving at Aspire Academy following Spain's 2010 triumph. Evaristo had no such spectacular training facilities at his disposal. But along with the experienced Brazilian the QFA brought in seven youth coaches from Brazil to work with various junior teams in the country for a year.

Upon his arrival in Doha, Evaristo began by scouting the talent he had on offer in a country of a significantly smaller size than his native Brazil, which had been producing footballing greats with apparent ease for many decades. Qatar at the time had just 220,000 inhabitants. Of those, there were an estimated 3,000 players in the age category which could be called upon for Australia 1981. The conclusion to which the former Barcelona and Brazil striker came after observing a number of matches was that there were indeed promising players at his disposal, although obviously not in the same numbers as he would find at home. But the Brazilian coach was happy with the raw skills of the players he had found. Now all that was needed was for their physical level to be brushed up to world standard. In addition, in the increasingly intense training sessions which took place in Doha, he worked on implementing a concerted attacking approach.

'I select players who are skilful and like to attack,' Evaristo noted at the time. 'My problem with Qatar youth players has been twofold: first to achieve a physical condition to play throughout a game at high tempo, and then to teach them how to play good football using skill and quickness of movement.'

In order to prepare Qatar's youngsters for what he was aware was the tough level of international competition awaiting them in Australia, Evaristo uprooted a large group of Qatari youth players from their comfort zone and took them to the other end of the globe. A month-long trip to his native Brazil was organised. Here the Qatari youngsters faced tough competition, but managed to win a few of their ten friendly matches. It was a much more thorough build-up than many other teams at the tournament had had, and they showed their skills by qualifying second from their group with a win and a draw.

If Al Ennabi had been underdogs in the previous three matches, then a new term was needed now to describe just how heavily favoured three-time World Cup winners Brazil were to reach the semi-finals against a country that had only recently gained independence. At 15:00 on 11 October 1981, a date that would go down in the history of Qatari football, the rank outsiders in white shirts and maroon shorts took to the pitch against the world-famous blue-and-yellow combination of their rivals at the International Sports Centre in Newcastle, New South Wales.

Coach Evaristo had plotted out the tactical approach carefully: full-out attack to surprise the favourites. And it worked. After just ten minutes Qatar took a shock lead. A low, drilled cross from the right found two Qatari players unmarked on the edge of the Brazilian area, and Ali Al Sada feigned skilfully to let his better-placed team-mate Khalid Al Mohamadi take the shot. The low, rifled finish was just what Qatar needed. 1-0 to the Maroons. The goal-scorer did a cartwheel of joy to celebrate. But if the Brazilians were astonished, they tried not to show it.

Just before the half hour, Ronaldo (not the famous one) levelled the score. The match would surely now swing in favour of the South Americans, the crowd in Newcastle must have thought at half-time. Again, Qatar surprised the world by retaking the lead in the 54th minute, Al Mohamadi notching a second goal as he slotted the ball past Pereira, making it 2-1. A sensation was taking shape in Newcastle. As the time trickled away and the Qatari team increasingly had possession of the ball, murmurs of appreciation went through the neutral crowd. But from an inswinging corner Ronaldo scored his second goal in the 78th minute.

Surely the Qatari dream was over now? Surely not. Rather than settle for a draw against the highly fancied opposition, Qatar went forward looking for a winner. A handball inside the Brazilian penalty area just three minutes before the end provided the perfect opportunity. But who would dare to take such an important penalty, with so much at stake? A miss might mean tragedy, while scoring would surely send Qatar through and turn you into a national hero overnight. It was left to Al Mohamadi to try to complete his hat-trick; he was clearly in fine form on the day. Pereira jumped left. And Al Mohamadi shot right to wrap up a sensational and historic hat-trick against Brazil.

It was some souvenir to take home to Qatar. This time there would be no reply. Qatar were through to the semi-finals. And the master tactician Evaristo had overseen the performance of a lifetime. His young team had outplayed and outscored his own beloved Brazil. For a summary of the importance of this tournament in Qatari football history, the following phrase, written at the time by FIFA observers, does the trick nicely: 'Brazil lost to the amazing Qatar.' Shouldn't it, according to all the form books and football traditions, have been 'Qatar lost to the amazing Brazil'? No. In this tournament the roles were reversed. Of course, it was 'only' an age-limited tournament, and not the senior sides. But in terms of the sentiments of a newly independent nation, Australia '81 might as well have been Spain '82. Qatar could beat Brazil on the football pitch. The birthplace of Qatar's underdog success story in world sports was not Doha but half a world away in Australia.

With a good enough plan and complete conviction in your strengths, anything seemed possible. The proof had just come on the pitch in Newcastle, where Mexican referee Antonio Marquez Ramirez had just blown the whistle for full time. A whole new nation, already mesmerised by the beautiful game, was now desperate to reach its first Cup final. Only the little matter of a semi-final at the Sydney Cricket Ground against England (who had, after all, only won the World Cup once) stood between Qatar and the World Youth Championship final at the same venue. Would beating the old colonial power provide an extra bit of satisfaction for the Qataris? Or were political matters, and feelings toward the nation that had relinquished power in Qatar just a decade earlier, entirely out of the picture?

Whatever the case, on 14 October 1981 at 20:00 Qatar marched confidently onto the pitch. They had, after all, beaten Brazil just three days earlier. The Qataris, in maroon shirts and white shorts, went on the offensive early on. The attacking approach soon paid off in the most spectacular way. If Qatar's opening goal of the tournament against Poland had been the freak deflected goal of the year, their opener against England was surely one of the best goals seen in world football in 1981.

A half-field cross from the left was curled in with seemingly little danger to the English goal. Having taken note of Qatar's spectacular offensive in their 3-2 win over Brazil, England had seven men in the penalty box defending. And the player to whom the cross was coming at shoulder height had his back to the goal. Keep calm and defend, the English must have thought. But the player in question was striker Badr Bilal, Qatar's Didier Drogba of Australia '81. In an act of improvisation bordering on the outrageous, Bilal took the ball directly out of the air and connected a bicycle kick with his left foot. The ball looped over the collection of English defenders and keeper Mark Kendall, who stretched out in vain. It was a goal that would have made Cristiano Ronaldo proud many years later. Qatar had taken an early lead again, and this time against the country that wrote the rules of the modern game.

England fought back with a series of opportunities that goalkeeper Younes Ahmed did well to smother. Acting as a de facto sweeper, in anticipation of the modern type of goalkeeping role Manuel Neuer would play in the winning German World Cup team of 2014, Ahmed often rushed out of his area to clear the ball when an English player beat the Qatari offside trap. Some twenty times English players were caught offside, causing increasing frustration for the highly favoured side.

Thirty-seven years later, I had the chance to ask Evaristo about his decision to make such play of the offside trap throughout the tournament.

'You see, we had to come up with very good strategies to beat these highly favoured teams,' he told me with a mischievous look in his eye. 'We did not have the best defenders in the world. But we had speed, players who were fast, and so we practised this tactic over and over, until everyone understood.'

The tactic worked extremely well for Qatar. England were quickly frustrated. When they did get through with a shot on goal, the cat-like Ahmed proved unbeatable. In his half-time talk in the stadium's catacombs, Evaristo reiterated that Qatar needed to continue attacking if they were to spring the next surprise and move into the final. He highlighted the absolute necessity of a second goal. Without it, the English would find their way back into the game. His players responded in style, with a fresh attacking surge at the start of the second half. In a brilliant display of individual skill, a solo run worthy of Lionel Messi ended in a fine strike by Ali Al Sada just after the hour to put Qatar 2-0 up.

The sensation was really happening. Could tiny Qatar really reach a World Cup final? England pulled a goal back through Michael Small in the 70th minute, but it was not to be enough. Qatar even had a chance to finish the match two goals up, but they missed a late penalty – though this did little to subdue the ecstatic celebrations at the final whistle. Qatar could not only beat Brazil but had just beaten England too. The Australian sky seemed the limit. The country which no one knew or expected to win a single game 'Down Under' had just reached the World Cup final.

'The best moment in my football life was my bicycle kick, and the moment we beat England and knew we were in the final,' Badr Bilal told me, sitting in the lobby of Al Sadd Sports Club in Doha three and a half decades later. All around him former team-mates and officials were busy playing cards at small glass tables, eagerly debating while playing a game called 'Brasileiro', named in honour of Evaristo. The famous coach brought the game to Doha, and it has been a part of Qatari popular culture ever since. Badr also belongs to the club of nostalgic players who believe that everything was better in the good old days. In this case, the result really couldn't have been better.

'At that time Poland were the best team in Europe, and we beat them in the group stages. Then we beat Brazil – the home nation of football – in the quarter-finals, and England in the semi-finals, which was a massive achievement.'

Whatever the outcome of the final against West Germany, the mere presence of Qatar in the title match indicated to FIFA observers that '[t]hey have clearly narrowed the gap at youth level between them and well-established soccer nations. The study group hopes that their approach to football of attacking fearlessly against stronger opponents will encourage others.'

It looked to some observers at the tournament as if West Germany, the two-time World Cup winners who had last won the senior edition on home soil just seven years earlier, might need some help from above if they wanted to avoid falling victim to this giant-killing Qatari side.

They got that 'help' when it starting raining heavily on the day of the final. If there's one thing you don't find much of in Qatar, it's rain. When it does rain, it's a special occasion; rain on your wedding day is a sign of good luck. My own marriage (in Aranjuez, an enchanting small town near Madrid) was also blessed with good luck and will therefore, surely, last forever. In the beige sands of the Qatari desert, rainfall is also a celebration of life, with little green desert plants springing up from the ground to form what looks like a lush and highly playable pitch hovering unexpectedly above the desert.

On 18 October at the Sydney Cricket Ground, though, the rainfall was not a good omen for Evaristo's team. The pitch was barely visible under a deep layer of water. It had rained so much that the area around the centre of the pitch was entirely waterlogged. The short passing style of attacking football practised by the Qataris could not be played successfully, with the ball getting stuck in puddles and pools of water. The Germans fared much better with their long balls towards their tall forwards.

Would the outcome of the final have been different on a sunny day?

Perhaps. Qatar might still have lost the match, but it would probably not have been as one-sided as the final turned out to be. Ralf Loose and the later Bayern Munich striker Roland Wohlfarth gave

West Germany a 2-0 lead at half-time, and a further strike from Loose as well as a late Holger Anthes goal made it a 4-0 final victory for the favourites.

It was nevertheless a resounding success for the new FIFA U-20 World Cup silver medallists. They received a triumphant welcome back home in Doha. Video footage of the time shows the team descending from the plane holding Qatari flags, and being welcomed by a mass of ecstatic people in a car cavalcade through Doha. The whole country came out to welcome its new heroes, lining the streets and dancing with joy at the sight of Qatar's footballing superstars. The future of football in Qatar seemed secure with this 'Amazing Australian' generation of players. And coach Evaristo had not just won a silver medal to go with the bronze he'd picked up with Brazil earlier, but also won a great many admirers along the way. He had set an extremely high standard for coaches in the region to follow in the coming years and decades. Gulf football coaches in general have over the years developed a reputation for extremely short stints in charge of clubs and national teams. One cause of this may be the phenomenal expectations raised by Brazilian coach Evaristo, who seemingly worked miracles in only a short space of time with Qatar.

In other disciplines, too, the country's sporting development was starting to take shape.

1982. KHALIFA INTERNATIONAL STADIUM
The athletes from Aladdin's lamp

In 1904, a German traveller by the name of Hermann Burchardt was the first person ever known to have taken photographs of Qatar, including one of a group of Bedouin tribesmen having tea from a beautiful traditional pot with a curved spout. Seventy-eight years later, on 13 February 1982, my German father set foot in Qatar for the first time. He must have felt just as much a pioneer as Burchardt had done all those years earlier, only he was here to stay.

'At first I thought I would stay one or two years, if everything went well maybe three,' my father later admitted. 'I had no idea how long it would turn out to be.'

His unusual move to Qatar made it into the tabloid press in Germany at the time. One late summer day in 2016, Grandpa Ulf went slowly down the spiral staircase with the low ceiling where he always cautioned you not to hit your head, and into his cellar, and came back up with a number of yellowing press clippings in a thin plastic folder which seemed on the verge of disintegrating. He sat down carefully in his favourite brown leather chair, which no one else was allowed to use, and pulled out the first clipping. It looked as old as one of Burchardt's early photos of Qatar. It was a sports story from February 1982 in Germany's leading tabloid paper, headlined, 'Athlete from Cologne tries his luck in the desert'. In the picture you can see my dad with a shot put ball, above the caption 'Joachim Krug heads to the desert for three years'. It turned out to be slightly longer than that: thirty-six years, and counting. In typical tabloid fashion, they wrote: 'Krug, who escaped from East Germany in 1972, feels like he is in a tale from the Thousand and One Nights, but he would have to be Aladdin with the magic lamp to turn the sons of the desert into world-class athletes.'

So my father packed his suitcase, adding in his favourite throwing shoes, and prepared to head out on his one-way flight to the desert. Grandpa read to us, with his unmistakable classic German pronunciation, the remainder of the story from the fading piece of paper which shook slightly in his ageing hands: 'Joachim Krug is a man who does not know fear of risk. He succeeded in an adventurous escape from East Germany in 1972, running through a minefield. The 19-year-old from Eisenach was a junior world record holder and one of the biggest talents in East Germany. One of the main reasons for the escape – a pretty girl from Cologne had stolen his heart.'

Now, after ten years in West Germany, and with a young family to support in Cologne, he had decided to hang up his competitive throwing shoes and move as an athletics coach to Qatar.

'The night before he flew to Doha, via Bahrain, he competed in his last competition in Germany,' Grandpa Ulf said, shifting slightly as the leather chair creaked under his worryingly light frame. The yellow newspaper clipping had been placed slowly back on the low wooden table in front of him. 'It was the German indoor championships in Dortmund, and he completed a hat-trick of German championships by winning the shot put event. Moments after getting the winner's medal around his neck, Joachim raced back to Cologne, and I drove him to the airport.'

It was to be a life-changing moment for the young athlete, who was in the prime of his career.

'Grandpa pressed a 100-Mark note into my hand, and said, "Take this with you, in case you need anything over there," Dad recalled. 'Then he wished me good luck and I got on the plane.'

On 13 February 1982, Joachim Krug landed in Qatar. There were no direct flights to Qatar in those days, and only three flights a week from Bahrain. Doha's tiny airport could hardly be called 'international' with the amount of traffic it received at the time. My father got off the plane and stood on the runway, observing for a few moments these new and unfamiliar surroundings. He waited for his suitcase to be unloaded from the airplane. It was much heavier than the others because of the big shot put ball buried beneath the clothes. The man handling the baggage gave him a puzzled look as he dragged it over with both hands. Joachim took the suitcase from him and easily lifted it with just one hand. Then he walked over into the airport building. Someone was waiting with a sign which had his name written on it. In the car he looked around as he was driven to the Ramada hotel, where he would be staying together with a handful of other German coaches for the first few months. It was one of only two hotels in Qatar when he arrived, as he would later explain to us on numerous occasions.

'The Corniche was then just a stretch of sand where people could swim; there were no walkways or palm trees, just sea and sand and some small roads,' he remembers of the city's now iconic seafront promenade.

The next morning he got up early and cleaned out the Ramada's breakfast buffet in order to prepare for his first full day in the new country, earning the sceptical looks of the hotel chef who had to cook extra food every morning from then on. Joachim then immediately took up training with his new athletes. None of them spoke English or German, 'except for one, who knew two words: "yes" and "no." So my father started to learn Arabic – one word at a time, using sign language to assist the learning process whenever needed. He also learned about the importance of other sports in the country. Alongside athletics, the Qataris were already on their way to building up an internationally competitive football team.

'Qatar had just the previous year achieved something miraculous in the World Youth Cup in Australia. The Brazilian coach Evaristo had a free hand after that success, and the football players were treated like kings. Football had a special place, and athletics had to move whenever football arrived,' he recounted. As a result, my father developed a deep-running phobia about football, because it supposedly takes the most talented youngsters away from athletics. Every now and then, over the years, he has made an effort to get over this phobia and watch football matches with me, because he knows how much I love the game.

He fondly remembered one incident where the new national heroes in Evaristo's team were almost in danger of losing their lives.

'Khalifa International Stadium already existed in the same place as today when I arrived, but it was no comparison to the outstanding facility today. Everything was very basic and the location was very far outside of Doha.'

His new team of athletes were training one afternoon when the football team showed up unexpectedly.

'There were no houses around the stadium, and only one little street leading up to it. Only this one stadium was available for training, but we had constant clashes with the football because of the timing and the grass. We had come to an agreement with the football federation that we would use the grass until 4.30 pm, at which time they would take over. Our athletes were throwing discuses, heavy metal discs which can cause serious injury, when the football players started walking onto the grass with their balls at 4.15.'

Anyone else might back down at the sight of the country's new sporting heroes, but my dad had other ideas: 'I told my athletes to keep throwing, because of the agreement. The next morning we had an official complaint: we were told not to bother the football players with our dangerous discus throwing.'

But on the whole Qatar's throwing and football coaches got on rather well; on weekends football matches were arranged between them. Evaristo, widely remembered as a 'fantastically fun guy', was always the centre of attention.

The next miracle was just around the corner.

Qatar wanted to go to the Olympics.

1984. HAMAD HOSPITAL
The Olympics, baby

'I was born in Qatar.'

I love telling people that. And seeing their reaction, somewhere between disbelief and shock. The man with the moustache in the lift going down from the office where I work, on the 33rd floor of one of Qatar's countless new skyscrapers – which were never there when we were youngsters playing football in the street – has just asked me how long I have been in Doha. It is a typical question among expatriates who want to compare how long they've lived and worked in Qatar. The problem for them is that no one can beat me on that question. Only my father can.

The man with the moustache probably has a name, actually he definitely does. Only I can't see it on the name-badge dangling from his belt because he is shaking with laughter from the hips up. He has a balding head, with a few wisps of white hair, and thick-rimmed glasses.

'Thirty-three years,' I reply to the disbelieving follow-up to my response. 'I was born here.'

The shaking moustache finally stops quivering long enough for him to ask me a few quick questions as the lift's display panel shows the numbers 6, 5, 4, 3, 2 ...

'What?'

'Yes.'

'What?'

'Yes.'

'Really?'
'Yes.'
'Are you joking?'
'No.'
'You landed on the moon?'
'No.'
'You were born in Doha?'
'Yes.'
'Do foreigners born in Qatar exist?'
'Yes, just like me.'

Then we reach ground level and, between the ebb and flow of people rushing in and out of the tower, one of the city's most important sports hubs, the man with the moustache is gone, never to be seen again, and I head off to my lunch break.

On my way out I cross paths with my father, that rare foreigner who can beat me at the 'how long have you lived in Qatar' game, who is rushing home from his own shift at work in a different sport – athletics. He has always been this way – always in a hurry, always busy, still with the same strong frame and perfect posture as when he first started working here thirty-six years ago. We now both work in the same high-rise building where many of Qatar's sports federations are housed. He works on the first floor of Al Bidda Tower – symbolically, perhaps, given that he was among the first foreign sports coaches to make their way to Doha. Some days there are so many foreigners running about that it feels like a new, 21st-century California gold rush, where men come to make a quick fortune and then head back home. For me, this country by the gently undulating waters of the Arabian Gulf is home. And it is not just because of the entry in my German passport, which reads: 'Place of birth: Doha, Qatar.'

The year was 1984, as in George Orwell's classic novel of that name. The means of transport: a battered old Mazda sports car with military markings, the first work car my father was ever given. The day: 21 April, with another hot summer fast approaching. At Hamad Hospital, a ten-minute drive from the Corniche, Doha's waterfront esplanade which would later sprout that spectacular skyline of high-rise towers as if by some magic rain shower, the old Mazda pulled up with screeching brakes outside the front entrance. It was late at night, and the doctors wheeled my mother in as my father went to park the car and have a quick, nervous, cigarette in the car park. By the time he was finished and had rushed inside, I was already lying in my mother's arms.

I was her third child, and her first pregnancy in Doha had just come to a concluding crescendo. By the time I was due to arrive, she had perfected the extremely difficult art of giving birth, to the extent that she went to the hospital at just the precise moment it was needed. In this case maybe Mom had stretched the 'just-in-time' concept a little too far, because by all accounts my father had to commit some serious red-light infringements to get her there on time. There were no traffic cameras around yet, however, so he simply dashed through the darkened streets in the middle of the night with the steely determination of a man who did not want to help deliver a baby in the car. He had not been in the delivery room for either of the first two births, and was not planning to make an exception on my arrival either. Jumping two walls with barbed wire on top and a minefield in between was all well and good, but helping his wife give birth was an altogether different sort of danger.

The fact that my mother chose to have me in Doha shows how quickly she too had adapted to her new surroundings. When she first landed in Doha in late 1982 with two small kids, she stepped out onto the tarmac and looked around in shock.

'I wanted to turn back straight away and return to Germany,' she said. 'Everything was so different. But I decided to stay and give it a go.'

Two years later, she was prepared to give having a baby in Qatar a go. She timed me to perfection, even though the dash through the streets of Doha must have caused my father a first few grey hairs.

Shortly thereafter, having spent just a few hours in hospital because she thought she was fine, my mom returned home with cute little me in her arms to our first street house in Doha.

At around the time I was born at Hamad Hospital in Doha, Qatar was already taking its first steps on the international football scene. Coach Evaristo was busy preparing his squad for what many in the country hoped would be yet another giant-killing spree. The football players were looking to win the country more international recognition at the very first Olympic Games in which Qatar took part – in Los Angeles in 1984. The Soviet Union and some other Communist countries boycotted the event in retaliation for Moscow 1980, but Qatar would not have missed it for the world.

Five members of the successful 1981 team were called up to the squad. As in Australia, the Qatari team was once again drawn into Group A – would it be a good omen? Their opening game saw the Qatari side take on reigning European champions France, on 29 July 1984 at 19:30 in the Navy–Marine Corps Memorial Stadium in Annapolis. Around 30,000 spectators were on hand to see a riveting encounter, another classic match-up between underdog and overwhelming favourite. After a first half in which each side attempted to control possession of the ball and no big chances were forthcoming, France took the lead just before the break, Patrice Garande notching the vital opener.

Qatar now needed to fight back. In the half-time team talk Evaristo explained some tactical changes: a sweeper was introduced as well as a second forward to go in search of goals. The second half was barely ten minutes old when Khalid Al Muhannadi raced into the French penalty area on the left and unleashed a perfect left-footed shot which rocketed into the top of the net.

If France were surprised, worse was to come. The same player scored another fine goal for Qatar on the hour mark. It looked as if Qatar were about to record another stunning win, but their lead was short-lived. From a set piece the French equalised just a minute later through Daniel Xuereb. Although Qatar were the better team in the final half hour and could well have won the match, it ended in a draw. Both teams remained in with a chance of going through to the knockout stage. The next round of matches would be crucial. But for Qatar, that 2-2 draw with France turned out to be the highlight of their first Olympic football experience. A 1-0 loss to Chile on 31 July, in a game in which Qatar had chances to score, meant that their final game, against Norway in Boston, would be decisive. The maroon-clad team lost 2-0, and their first Olympic appearance ended in a first-round exit. France went on to win the Olympic tournament. In Qatar's first appearance in the athletics disciplines for which my father had come to Doha, Mansour Salah finished in 21st position in the decathlon. It was a promising start which in subsequent Olympics would culminate in a number of medals for the Qatari athletics team, confounding the clever tabloid journalist with his cheeky comment about 'needing Aladdin's lamp to turn the sons of the desert into world-class athletes'.

As Qatar began to participate more frequently in regional and international sporting events, my father would travel regularly to competitions and training camps with his athletes.

'At first, when he was told by his boss that there was no reason to take an athlete with such a meagre personal best to a regional competition, he paid for trips from his own pocket,' my mother remembered. 'He argued that without exposure to top competitions they would not improve. They started seeing the point of this and competing and travelling even internationally.'

At a regional competition in Bahrain in 1984, his belief in the Qatari athletes paid off. The best shot putter in the group, Abdullah Saad, threw the heavy metal ball 14.40 metres to win the competition and set a new Qatari record. In 1982 my dad had won the German indoor championship with a throw of 18.80 metres, but now he was beginning to find the right approach to get his athletes to throw further and train harder. In an interview with a local newspaper during his summer holiday in Germany that year, he said: 'The most important thing is to know how to handle your athletes in a personal manner. If you do, they are just as motivated and want to achieve results as much as the athletes in Germany. None of my athletes have missed their training sessions.'

Training in the hot summer months was difficult in Qatar, so training camps were organised abroad in Europe. One black-and-white photo which Dad pulled out of the many dusty grey metal boxes in the garage shows his team, around fifteen smiling Qatari athletes with stylish '80s hair-dos, visiting the Bayer factory in Leverkusen. Another trip to Germany particularly sticks in my mind, when he took his shot putters and discus throwers to a training camp in Dusseldorf, and my elder brother Hans and I were allowed to join them on the bus ride. There could be nothing more exciting for us boys than being with the athletes in that bus as we headed to their training camp with its green fields and perfect facilities. The athletes sang on the way to training. We joined in the chant, even though we didn't know the Arabic words. Then we watched as Dad put them through their paces on the training fields.

'Watch out, kids, don't walk on the fields when they are throwing,' he warned us, as he must have warned Evaristo's players a few years earlier. We were always careful to comply, having heard the story of the football stars who almost got hit by flying metal discs.

Back in Doha there were also still many challenges, from families not wanting their sons to be involved in sports, to basics such as the sporting attire the athletes wore.

'Sport in those days was done mostly in closed spaces in the stadium, and the general public was not really aware of the benefits,' my father remembers. 'The exposure to the public changed with athletics, since our middle- and long-distance runners had to use the roads for training. Especially in the hot climate they ran in shorts, which angered many people passing in cars. They used their horns to express their anger and sometimes they even tried to run over the athletes with their cars.'

A solution to this unusual problem was found in the end, even if the compromise gradually became unnecessary. 'Finally we had to oblige all athletes to wear long trousers if they used the road for training. The background for this behaviour was that by tradition you should not expose skin to other people. Some of the athletes also refused in the beginning to train in short trousers or wear t-shirts.'

My father's job was often pioneering work. Sometimes it meant actually getting a bag of cement and building something new with his own hands. My father built the first throwing ring in Qatar together with his athletes, bringing the cement in a big sack and creating the circular space, with a small ledge as boundary, from which the shot put and discus are thrown into the distance.

'So, boys, today we are going to build a throwing ring,' my dad said in his heavily German-accented English at one of those early practice sessions.

He got a lot of confused looks and puzzled glances at the bag of cement which he had hanging casually over his shoulder.

'Let's build a house,' he said to them in broken Arabic.

'A house, are you sure?' they asked him – also in Arabic.

It was all as clear as mud, so he started mixing the cement and they all joined in to build the throwing ring with him.

'This is not a house, but it looks good,' one of his athletes said afterwards. They shook hands and started using their newly created throwing ring.

Slowly but surely, brick by successful brick, the young sporting nation of Qatar was building the foundations for a major breakthrough. Having missed out on qualification for the 1986 World Cup in Mexico, the 1990 edition in Italy now beckoned.

1989. SINGAPORE
Miracle men wear maroon

In football, there is something about the colour of a shirt which can take on magical qualities. If you wear it your way, and make it your own, you become known for it and associated with it. The Dutch are outrageous orange. The French beautiful blue. The Spanish tiki-taka red. The Germans winning white. And the Brazilians are wonderful yellow. That one game where Qatar wore yellow shirts was merely an exception, despite the 'Brazilians of the Gulf' nickname, which they probably didn't mind very much. But there was really only ever one colour the Qatari team could make their own. The maroon shirt. Miracle men wear maroon.

There was one player in particular who was making that shirt and that colour his own during Qatar's next phase of football development. If during the early days of football in Qatar Khattab Al Daffa was admired for his displays in maroon, during the 1980s there was a single, skilful striker who was the key to the country's footballing dreams. Mansour Muftah was not tall for a forward, coming in at around 1.78 metres. He just knew exactly how to get the ball into the back of the net, from every angle and every position. He was Qatar's equivalent of Gerd Muller, the famed German striker. When Muftah eventually retired from international football in 1990 at the age of 35, he had made his name as *the* man in maroon. In eighty-nine games for his country, he is said to have scored fifty-three goals wearing the maroon shirt. He helped his country to the final of the 1981 World Military Cup, also hosted by Qatar, and twice finished as runner-up in the Gulf Cup: in 1984 and 1990, the former a heartbreaking penalty shoot-out loss in the decisive game against Iraq after Muftah had scored four goals in the tournament, including the equaliser in extra time in the final. Brazilian coach Evaristo was an important mentor throughout his glittering career, as Muftah commented: 'He was undoubtedly the most influential person in my playing career.'

As that long and illustrious career came slowly to a close, Muftah had some more real highlights on home soil to look forward to: in 1988 the Asian Cup was held in Qatar for the first time. This continental tournament brought together the top teams in Asia and was held in December 1988 at two venues in Doha. In a tough five-team group from which only two would progress to the semi-finals, Muftah scored twice for Qatar, including in the final match in which they beat Japan with a convincing 3-0 scoreline. He also handed out three assists to his team-mates, but they finished a point behind Iran and did not reach the semi-finals.

Qatar was gaining important hosting experience, but the crowning moment to Muftah's unique career was still proving elusive. Fourteen trophies in national football, countless scoring records and four Qatari golden boot trophies stood in his glittering cabinet (including a hat-trick of top scorer trophies from 1981-1984, an award which has since been named after him in recognition of his contribution to Qatari football), but he craved a big success with his beloved national team. It almost came the year after the Doha Asian Games, in 1989. I was just five at the time, and had not yet become as hopelessly addicted to football as I would be a few years later.

The World Cup the following year in Italy would have just two Asian teams competing. Qatar had reached the final round of the Asian qualifiers, held in Singapore in October 1989. Never had Qatar, which had been attempting to reach the World Cup since Argentina 1978, been so close to that elusive dream. Ahead of Mexico 1986 they had been edged out by Iraq, but they left that team behind them now and progressed to the six-team round-robin final stage. A goalless draw with eventual qualifiers South Korea was followed three days later by a 1-1 draw against Saudi Arabia, in which Muftah notched Qatar's goal and kept alive the World Cup dream. There followed a loss to North Korea and a draw with the UAE, and so the next game against China absolutely needed to be won for Qatar to remain in the race. Qatar trailed behind after a late goal for China, but first Mahmoud Soufi, and then Muftah with a dramatic late winner, had Al Ennabi agonisingly close to Italia 1990. If the UAE lost at the same time to South Korea, then Qatar was going to the World Cup. But that game ended in a draw; Qatar had needed just a single point more to qualify. It was a heart-breaking way for Qatar's fans to end a decade which had begun in such spectacular fashion in Australia. The Maroons had almost achieved their second miracle, but they would need to wait two more years for it to come to pass.

'The sports development in the '80s was slow but steady,' my father said, looking back on his early days as a coaching pioneer in Qatar. 'But one factor was there right from the beginning, and I think it was important for the developments that followed. His Highness Sheikh Hamad, in those days the Heir Apparent (Crown Prince) of Qatar and soon to become Amir, or ruler, was very interested in sport, and continuously and in many ways encouraged the developments we see today. He opened up the military for sport in order to draw from a bigger pool of potential athletes, and his keen interest was manifested as well in the fact that he knew all our athletes by name.'

Plenty of new names were just waiting to emerge in the coming years. Football in particular had come a long way since the early days of Al Daffa's first kicks of the socks ball. The Maroons had come within an inch of qualifying for Italia 1990, but the next decade would be a golden one for sports in Qatar. It was ironic, then, that precisely at this most promising of times we were packing our suitcases once more, this time heading for a country even smaller than Qatar. Our time in Doha, the city where I was born in 1984, had come to a premature end.

For the first six years of my life, Qatar and the Middle East were a safe and secure home, filled with the relaxed sounds of childhood laughter, camels munching rhythmically in the desert, and the softly lapping waves of the Arabian Gulf. All that changed in 1990, when we moved the short distance across the sea to the tiny island state of Bahrain. Within months, the background sounds in my life were those of air raid sirens, the shuffling shoes of my classmates heading down into the air raid shelter, and the hectic screeching of tape being stretched over the glass of our windows at home as we feared the worst from Saddam Hussein's Scud missiles. We learned who Iraq's dictator was from the television. There was 24/7 news coverage of the war, which seemed to come knocking right at our door. We heard that Saddam was looking to take over other countries like Kuwait, and discovered that Bahrain was well within range of his dreaded missiles. As young kids, we were shocked to hear that there was every possibility of there being gas inside those Scud missiles. So yes, moving country at the age of just six was quite a change for me in every way.

We moved to the Bahraini capital, Manama, just before the first Gulf War broke out, because my dad had lost his job in Doha. Along with a number of other foreign coaches, he had been asked to leave as part of a change of management, although as a youngster I did not understand much of the reasoning behind it. After a few months in Germany living with Grandpa and Grandma, Dad quickly found a new job with Bahrain's national athletics team.

The six Krug family members arrived in Bahrain with a colourful collection of suitcases and boxes and moved into a hotel in the centre of the city, where Dad once again liked to clear the morning buffet with his giant appetite. The hotel management must have noticed and complained, because we soon moved out to a residential area surrounded by high walls – a 'compound' – by the sea. There was a tennis court in our compound where Mom and Dad used to play sometimes, and we would watch them hit the ball back and forth over the white net and laugh at missed shots. If we were lucky we'd get to hit a few balls ourselves when they were having a break. On one side of the compound there was a long, winding road which led to the city. On the other two sides there was the coastline, with a beautiful array of little crystalline pools above the rocky shore containing tiny crabs that scuttled away quickly before we could nab them. At the back of the compound was an adventurous-looking mangrove swamp with thick vegetation that we'd never seen in Qatar.

There was a skateboard ramp in the middle of the compound, and the four of us kids became expert skateboarders, taking it in turns to race up and down the ramp and launch up into the sunny sky. My elder brother Hans was always the first to excel at any new sport we took up, while Tomi eagerly tried to copy his every move with the energy and enthusiasm of the youngest-born who wants to be involved in everything. On the skateboard ramp Hans started to drop in right from the top, and of course Tomi wanted to try the same. The outcome was often painful, but to his credit he never gave up. Meanwhile, my elder sister Anna led exploratory trips outside the compound which took us right into the middle of the expansive mangroves. We took to exploring the entire area, including the seashore, where we admired the crabs moving about in the crystal-clear pools of water.

Ours has always been a sporting family. Over the years, we have played almost as many different sports as we have lived in different houses. Anna would become the best squash player in the family, and was always out and about with her friends, getting involved in whatever was 'cool' at the time, while between us three brothers a healthy sporting competitiveness began to develop. We all took up the same sports at more or less the same time – perhaps, more than anything else, it was just practical for our parents to buy sporting equipment for the three of us in one fell swoop. And of course everyone wanted to excel at the same sport, whether it was skateboarding or tennis or football or table tennis. Hans was growing up to be the tallest of us, and he had the most innate sporting talent from an early age, while Tomi was the one who entered the fray with the fiercest determination, always starting with the disadvantage of being the youngest by three years and yet wanting to win all the time. In later years, when we all took to playing tennis competitively, it would mean direct match-ups on court between us. But for now it was playing and running and kicking in each other's company.

I started school in Bahrain at the age of six. When I walked into class on the first day I could understand virtually nothing. The lessons were in English. We'd been speaking German at home.

'This afternoon is your Arabic class too,' the teacher said, and it was like hearing Chinese.

I learned English very quickly, though, and loved reading the books assigned to us as homework. There was the book about the hungry crocodile which I'd read at home with Dad – he would read it with a German accent, and I'd re-read it with the English accent they taught us at school.

It was an idyllic family life in Bahrain, with beach trips and school routines and exploratory excursions to the mangroves, until the first Gulf War began. The images of Iraqi troops marching into Kuwait flickered across our television set one evening, and we realised a war had begun. Soon the Americans were starting to bomb Iraq with their vast array of warplanes, and sending troops to liberate Kuwait from occupation by Saddam Hussein's forces. The danger associated in the West with living in the Middle East had never worried us before. Now it came right to our doorstep and knocked ominously at our taped-up windows.

Saddam's Scud missiles were a threat to the entire region. Since they were said to contain chemical gas, we were told to tape up all of our windows in case any missiles came flying our way. Mom and Dad quickly pulled duct tape across all our windows and bought us a gas mask each, as recommended by the government. There we were, then, four little kids and our parents, all sitting hunched in the living room with our alien-like gas masks on. The wailing warning siren went off on a regular basis, meaning everyone had to run inside from wherever we were in the compound and take cover. On school days it was particularly daunting. Whenever the air raid siren went off the teacher said: 'OK, kids, let's quickly leave what we're doing and head down into the bomb shelter.'

We were all rushed into the bunker underneath the school building. There we crouched and read English comic magazines or played games until the all-clear siren went and we were allowed to come up into the daylight again. It was a nerve-wracking time, and one moment in particular got to me that year.

We had been playing on the skateboard ramp one afternoon when the siren went off. Hans was at the top of the ramp and casually dropped down to where we were standing and we all raced home. Dad shut up the doors, replaced the tape which had peeled off, and then counted the kids – we were all there. But someone was missing. Mom was not home.

'But where is Mom?' I asked, incredulous. We'd been told so many nightmarish stories of the missiles which were surely flying in our direction that there was no way I could accept my mother being out there alone.

'She's still at the fitness club; she was teaching a class, and I guess she is taking shelter there, unless she is already on her way,' Dad said.

'Can't you call her at the fitness centre?' I asked, monitoring the sky for any incoming missiles from Saddam Hussein's seemingly endless arsenal.

'I've tried about five times, but no one is answering,' he said. 'I'm sure it will be fine.'

In best Grandpa Ulf fashion, though, I was already imagining a thousand things which might possibly have happened and why they weren't answering the phone at the fitness club where my mom worked.

It was an agonising wait until she finally pulled into the driveway and we were all together in the supposed safety of the duct-taped house. Six members of the Krug family, all hoping that none of the wicked Scud missiles would drop from the sky anywhere near where we were sitting, gazing at each other with the long-nosed gas masks making us look like a family of aliens. We grew accustomed that year, 1990, to watching the news every night and seeing the latest images of the bombings and the troops moving across Kuwait to liberate the country. Then one day it was all over. In total only a few missiles had landed in Bahrain, but it was a frightening brush with a war which had ramifications across the entire region.

The devastating side effects of the first Gulf War also came washing up to the pools of formerly crystalline water outside our compound. The retreating Iraqi troops had set ablaze oil rigs en masse in Kuwait, and the sea outside our house was filled with black pools of oil, which found its way even into the small rocky ledge where the crabs now shuffled about uneasily. Hundreds of thousands of fish and sea animals died and were washed ashore, their joints clogged by the oil released by the retreating Iraqi army.

After a war-torn year in Bahrain, our family was uneasily looking to move again. It was as if the restless genes of the Bedouins had somehow found their way into our bones in those first years in Qatar. We'd never really grown accustomed to the little island state of Bahrain, and the war certainly didn't help to make us feel at home. Some families might have seen this as an ideal point to head back to the supposed safety of Europe. Instead, we were packing out suitcases and boxes again for a familiar destination. It was as if some magnetic force was pulling us all back to Doha, the sports capital in the making, which was attracting a sporting family magically back to its shores.

At around the time we were packing our boxes in Bahrain, Qatar's youngsters were again trying to make their mark on world football. Qatar's under-17 team had almost no expectations to live up to as they prepared for the 1991 FIFA U-17 World Championship in Tuscany, in beautiful Italy. Sure, their under-20 counterparts had reached the final in Australia ten years earlier, but many in the international football community still saw that as a freak result rather than the product of an ambitious and fast-developing sporting nation with a real passion for football.

Right at the start of the new decade, Qatar was about to take the next step on its sporting journey. The 1990s were for Qatar's later global sporting ambitions what a budding sportsman might call the formative years. Silky skills first became evident. Stamina and consistency were still to be fully developed. And much experience needed to be gathered in the coming decade. While far from the finished product, the first signs of Qatar's later spectacular development into a major sporting player began to emerge in the early 1990s.

It was around this time that I first represented my school at football – competing against kids from Qatar and a host of other nations as we played a three-school annual tournament. Football was the ideal way to settle back into the relaxing rhythm of life in Doha. We won the final by a single goal scored by my Jordanian school friend Mazen, a skilful player who was the star midfielder of our team. He swung in a right-footed corner which I can still see in my mind as it temptingly curled in from the left, and it was my job, positioned in the penalty box as the team's big striker, to have a swing at the ball. It may not have been much of a touch on the ball, or indeed any touch at all, but in best opportunistic striker fashion I claimed it anyway, running around with my arms up high in the universal gesture of celebration. We'd won the local three-school tournament. I was on top of the world.

In Italy, Qatar's youngsters also took to the pitch in search of sweet celebrations, preferably for goals they had actually scored themselves rather than just claimed to have scored. In their first group game, against Congo on 17 August 1991, Qatar didn't manage to get on the scoresheet, but they earned their first point of the tournament by holding the African side to a 0-0 draw. Only a game later, though, the Qataris were in trouble as an early goal from Jorge Toledano gave group favourites Mexico a 1-0 win. The maroon-clad youth team therefore had to win their last group game, against Australia, to stand a chance of progressing. The pressure was palpable but they did just that, hitting the post twice before Jassim Al Tamimi notched the vital late goal in the 76th minute to let Qatar advance to the quarter-finals. He celebrated in style just as I had done in my little school tournament. Clearly Qatar's young footballers dealt well with pressure at the crucial moments.

That was again the case in the quarter-finals. Here, the favoured USA awaited. The Americans had won all three of their group-stage matches against top opposition, including Argentina and hosts Italy. No one expected the underdogs from Qatar to seriously challenge them for a place in the semi-finals. It turned out to be another stunning triumph for the Al Ennabi juniors. Ahmed Saif Bu-Hendi curled in a magnificent free kick on the quarter-hour mark to equalise Brian Kelly's third-minute opener for the Americans. Qatar's youngsters were clearly the more comfortable team on the ball, honouring their nickname of 'Brazilians of the Gulf'. A fantastic picture taken precisely the moment after the equaliser shows the boys in maroon celebrating in a jumping and ecstatic bundle, while an isolated American defender looks around in desperate search of an explanation. None would be forthcoming. Qatar won the game on penalty kicks and was now just a step away from another final.

The football world would once again take note of Qatar's youngsters. A difficult game against Ghana awaited. The African side had upset Brazil in the previous match, but Qatar held their own against the highly praised Ghanaian team for much of the game. It ended in a goalless draw, and once again it was a penalty shoot-out that decided the outcome. This time though, luck was not on Qatar's side. They missed two spot kicks and eventually finished the tournament in fourth place. Still, to finish in the top four U-17 nations in the world was another major success for a small nation like Qatar. It had been a fine start to what would turn out to be a golden sporting decade. Now what was needed and desired was for that junior success to be translated to the senior level.

Just a short flight away from Italy, FC Barcelona were starting to shape a new era as they put in place the foundations of a future footballing philosophy. Dutch coach Johan Cruyff won the Spanish league with the Catalan club that year. It was in Barcelona that the next major success for Qatari football would take place a year later. It was to be perhaps their biggest international triumph.

1992. BARCELONA
Mubarak Mustafa's golden header

My father seemed to sense that Qatar was the place for a sporting family to be. After that troubling year in Bahrain, he had been offered a job leading the sports clubs run by the country's state-owned oil company in Doha, and he gladly accepted the offer. When people ask me nowadays what else I have seen of the region, the answer is that that brief stint in Bahrain was in fact our only foray into any of the neighbouring countries. I have never been to Dubai or Abu Dhabi, and don't intend to go any time soon.

It is as if the rivalry between Gulf cities and states has led each to develop its own particular skillset, and Qatar has decided to make sport its calling card. Aside from Bahrain, the only Middle Eastern country I have been to is Jordan, where I was sent by work in 2015 to attend a football conference next to the Dead Sea. The rustic surroundings on the road trip to the conference reminded me of our earliest days in Doha. Back in the days when things were simple and there was nothing much to do aside from head to the beach every weekend in Dad's old blue Toyota Land Cruiser, which he'd had for so many years that it seemed like part of the very architecture of the city.

Fleeting visitors to Qatar often fail to see the real essence of this country I call home. They might see an array of shiny Italian, English and German sports cars in a rainbow of flashy colours driving up and down Doha's waterfront Corniche, or the nearby man-made island called The Pearl, and believe those sports cars to be representative of the entire country. When I think of our quintessential Qatari car it is that faded blue Toyota Land Cruiser with the white stripes along the side, which Dad held on to for far too long. It is not the glitz and glamour which makes this country so special, but the remarkable little human stories of every shape and size and colour which you find around every street corner. One visiting British diplomat put it quite aptly when he called Doha 'the greatest melting pot on earth'. So in those exciting early '90s years we were melting comfortably back into the fascinating Arabian teapot that was Doha. With the unwanted drama of the Gulf War slowly subsiding there was precious little to do. This was around the time that Qatar was labelled 'one of the most boring places on earth' by a renowned travel guide, but as young kids we didn't have any problems at all with the quirky places our father used to take us for trips when Mom (understandably, with four kids) wanted everyone out of the house as quickly as possible.

'Off you go, then,' Mom would call through the house at the Al Messilah compound where we now lived, near the fittingly named Sports Roundabout – the same compound Evaristo had lived in early on in his Doha career, as he would remind me many years later as I drove him through the completely transformed city.

It always seemed to be that faithful old car which took us places. One day it drove us out to Doha Zoo with Dad's mother Dora, who was visiting us from the now unified Germany. The four of us kids piled excitedly out of the back of the car and into the zoo, where an ageing lion kindly decided to pee all over me from the safety of his cage. I screamed heartily, but at least all the others got a good laugh out of it, and of course Dad captured it all on his trusty shoulder-mount camera for some classic family viewing.

Another year the blue Land Cruiser took us up north to visit an Arabian horse farm with Grandpa Ulf, who was visiting us from Cologne. He had always loved horses, so my dad arranged for us to visit the stable where his Qatari friend kept his collection, and where

Grandpa could stroke their beautiful black noses and feed them little sugar cubes just as he did in Germany. In this way the years passed, and the trusty old blue car remained with us, chugging along reliably until the first warning signs started to appear on the dashboard. At least once a week we'd go on our customary beach trips to the south. But after a number of years the car engine started to heat up too quickly, and a red warning sign would light up on the dashboard.

'It's giving me the flashing red light again,' Dad would state matter-of-factly. 'We may have to pull over and give the engine some time to recover.'

So he'd pull over on the side of the long road, where there was nothing to either left or right but endless, utterly beautiful desert.

'Dad, is the engine going to explode again?' Anna asked, only slightly concerned.

'Don't worry, I just need to pour in some more cooling water,' Dad replied, and got out to yank up the bonnet and give his beloved car a quick sip of water.

'Dad, why don't we just buy a new car?' Tomi asked, succinct as always, from the back seat, his baseball cap on backwards.

'No, we don't need a new car. This one takes us places just fine,' Dad replied stubbornly.

That trusty car did indeed always get us to exotic locations – it took us over flowing sand dunes and through rocky terrain on fossil hunts – and it took us to school and to the Falcon Club, the sports club where my parents now worked in the fitness centre. It never stopped driving. Despite occasional problems when the engine overheated, that car had probably covered the length of Qatar a thousand and one times over. That was why my dad never wanted to get rid of it, even though we all teased him about it, as I'm sure did many others. But he stayed the course with it, and took it, with us, to his favourite mechanic in the Industrial Area when it needed to be fixed again, as it always did. He trusted it innately, as he would a brother.

On one occasion we had to leave the car in the Industrial Area garage overnight, and they gave us a Mercedes as a replacement. It felt strangely unnatural as we drove home in a car seen all over the world as quintessentially German. Dad looked completely out of place driving it. It was with some relief that he got back into his old blue Toyota a few days later and headed to work at Khalifa Stadium with a toot of the horn.

'So long, kids,' he shouted out of the window. 'Be nice to Mom or she'll send us on another desert trip. And we all know this car can't handle many more of those before it finally retires.'

It was this kind of trusting relationship that Qatar called upon when looking ahead to the Barcelona Olympics in 1992, another opportunity to drive forward the country's sporting ambitions. Although the Olympic football format can be somewhat confusing to outside observers, the prestige of the Olympics undoubtedly gives the tournament a special standing. The current rule restricting teams to fielding only under-23 players, with a maximum of three overage players allowed, was first introduced at the Barcelona Olympics. Qatar, having qualified in style as one of only three Asian representatives, was now eager to improve on its only other showing, the first-round exit in Los Angeles in 1984, the year I was born in Doha.

So a trusted name was commissioned to deliver something special in Barcelona, a name associated with many of Qatar's early football successes: Evaristo de Macedo. The widely respected Brazilian had had brief stints coaching other teams, including Iraq at the 1986 World Cup in Mexico, but was now working hard once more to get the 'Brazilians of the Gulf' into top form entering the tournament. And they entered it with a bang. In a tricky-looking group including hosts Spain and flamboyant Colombia, the Qataris opened their campaign with a 1-0 victory over Egypt in the Barcelona suburb of Sabadell on 24 July 1992. The sporting hero of the day was Mubarak Mustafa, who would go on to become the next great goal-scorer for the Qatari national team. Mustafa can be seen, by way of comparison, as Qatar's Thierry Henry. Mustafa was the graceful gazelle, dashing through the penalty box and scoring goals before the defenders could even locate him.

'My greatest skills as a footballer were my speed and an eye for the goal,' Mustafa told me many years later. 'But I also had the quality to make opportunities for others.'

On this occasion Mustafa showed his goal-scoring touch at a critical moment. The skilful, rapid striker popped up in exactly the right spot just fifteen minutes before the end of the game against Egypt to hand Qatar a famous victory. A perfectly weighted cross from the left wing was met with a majestic jump and pragmatic downward header. It was textbook stuff. Mustafa then easily outpaced all his team-mates across half the pitch to celebrate with the coaching staff. It was perhaps one of the most important goals in Qatar's football history, and Mustafa knew it.

With two points under their belts (the three points per win rule had yet to be introduced at this stage in world football), coach Evaristo stressed the vital importance of the next game against Colombia just three days later in the same stadium. Colombia had received a 4-0 thrashing from hosts Spain in Valencia a few days earlier. In that match, a young Pep Guardiola scored Spain's opener from an indirect free kick after just ten minutes. This was the tournament where the back-pass rule was first introduced, no longer allowing goalkeepers to pick up with their hands a back-pass from one of their own team's players. This caused some initial confusion among the players and led to three goals from indirect free kicks, including this goal by Guardiola.

Football would later bring the Catalan midfielder to the shores of Qatar, just before he embarked on the most successful four-year coaching stint in FC Barcelona's history. But for now Guardiola was just a young player showing signs of great promise at his home Olympics. And astute coach Evaristo was aware that a result in

Qatar's last game, against the highly fancied Spaniards, would be a difficult undertaking.

The entire Qatar expedition was focused on the Colombia match. In a tense encounter in which Colombia relied on flashes of brilliance from Faustino Asprilla, the skilful forward who would make his name in world football at Parma and Newcastle United, the South Americans took the lead just after the hour mark. The goal was scored by Victor Aristizabal, who also became a fine player for Colombia's national team and later joined Spanish side Valencia just down the road from Barcelona.

Clearly the Colombian team had plenty of talent, but Qatar's golden generation believed in their skills too. As the clock wound down and only minutes remained to look for an equaliser, Qatar needed to draw once more upon steely reserves of self-conviction. A minnow in world football might have been content to keep a respectable scoreline against the talented Colombians. But Qatar's mentality was not that of a minnow. Perhaps buoyed by memories of the country's 1981 and 1991 youth team successes, they went in search of an equaliser. It came just two minutes before the final whistle. Mahmoud Soufi, another key member of the successful Al Ennabi team of the next decade, sent the Colombian side into shock with his late goal. The South Americans would lose their last match to Egypt, while Qatar ended the group stage with a respectable 2-0 loss to Guardiola's Spain. It was enough for Evaristo's team to progress to the quarter-finals.

A year after their youth success dubbed the 'Wonder of Tuscany', Qatar now had the 'Miracle of Barcelona'. Qatar was among the eight top nations in world football at these Olympics. Some statisticians even placed the team at number six, taking goal difference into account. In the quarter-final match that followed, Evaristo's team took on Poland. By all accounts they gave another spirited performance against the powerful Poles, who would later reach the final and come within a whisker of winning the tournament.

The first of August 1992 saw the Qataris run out through the tunnel and up into the legendary Camp Nou Stadium in Barcelona, one of the most renowned football grounds in the world. Some twenty years later the names of first Qatar Foundation and then Qatar Airways would be printed across the iconic blue-and-red striped FC Barcelona football shirts and the stadium itself thanks to the most lucrative sponsorship deal in the world. This was to be the scene of a tactical battle of grand proportions.

In 2010 I drove from Valencia to Barcelona and back in an epic single-day road trip with my lovely Colombian family-in-law, my wife and grandmother-in-law in the back seat and Uncle Pacho driving at, and even beyond, the speed limit so we could make it to Camp Nou in time for kick-off. It was totally crazy, something that could only have been brought about by my longstanding obsession with football, and my desire to see a live game at this legendary stadium for the first time. Entering the stadium is an awesome experience. From the outside, Camp Nou looks almost small, somehow in contrast to everything you have heard about it. On the inside, however, it shatters your every expectation. Walking up the stairs and arriving inside, the sheer height of the stands makes you shudder – they seem to reach all the way up to the golden-blue sky.

You need to blink a few times to take it all in: the green pitch, the grandeur of the biggest sporting occasion you have ever experienced, the chants which reverberate through the stadium at a 21:30 late-night kick-off in the balmy Barcelona evening. Spanish life starts up again late in the evening. The exciting Barcelona day is fading magically into night, and the stadium is awash with a million tiny colours, all fighting for your recognition.

Qatar was ready to walk out into the biggest match of its young sporting history.

Opposing styles came face to face that night. The Polish team was the expected highly organised and well-oiled unit, while Qatar put forward their own skilful set of players, whom coach Evaristo had once more shaped into a formidable side. According to the official technical report, there followed a match which contained 'the brilliant efforts of Qatar's outstanding individual players. A fascinating battle ensued in which the Arabs held their own surprisingly well until a Wojciech Kowalczyk goal just before half-time heralded the decision.'

The only surprise for coach Evaristo that day was that his team did not find the equaliser, as they had done against Colombia some days earlier. Qatar again showed that they were more than ready for the biggest sporting occasion on the grandest stage possible, pressing the Polish team back into their own half and unleashing a period of prolonged pressure that could well have brought about the equaliser. It did not, however, and the Polish side countered well to settle the match after 74 minutes, Marcin Jalocha scoring the crucial second goal to make it 2-0. The Olympic medal dream was over for Qatar's football team. But along the way they had impressed many in world football with their clever, spirited style of play. The Poles were also an outstanding side, as they proved again by dispatching Australia to the tune of 6-1 in the semi-finals. Later they came agonisingly close to winning the final against Spain, only to lose out at the very last minute to the ecstatic hosts. Pep had found his Barcelona gold.

For Barcelona as a city, the hosting experience transformed not just the heart of the Catalan capital but also the city's entire image, marking it out as a hip, desirable destination for years to come. Doha, the city where Evaristo's team received a hero's welcome upon their return in 1992, was at the time still a quiet town with a single small shopping mall in addition to its traditional markets. But thirty years later, in 2022, Doha will be looking for the same transformative effect on both city and image after its own mega event.

In the whole Olympic tournament Qatar had lost only to the two finalists. It was an outstanding result for the country. The pride of its successful football team returning home was doubled by Qatar's first-ever Olympic medal, won by 1500-metre runner Mohamed Suleiman. The small-framed middle-distance runner put in an impressive dash to the finish line to claim a much-celebrated bronze medal for Qatar. The sporting decade had begun in the best possible manner for our adopted home nation. Here was that success at world level which the German tabloid just a decade earlier had dismissed as a distant dream needing the help of 'Aladdin's magic lamp'. It seemed that all we needed was hard work and the meticulous planning which gives you a sporting chance in any arena.

Now, coming up, we had the perfect opportunity to transform those age-restricted successes into senior team triumphs in the regional sphere: the 1992 Gulf Cup in Qatar.

1992. DOHA
The falcon that swooped from the mountains

Meeting Mubarak Mustafa for the writing of this book was an inspirational moment, not only for the depth of knowledge and insight he gave, but also because of his wise and gracious manner. We met one warm day at Katara Cultural Village in Doha, next to the mosque and just a short walk away from the football history exhibition he had been proudly showing me that day. It contained his most important football memorabilia, as well as that of some of his former team-mates, and included a classic maroon Qatar shirt he had worn with the number 20 on the back.

Mubarak spoke in Arabic, but by then I had learned enough of the language to have short exchanges with him and he smiled at this, as he did at the fact that I had been born in Doha and watched him play numerous times as a youngster. It seemed somehow magical to him, as did the fact that I was writing a book about Qatar's football history. He gave me all the time I needed and answered every one of the many questions I put to him.

We walked around the exhibition, and at times he pointed out names and photos of players in the team of the legendary coach Evaristo, or 'Fra-risto', as he pronounced it with a nostalgic smile.

Before we started our interview, Mustafa proudly showed me one of the many medals he had won — one for athletics rather than football.

'When I was young, I did both, athletics and football,' he recalled. 'Sometimes I even trained in both sports on the same day — until the president of the football club found out, and then he got very angry, and that was when I focused only on football.'

I told him of my father's journey as an athletics coach in the country as we settled down in the low red sofas across from each other.

'I'd like to thank you for this, and your father for what he has contributed to sport in the country,' Mustafa said. 'It feels like you are one of us, a real sporting family.'

Then he began speaking about his earliest days in football in Qatar, and said, with eyes wide open to show just how important the sport already was back then, that the game was 'hugely popular in the country'.

'I went to school near Al Arabi Club, and back then the clubs played and trained in schools because they had better facilities for football. We used to play with the club for training sessions, and the best players were presented with small booklets containing information about some of the Brazilian legends of the game. When I first joined the team I had an Egyptian coach, and he gave me the chance to play one day. In my first game, I scored six goals. From then on, the club believed in me.'

The young Mustafa rose through the ranks at his club and soon caught the eye of coach Evaristo, who selected him for the Olympic team which qualified for the 1992 Barcelona Olympics. The tournament was Mustafa's first for Qatar, and he subsequently became a national hero as he scored that headed winner against Egypt in Sabadell which allowed his side to reach the quarter-finals at Camp Nou.

'Evaristo was very important in my career, because he built a strong personality within me; he instilled in me courage and independence, and no player under him left the pitch without having given it their all,' the former Qatar striker reminisced about his first national team coach.

'To reach Camp Nou as the team from Qatar, where we had a

small population and were not a famous country at the time, to play there was a very significant achievement for us all.'

After Mustafa and the team returned to Doha that summer, his family was visited by local newspaper journalists who wanted to hear all about the new goal-scoring hero. As our conversation moved from the past to the future I asked the graceful striker whether he thought the young team being prepared by Qatar for 2022 would also stand a chance of surprising the world, as his team had done thirty years previously in Barcelona.

'Do you know what you will eat in 2022?' he asked me with a mischievous smile. 'In football it is very hard to predict how well a team will do in the future. What I know for sure is that Qatar will have a competitive team which will honour the name of this country. I can also guarantee that in terms of organisation and facilities, everything will be spectacular. People will remember Qatar fondly after the World Cup.'

People in Qatar remember Mustafa fondly too. In the tournament which was just on the horizon after Barcelona 1992, he would gain the nickname which stayed with him for the remainder of his career.

'I became known as "Senyari", a type of falcon which is very rare and beautiful, and can only be found at the top of mountains. A commentator who is very famous in Qatar gave me the nickname after one game where I scored a lot of goals for Qatar, and ever since then it has stuck. I've won a lot of awards in my career, even been awarded the IOC lifetime Fair Play award for not receiving a single yellow card in my career. My philosophy throughout my career was always very simple. You need to have dedication and love what you do.'

As 1992 came to an end, Qatar's goal-scoring falcon was about to land one of his most important titles, and the country's first-ever football title at senior level.

1992. KHALIFA INTERNATIONAL STADIUM
Evaristo's legacy

History was always one of my favourite subjects at school. From the time we entered primary school at Doha Independent School, the small white single-storey building with the curly-haired headmistress called Mrs Williams, I took a liking to the subject. According to Mom there was a split right down the middle in our family when it came to enjoying school: Anna and I were always extremely eager to go along and learn new things, while Tomi and Hans preferred the days when they could stay at home and plan impromptu excursions. It went to such extremes that in the early days my father was regularly called back in to school to try and find Tomi, who had snuck out of class to try and run back home. He never got very far, but to his credit he kept trying.

Meanwhile, I was fascinated by the breadth of topics we were taught in that first school in Qatar. We were assigned a project about ancient Egypt, and I put an incredible amount of work into making sure that the booklet I produced was as close as I could get to a perfect impression of life under Tutankhamun.

Later, as we four Krug kids gradually migrated the hundred steps or so across to the two-storey secondary school building of Doha College, my love for the subject continued. I had a teacher of history who was entirely crazy about football, which was a perfect combination for me. His name was Mr Green, but he was a Red. A fanatical Liverpool fan, he made sure everyone knew about his passion. His other passion was history; without it, he used to say, you cannot seriously draw any conclusions about the present day. The very same school, just a few hundred metres away from Al Sadd Sports Club, turned out to be something of an incubator for Qatar's young generation leading the preparations for FIFA World Cup Qatar 2022™ some two decades later, including the Secretary-General of the Supreme Committee for Delivery and Legacy, Hassan Al Thawadi. While all that still lay in the distant future, Qatar was beginning to take a liking to hosting major events.

The Gulf Cup held at Khalifa International Stadium in 1992 represented a chance to bring together sporting and hosting success, at the venue which had come to symbolise Qatar's increasingly global sporting ambitions.

Some months had passed since the historic summer in Barcelona. The cooler winter months were the time when the tournament was to begin in Doha, with the opening match between Qatar and Oman set for 27 November. At the last Gulf Cup, in 1990, a German coach named Uli Maslo, who had managed Dortmund a decade earlier, had been in charge. But for this tournament, on home soil, there was a real expectation that the team Evaristo had formed into a winning unit at the Barcelona Olympics could do something special.

The tournament featured six regional teams, with politics playing a hand in reducing the number of teams by one. Iraq was excluded from the tournament for its 1990 invasion of Kuwait, which had caused the 1991 Gulf War that had us scampering into bunkers and taping up the windows in Bahrain.

That 1992 Gulf Cup was to be the last major legacy of a man who has found a permanent place in the hearts of the Qatari people. When I asked Obaid Juma, the legendary Al Sadd defender, and later commentator with Al Kass sports television in Doha before he sadly passed away in November 2018, his opinion on who was the best Qatar national team coach of all time, the answer came automatically, without the need to consider any other options: Evaristo de Macedo. Or, as they pronounce it here in Qatar, Fra-risto.

'I assisted him for some time before the 1981 finals in Australia,' Juma recalled between long, furious puffs on his customary cigarette. 'When he called the boys for training, he made them practise something over and over again. Until they had it automatised in their brain. I remember he used to make them practise the offside trap for one hour. When he was finished, no one forgot it.'

It was the same kind of obsessive attention to detail which would mark Pep Guardiola's rise to the top of the world coaching pyramid a few decades later. For now, the home side trained obsessively to win a trophy which Qatar had never lifted before.

Qatar opened the tournament with a convincing 2-0 win over Oman at Khalifa Stadium on 27 November, and then went on an impressive winning streak. Their sixth-place finish at the Barcelona Olympics had worked wonders for the confidence of the team, and most notably for star striker Mubarak Mustafa. Three days later, they edged out neighbours Bahrain 1-0, followed by a thumping 4-0 win over Kuwait and a 1-0 victory over the UAE. By the time their last match, against Saudi Arabia, came around on 10 December, Qatar had yet to concede a goal in the tournament and were already champions in the purely round-robin format that was used that year. A 1-0 loss to Qatar's big neighbour could not dampen the ecstatic celebrations that took place in Doha for the new Gulf Cup champions. Qatar lifted the trophy for the first time ever at Khalifa International Stadium, which was fast earning itself a special place in Qatari sporting history.

The graceful striker Mustafa picked up both best player and top scorer trophies, and goalkeeper Ahmed Khalil completed the Qatari clean sweep by taking home the best keeper award.

Qatar had put itself on the regional map by winning the tournament. Its outstanding results that year also helped to propel the country up the FIFA world rankings. In August 1993, the country was ranked as high as 51st by FIFA. But Qatar wanted more than that. The country's leaders were developing an ambitious sports strategy that incorporated more than just football. Just a few months after Qatar winning the Gulf Cup football tournament on home soil, the world's top tennis stars visited Qatar for the first time, for the first ATP Qatar Open.

For the people of Qatar, their team's triumph in the 1992 Gulf Cup at home meant only one thing – wild celebrations. And there is only one way of celebrating a major football triumph in Qatar – people get into their cars, or rather on top of them, or start doing wild gymnastics leaning out of their car windows, and start honking wildly, playing loudly blaring music, waving flags and shouting for joy as they drive along the Doha Corniche at about two miles per hour. This is unfortunate for anyone in a hurry to get anywhere important on such a night, but a great deal of fun for anyone as intoxicated as most people here are by the game of football. There is one famous fan who has decorated his whole car in Qatar colours and memorabilia, and blasts out loud traditional music as he waves his sword out of the window. It is pure passion.

We've been caught up in a few such celebrations ourselves. One of those was in my dad's old ride, the trusty blue Toyota Land Cruiser, chugging slowly along the palm tree-lined road which he had first seen as an empty stretch of sand when he arrived in Doha. People all around us were waving Qatari flags, shouting out in joy and blasting their horns at an imaginary football god who might just have come on the long and unlikely journey halfway across the world from Brazil.

'Hey, Dad, is it the cooling water again, or why are we going so slow?' Tomi asked, tongue in cheek, from the back seat.

But this time it wasn't the engine's cooling water holding up our progress. It was a young nation celebrating its first-ever senior football triumph. Would more football triumphs follow for the boys in maroon? My dad honked the horn of his reliable blue 4x4, hoping instead that all the talented youngsters would make their way to his athletics team.

1994. KHALIFA TENNIS COMPLEX
Boris Becker and his sweaty towels

While the different houses we lived in throughout the years in Qatar were all enchanting in their different ways, we always had a major issue at home with the size of our shoe shelves. As a large sporting family, we had countless pairs of sports shoes fighting for limited space on the shelf. Some would inevitably be jammed in over others in the most haphazard way, resulting in shoes dropping out and consequently being shifted to an upstairs cupboard – the worst possible outcome, since you'd have to climb the stairs each time you wanted to wear them.

The traditional Qatari shoes for men, worn with the white thobe, are brown or black sandals with a single thick strap across the front, to which entire shops are dedicated in Doha. We didn't go to such stores, but for our shoes headed to Olympic Sports, a shop where Dad knew the owner and Mom would sit us down, one after another, to get us the trainers we needed.

On our parents' side there were Mom's purple and blue trainers which she wore to give aerobics classes in the women's gym at the Falcon Club, and in which she walked our numerous pets, did the shopping with us at Family Food Centre and generally did magical things to keep a six-person family ticking over on a daily basis. Then there were Dad's plain black throwing shoes with the flat-bottomed soles which he put on when he headed to the men's section of the fitness centre for training in the evenings. He also laced them up at weekends when he pulled on the shirt of Al Sadd Sports Club for athletics competitions, at which he still regularly won the shot put competition, even in his early forties. These shoes had no cushioning at all, because they were designed to optimise his centre of gravity and stability for those throws my father had perfected over the years.

We four kids started with a whole variety of general jogging shoes, of which I still seem to remember a model called 'Pumps', which had a large red button that apparently had some performance-enhancing effect if you pushed it often enough, but was actually probably just a smart marketing exercise. After a few years back in Doha, a new type of sports shoe was added to the family collection.

I was given my first tennis shoes as a gift for being a ball boy at the Qatar Open. They were standard-issue white shoes with a few blue stripes across the side.

Catch. One of the earliest sporting skills you learn as a youngster. There I stood at the baseline, next to the linesman. A towel was flying my way, drenched in sweat. As a wide-eyed ball boy I caught it gratefully, because it was the towel of Boris Becker, my first sporting idol.

Normally I read about his exploits in the newspaper on the way to school. My father has always loved reading the *Gulf Times*, Qatar's first English-language newspaper. He's been getting it since 1982 and still has it delivered to his house every day, to read with his morning coffee and bread from the Arab pastry shop on the corner of the petrol station next door. The *Gulf Times* started in 1978, initially as a weekly, but by February 1981 it had gone daily, and the following year my dad arrived and started reading it. Two decades later I would join the paper as an 18-year-old cub reporter with a keen interest in finding sports stories. But back in the days of the first Qatar Open tennis tournament I was a young schoolboy who idolised Boris Becker. In an age when instant results on the internet were still a far-off prospect, I'd wait eagerly until the trip to school each morning to read the news about Becker's latest feat in some tournament in Rome, Amsterdam, Tokyo or London.

If you wanted the news first on these school trips, it was crucial to grab the right seat in the old Toyota Land Cruiser. As we four kids piled into the car each morning, there was a certain magic about getting the front seat, not only for the usual bragging rights of sitting beside my father as he drove us to school, but also because of the newspaper. In those days there was no home delivery, so newspapers were bought from newspaper sellers who stood at traffic lights holding large bundles of papers bound up with criss-crossing string. My father paid the one Qatari riyal which the newspaper cost in those days, then as the lights changed he chucked it nonchalantly onto the top of the dashboard. Within an instant it had already been divided into four sections, not without the occasional heated argument.

I always tried to get my hands on the sports section first. And there it was, the news item which stated that Boris Becker had beaten Pete Sampras in the World Tour final in Frankfurt, or Stefan Edberg at the Australian Open, or some other great player in another famous triumph where he had 'employed his booming serve to great effect'. There would be a picture of him going for his famous diving volley. And then one day Boris Becker wandered out of the pages of the newspaper and onto Centre Court in Doha.

In January 1993, I was an enthralled spectator on a sold-out Centre Court at the Khalifa International Tennis and Squash Complex for the final match of the inaugural Qatar Open. Boris Becker and his Swedish rival Stefan Edberg had rocked into town like the superstars they were at the time, posing with camels and falcons. Becker did more than pose for photos and went on to win the tournament, lifting the golden trophy in the shape of a falcon. My English school friend Richard had got hold of some tickets and had one spare.

'Do you want to come and watch the final?' he asked, as we headed home from school one day in his father's green Range Rover.

Of course I did. We took our seats that evening close to the court and I marvelled at the players' skills.

'Look what they're doing with just a racket and their bare hands,' I whispered to Richard in the middle of a particularly impressive point.

'Wouldn't it be awesome if we could play like them?' Richard agreed, nodding as we watched the ball fly back and forth across the net. I decided that it would, and that I'd try it myself at the earliest opportunity.

It was an incredibly close final. Becker edged out Croatia's big-serving Goran Ivanisevic in three sets, with each set going right down to the wire. Then it was all over and the hugely popular German champion lifted the falcon trophy into the night sky. It was a momentous occasion for Qatar too, because it signalled the start of a concerted approach to bringing the world's best athletes and events to Doha on an annual basis.

A year later, instead of sitting in the stands or trying to catch the flying newspaper to find out about Becker's latest victories on court in exotic-sounding parts of the world, I decided I wanted to be there myself, on the Centre Court of the Khalifa Tennis Complex in Doha. Someone from the tournament had passed by our school inviting kids to sign up if they were interested in joining the teams of ball boys and girls for the event. I put my name down and was one of the youngest to do so, but I absolutely loved every minute of the experience. We'd had plenty of opportunities to learn the basic sporting skills in our family, and out on the practice court I was immediately identified as one of the most skilful catchers and throwers of the ball.

'Right, you're on one of our top teams, you go on the baseline and just keep catching the ball as reliably as you do,' Beryl, the woman in charge of selecting the teams, told me the day before the start of the 1994 Qatar Open tennis tournament. 'You're going to be on Centre Court. Just don't get nervous. You'll do a great job.'

The first matches, during the qualifying rounds, were on the outside courts. Then we were called in by Beryl.

'It's time. There's the door. Out you go, and do a good job as always.'

In my first pair of tennis shoes I walked onto the Centre Court and took my place on the baseline. Then Boris Becker walked out onto the court. In front of a sell-out crowd, and with spectators lining even the walkways to catch a glimpse of the German legend, I tossed him the ball when he nodded nonchalantly my way, or ran to bring him his sweaty towel when he did the swiping motion with his hand after a particularly difficult point.

At one stage I looked up, and there was my dad, nodding to me from a vantage point in the stands.

'How was it, son?' he asked in the car on the drive back home.

'Incredible – I've never felt anything like that atmosphere in my life. He was right there in front of me, and I tossed him the ball.'

'It was great to see you out there,' he said, and shifted the long gear stick forward. 'And it's getting kind of late. Maybe you should take the day off school tomorrow.'

We had always been a sporting family, but it was the coincidence of my friend's spare ticket and that early ball-boying experience which drew all four of us Krug kids toward the tennis courts, with their white lines and the black net separating adversaries. But in fact we had started out as a gymnastics family, wearing no shoes at all.

When we were still only small giant Germans, my father used to lie down on his back in the living room and bellow out in his deep voice: 'Anyone want to do some gymnastics today?'

Then it was always a race among the four of us to see who'd get to the living room first. Gymnastics basically consisted of us climbing all over him and being spun around like acrobats in a circus. Sometimes he would have two of us on each arm, and call out to Mom that he could lift her too. No one doubted this. It was all enormous fun. We'd take turns climbing up and down his strong arms, and then he'd say enough was enough and we'd all have to go to bed. He was always strict about bedtime and going to school. Mom would often let us stay home if we feigned sickness well enough to convince our dad.

'If you don't feel like going to school, stay home with me,' Mom said. Anna pushed this to the limit one day when she took a note to her teacher which she had seen in a joke book. It read: 'Anna missed school yesterday because her aim was bad.' The signature seemed to be that of my mother. The teacher compared it various times with previous genuine signatures from Mom, and they all seemed to confirm that either my sister was good at forging signatures or, as had indeed been the case, my mother had a sense of humour. Having received such an unusual note, the teacher in question – who, just to make matters worse, was of a mathematical bent and didn't deal much in the currency of humour – didn't know whether to laugh or cry. In the end he left it at a very British formal scolding and a note back home to my parents.

We loved Mom for letting us stay home when we wanted, but on the other hand she had a strict sense of morality and values. There was nothing wrong with staying home from school for a day if you wanted. But she always taught us to be honest, good-natured and humble human beings.

After having briefly been a skateboarding family during our year in Bahrain, we had returned to Doha and a city starting to put itself on the world's sporting map in a variety of disciplines. Soon we started entering, and winning, local junior tennis tournaments in Qatar. It was usually a Krug family clean sweep in the trophy ceremonies for the different age groups, so much so that the *Gulf Times* started writing about us as the 'family with the golden touch'.

'Courting success is family affair for the Krugs,' wrote local sports writer Anil John in the headline of a *Gulf Times* article about our family. Some years later he'd be my first boss in journalism when I started my apprenticeship with the paper. That year, the bespectacled journalist visited us at a training session at the Al Ahli compound tennis courts to write a piece in which he highlighted my father's enormous biceps, and his methodical planning of our tennis careers.

Dad certainly knew how to plan for success, just as he had done with his athletes over the years. Whenever a new tournament draw came out, my father would print it out and hang it on the fridge, with the route to the final already highlighted in yellow, and all the playing dates and times underlined so we wouldn't forget them.

'I've already highlighted your respective paths to the final,' he would say at lunch that day, putting the *Gulf Times* aside for a while to add: 'This year you have some difficult opponents, but I don't doubt that you can win everything again.'

I guess you never lose your competitive spirit, and he was always there in the stands at tournaments to support us and give us his tips: 'Just play your game, don't get distracted.'

And we didn't; the family built up an impressive trophy collection over those years, which eventually ended up as a heap of rusting metal in the storage room because they got too numerous and bulky. While we were lifting our first trophies on the tennis court, Qatar was starting to enter the international sports hosting scene. The Qatar Open tennis tournament marked the first of a wide range of annual international sports competitions that Qatar began to organise in the 1990s.

As a sporting country, Qatar must have felt as I did walking out onto the Centre Court and seeing Boris Becker sitting there on the bench: starry-eyed, excited, and learning eagerly as it went along. To be a good ball boy or girl you need a couple of essential qualities. In the weeks of training before the big tournament every year we were drilled in what we should and shouldn't do out on Centre Court, the holy grail of the tennis world, for which only the best ball boys and girls were selected. You need coordination, safe hands on the ball, a sense of where the game is going, and above all to be almost invisible.

Like a good holding midfielder in football, ball boys in tennis are at their best when they aren't noticed at all. No tripping over flailing feet, no dropping balls when they come flying or rolling your way, and always have balls or towels ready for whenever the player needs them. In a way, this is what the hosting of a sporting event is also about – good coordination, safety, and a sense of what the sport is about, as well as being almost invisible. The sign of success for the host is if the conversation is all about the action on the court or pitch. And while I tried to find my feet on the tennis court, my father was helping the athletics federation get ready for the best athletes in the world to come to Doha every year.

The Qatar Athletic Grand Prix started up in the mid-1990s, and was held on a yearly basis. It was to become an annual moment of family excitement, as all of us headed together to sit in the stands on the large concrete slabs of the mighty Khalifa Stadium and look down at the athletes running, jumping and throwing their way into Qatar's sporting history books. To our left and right were groups of local fans, chewing on the salty 'haeb' nuts which were sold by vendors in little plastic bags. Sometimes some nut shells would fly our way, and we had to wave kindly and turn back to the action on the grass below. We were never allowed to eat any of those nuts ourselves because Mom was as meticulous about hygiene standards as she was about morals, and those plastic bags full of nuts didn't look anywhere near clean enough for her. We'd have a fantastic time anyway, my father popping along when he was not busy on the track, to explain what new personal or season's best this or that athlete had just achieved.

As the resident sports nerd in the family, I would nod in agreement and say 'ah, yes, Dad, that is impressive', even though I had no idea what he was talking about.

Tennis and athletics were just to be the start of Qatar's sports hosting offensive, an approach which had its origins in the early visits of Pele in 1973 and Muhammad Ali in 1971 to Doha Stadium.

Qatar as a country wanted to put itself on the map in a region which was still more often in the news because of conflict than for anything positive. Sport was a way to change such negative perceptions, and in a region where tiny Kuwait – only slightly bigger than Qatar – had so recently been briefly swallowed up by its big bullying neighbour Iraq, it was also a way of making people aware that the country existed. In the early 1990s Qatar had still to be discovered in the sports world, and even in general public awareness it barely existed. I remember vividly one remark from a snarky kid in Germany one summer, asking whether 'Qatar' was 'a washing powder'. The best way to describe it to those who did not know was by saying 'it's next to Saudi Arabia'. Even then some were confused.

The only thing clear to me at the time I was a ball boy was that I was in a very fortunate position, seeing my *Gulf Times* sporting idols in person at such close quarters. It didn't even matter getting hit by a tennis ball or two. A hugely powerful serve from Goran Ivanisevic – later to become Wimbledon champion right at the end of his career – hit me on the thigh in one match, but of course I didn't make a sound. It was, after all, an ace from the mighty Croatian. And the sweaty towel flying my way was a towel from Boris Becker.

We were all inspired. We played day and night. At our house in the Al Sadd area next to the villa of Khattab Al Daffa, the former football star, my father built us a makeshift tennis court in the front yard, and we hit the ball to each other across a loosely fixed net. It was our Wimbledon in the desert, and we were happy. Sometimes Khattab would come over as Boris Becker was mounting a heroic comeback from two sets down at Wimbledon, and my father would proudly explain to him that the German player was the best in the world, and would surely go on at least to reach the final.

I tried several times to meet Boris Becker while doing my research for this book, but it never quite materialised. Sometimes you meet your idols on the court but not in person, even many years later. When I saw him walking off Centre Court in Doha that year, with his trademark swagger and the Lotto shirt and ridiculously short shorts slowly disappearing from view, I made a vow to become a tennis player when I was big. But as always, life had plenty of surprises in store. One such surprise, a real underdog story which no one could have expected, would pull me away from the individual sport of tennis and toward the greatest team sport in the world.

In the middle of all this tennis mania sweeping through our family, I went to my first football match in April 1995. It was a game Dad took us to, and at the age of 11 I was suddenly inspired by a second sport. At the same time, just as our shoe shelf was filling up with tennis shoes, Qatar's sporting schedule was adding ever more types of footwear to the collection. The month I turned 11, April 1995, some of the best young footballers in the world were lacing their boots getting ready to take to the pitches of Qatar.

1995. AL AHLI STADIUM
The stars of the future arrive in Doha

The first game you attend with your father at a sport you love is always something special, and mine was all the more special given that it was a World Cup match in my hometown, and with the team that I supported playing. Even though it was 'just' the juniors, it might as well have been 1990 World Cup-winning captain Lothar Matthaus personally coming to visit.

'Hey, Dad, do you still remember that first game of football we ever attended together, back in 1995?' I asked my father recently.

'No,' he said, rather too honestly.

'Yes, you remember, we went to the under-20 World Cup, it was in Doha in April that year. Germany played. Against Costa Rica. You remember? At Al Ahli Stadium?'

'No, who won?' he said with a laugh. In his defence, he's held that lifelong grudge against football for taking the best athletes away from his beloved shot put and discus. And he's only ever watched football games with me because he knows I'm a football nutter. He'll even make expert observations to me about the game or the players, or the tactics employed by the coach, in order to feign interest. But that year, even though he did not remember it twenty-something years later, he did take me to my first game of football in the home of Doha's oldest club: Al Ahli Stadium.

Three weeks before it was due to host the 1995 FIFA World Youth Championship, Nigeria was hit by an outbreak of meningitis which meant it could not welcome the best young footballers in the world. FIFA now had a dilemma, with very little time to find a replacement venue. The budding sports nation of Qatar stepped in with a solution and offered to host the tournament. By this time I was already well on my way to becoming an addict, having been a nervous wreck watching USA 1994 on television, but going to my first live football game that April 1995 probably helped tip me over the edge.

It is difficult to look back and pinpoint the exact moment you became a football nutter, the type that makes summer travel plans based on the timetables of major football tournaments while pretending this is not the case. I don't think I can reasonably say there was a single match or moment in time that did it and left me irreversibly infected with madness for the round ball for the rest of my life. I suppose it is like falling in love – although you have an initial crush, and there are early signs that it could work out, it's the little tricks and goals and sliding tackles and step-overs along the way that eventually get you to the point where you can think of nothing and no one else but your team's next game against that third division side in the first round of the League Cup which no one else really cares about – and in all fairness you probably shouldn't either, but you do.

So instead of going straight back to the very first football game I ever attended, I'd like to look a little further back to diagnose the earliest signs of some kind of 'football disease', as my mother later jokingly called it, starting to seep into my brain. The very first symptom was triggered by some news that came over the airwaves through a car radio. It was on a warm summer day in 1990 when my father had taken us to his training session with the athletes. The venue was a few green fields in the middle of the desert, with Khalifa Stadium behind us. There was the old throwing ground with the small gym in the white bungalow to one side, and the pot-holed training pitch for my father's athletes to the left. Some beautifully lush, well-kept football pitches had been built to the right.

Sometimes we would go there to kick a ball around on those new football pitches and marvel at the fantastic state of the grass, hoping we wouldn't be told off for playing on it. There were no guards around, though, so we played as much as we wanted on those perfect green pitches. Much later, Qatar's futuristic Aspire Academy would be built on the very same plot of land to train and nurture the country's best sporting talents, but just then we were probably the most talented kids on that particular pitch. There was not much of a parking area – it was just a patch of dust with a few rocks dotted about. Just then the English news bulletin on QBS (Qatar Broadcasting Service) Radio was coming to a close, and the sports news was read out.

Something caught my attention.

'Wait, Dad, don't turn the radio off yet,' I said quickly, and he turned it up a notch on the little black dial.

'In sports news, the World Cup final has been played today between West Germany and Argentina in Rome, Italy,' the announcer read from his sheet, and the entire car fell silent, as the bustle and nagging and poking always involved with four siblings suddenly stopped. An expectant hush descended. Then: 'West Germany has won the final 1-0, with a penalty from Andreas Brehme marking the difference. It is their third World Cup triumph.'

The car erupted in a concert of hoots and cheers. We were the Champions of the World, without us even having known that the match was being played that day. The result clearly gave us wings out on the newly laid football pitches, as we re-enacted the match in Rome. We plucked the tattered football from the back of the car, chucked it out onto the pitch and ran after it, much to the despair of our father.

'Kids, that's not how you do it, let me show you how you play football,' he shouted, and we all ran after the ball together. He must have realised that there was no way he was going to turn us into mini shot putters on that monumental day for German football. 'Did I ever tell you that I was a goalkeeper in my university days, and that no one got a ball past me?'

'Well, watch this shot from Maradona,' Tomi shouted, hitting the ball high and long and into the dirt pit beside the pristine green of the pitches.

Looking back, I wonder why we were not aware of the World Cup final taking place. For a six-year-old, it surely wasn't too early to watch the game on television. Maybe we didn't have the channel which was showing the match? Maybe Dad wanted to make sure we didn't have it, so that we made it to the athletics training pitch on time. Whatever the case, we were all Andreas Brehme that day on the pitch. And my fascination with football, as well as my love for the German national team – even though we had never lived in Germany – had begun in earnest.

A few years later, then, when in April 1995 I turned 11 years old, I'd still not been to a football stadium, but quite suddenly an unlikely opportunity presented itself. Qatar unexpectedly turned World Cup host that year, the first time an event on such a global scale had made its way to our quiet and peaceful hometown.

I read about it in the *Gulf Times* one morning. Germany were coming! Not only our team, but all of the world's best young players. Spain, Brazil, Argentina – you name it. They were all headed to Doha. Dad must have sensed the opportunity to make us happy – and no one more so than the emerging football freak in the family – because one day shortly before my birthday he announced one of his famous family excursions. Instead of going to a pigeon farm in the desert, a sheikh's tent, an Arabian horse show or a camel race, we were headed to the rather more ordinary setting of a football stadium and a World Cup match.

The match in question was Germany against Costa Rica. Intelligently, I thought, Dad had chosen a game where Germany were sure to win. We headed out to Al Ahli Stadium for the evening kick-off on 17 April and got ready to celebrate at least a handful of German goals. Germany had drawn 1-1 with Cameroon on their first outing, so this one took on an additional level of importance. A win and we'd be through. A loss and Germany would be out. We didn't even contemplate a draw, though, much less anything as shocking as defeat. There was a lively atmosphere around the stadium as we found a parking space and walked towards the stands past a sprinkling of Costa Rica fans and some neutral Qataris in their white thobes.

'Your tickets, please?' asked a friendly volunteer, and Dad pulled them out of his Qatar sports jacket, which was becoming his trademark. He'd got the tickets from a friend at work and showed them proudly now.

'Six Germans,' Dad said with his usual patriotic fervour, 'expecting a big win today.'

'On you go, enjoy your match,' the volunteer said, and waved us through.

Each step up those spiralling stairs weighed heavy with expectation. How would this game turn out? I'd been mesmerised by the electric energy of a Centre Court packed to the roof with fans cheering on Boris Becker a year earlier. The crowd here was decidedly more relaxed as we heard the German national anthem ring out across the ground. The Al Ahli Stadium in Doha is a small stadium, holding about 15,000 spectators. A few years later a certain Pep Guardiola would play out the last days of his professional football career here. On that day, though, the stadium was about a quarter full. We had created posters cheering our team on, and proudly waved them about. Dad sat down next to us and had a quick cigarette to one side, and then my first-ever live game kicked off.

The tournament had started a few days earlier, on 13 April, with 65,000 spectators packed into Khalifa International Stadium to see hosts Qatar earn a 1-1 draw with Russia. Germany's Hermann Albrecht had refereed that one. Now Frenchman Alain Sars put the whistle to his lips and gave a short, shrill blast, and we were under way. The excitement was palpable. My heart was beating wildly, as it had done during USA 1994, as the German players sprinted efficiently across the green blades of grass, the ball passing crisply between the players in their white-and-black kits. It was all looking good – almost too good. Just before half-time, the French referee pointed to the spot. Penalty for Costa Rica. Maybe a miraculous save from the goalkeeper? No. It was 1-0 to the underdogs, with Jewison Bennett the scorer.

'Don't worry,' Dad said with stoic calm, lighting another cigarette at half-time. 'We'll get back into this one.'

A few minutes after half-time it started looking even worse. Another goal, this one by Jafet Soto, again for the opposing team. Germany got a late consolation goal in the 90th minute through Jan Walle, and we at last got up and had something to cheer about. We waved our banners about, hoping for a late miracle.

'Germans never give up,' Dad said, pulling his Qatar tracksuit up in preparation for the final whistle. 'We're known for these very late goals.'

But this time there were no more goals in the match. The referee blew three times for full time, and I left the ground disappointed. My first football game had ended in defeat to the rank outsiders from Costa Rica. I headed back home dejected. Perhaps tennis was the best sport for us after all, I thought as we drove back through the quiet streets of late-night Doha. Germany drew their final group game against a Mark Viduka-inspired Australia and headed home early from the tournament. We didn't return to see another football match until the final on 28 April, when Dad took us to see one of the biggest rivalries in world football – Argentina against Brazil.

Despite my early disappointment, the tournament showed a different side of Qatar's sporting strategy. While fourteen years earlier it had been the young football players who had provided the highlights by reaching the U-20 final in Australia, this time it was the organisational side which excelled. Even though it had been handed to Qatar just three weeks before the start, the event was a big success. Crowds showed up in big numbers. An average of almost 15,000 fans per game attended, and another sell-out of 65,000 was recorded for the final. And again we were there among them, listening to the national anthems before kick-off. This time, in the enormous Khalifa International Stadium, the atmosphere was exciting and pulsating. Everyone had come to see who would lift the trophy. It was a tournament that had introduced many new stars, from the likes of Portugal's Nuno Gomes to future Real Madrid stars Fernando Morientes, Raul Gonzalez and Michel Salgado, who helped Spain reach the semi-finals in Doha that year.

For the writing of this book, I met Salgado, the right-back counterpart to the famous Roberto Carlos in the 'galacticos' era. He remembered Doha fondly as a stepping-stone to his senior career. He also recalled a place which had few entertainment options for the players in those days. 'There was one burger joint where we always went at night to hang out with the guys,' the Spaniard said with a laugh. 'Incredible how Doha has developed since then. Look at it now.'

We looked out across the city from the top of one of the many skyscrapers which had sprung up in the West Bay district since then.

'For me it was amazing to come here as a 19-year-old, and then not only playing the tournament but after that watching the country developing.'

Again I marvelled at the energy welling up through the crowd every time the ball reached the penalty area. I had never experienced anything quite like the collective roar and buzz of the crowd, and I loved every minute of it. It was 28 April (coincidentally also the date of my wedding a good many years later) and a week after my 11th birthday, but it felt like a belated birthday gift to watch

Argentina score once in each half to claim their second youth title. The disappointment of Germany's early exit had long since dissipated, making way for a renewed fascination with this game which had my stomach in knots. As we walked home that night I told my father that I wouldn't mind going to plenty more such games.

'Sure,' he said in his easy, laughing, manner. 'Maybe one day you'll go to a senior World Cup match too.'

And then he went and forgot about the game all those years later.

Qatar, meanwhile, was also dreaming about the World Cup. Two years later, the young nation was on the verge of qualifying for its first-ever senior tournament, needing just a single win to reach the 1998 FIFA World Cup™ finals in France.

At the seafront Doha Club there was an annual tennis tournament, and one afternoon in 1997, after coming off court as a winner once more, I looked over at the giant TV screen which had been set up nearby for people to watch our country's vital game. It was our last World Cup qualifier, against Saudi Arabia. Qatar needed only a win at home, in front of a packed and expectant crowd at Khalifa Stadium, to qualify for their first-ever World Cup finals. Would that be enough against their big neighbours?

Qatar had previously come close to qualifying for Italia 1990, missing out by just a single point. So now seemed the perfect opportunity to make amends. We just needed a goal or two from Mubarak Mustafa, then we would be fine. I waited around with my big red Wilson tennis bag slung across my shoulders to see what would happen. My hopes were high that the home team, my home team, would win the crucial game. It was a single game they needed to win, against a difficult but manageable opponent. Qatar lost that night by a single goal, and the whole nation sighed in collective disappointment. Saudi Arabia went to the World Cup in France in 1998. Again the sporting underdog had come within ninety minutes of qualifying for football's greatest tournament.

In the summer of 2000 the Olympic Games took place in Sydney, Australia, and Dad had been nominated to go along with the Qatar team, of which he was now the head athletics coach. He flew over with the team ahead of the Olympics, and the rest of us readied ourselves in Doha to watch the multitude of sports on television with the chocolate chip cookies Mom baked for us, which you always ate too many of because they were so good. It was warm in Doha at that time, so we watched the Olympics for most of each morning. The opening ceremony had a special moment in store for all of us. We gathered around the sofa to see the teams marching in.

'Where's Dad, where's Dad?' Tomi shouted, excited as only a 13-year-old kid waiting to see his father on television could be.

'Is he on yet?' Mom shouted from somewhere around the house.

We had to wait a while as the countries entered Sydney's Olympic stadium in alphabetical order. Germany passed, and then it came to the letter P, Pakistan and Poland and all of the P's were finished, and then in marched Qatar.

'There he is, there he is, that's him,' Tomi shouted, and sure enough, there was Dad, marching in his beloved Qatar tracksuit and waving the maroon-and-white flag, inside the Olympic stadium. I felt a surge of pride as he walked, straight as an arrow as he always did with his impeccable posture, into Sydney's Olympic stadium along with the athletes from the team. In the same country where Qatar had first made a sporting impression on the world almost two decades earlier, my father was now writing his own sporting history with Qatar, fulfilling the Olympic dream which the Western boycott of Moscow 1980 had snatched away from him. We shouted and jumped, and he waved to the crowd, and then it was the next countries marching in, the ones beginning with R.

Those were some of the happiest years we spent in Qatar. Two years flew by and before I knew it I was preparing for my final exams at school, with a whole new life ahead of me. While everyone else was busy completing applications for universities abroad, I was more fascinated by the first World Cup in Asia, which was just around the corner in South Korea and Japan. For Qatar, the tournament itself would be an important one, because although the Qatar team had not qualified, this was the first time the tournament was being hosted outside Europe and the Americas.

I had no intention of going to university just yet, reasoning that I did not need to follow the conventional factory production line career path as I figured out what to do with my life.

The final exam revision period came just at the right time that summer. I pre-played Germany's entire tournament on the PlayStation before the first ball had been kicked in the Far East. When it did start, Germany got off to a flyer, hitting eight goals past our big neighbour Saudi Arabia, including a hat-trick from Miroslav Klose. After each goal I jumped for joy in front of the television which I'd had specially installed in my upstairs room. Fourteen years later I would be in the stadium watching Klose notch his record-breaking sixteenth goal against Brazil, overtaking Ronaldo's record in his own country.

But it was just that Ronaldo-inspired team which ruined Germany's first chance of a World Cup win since the victory we heard about on the car radio back in 1990. We made our way to the final in typical German fashion, winning games by single goals and with Oliver Kahn making some stunning saves. Together with all of my family, I watched as star midfielder Michael Ballack got his second yellow card of the tournament in the semi-final win over South Korea, and had to sit out the final. Along the way I had managed to pull off the balancing act of passing all my exams with ease while still watching every single minute of every single game of the tournament. My family knew that for this month no one should bother me.

Oliver Kahn, the goalkeeping hero of the hour, could surely keep out the star-studded side of Felipe Scolari with Ronaldo, Rivaldo and Ronaldinho in the final? He could not. I watched aghast as Kahn made his first mistake of the tournament and Ronaldo, with his strange semi-circular haircut, was in, scoring a goal and breaking German hearts all over again. Oliver Kahn had been the hero all the way up to the final, getting us there in the first place, so it was difficult to blame him now. Then Ronaldo added a second goal for Brazil, and I was in my usual dark post-football-defeat depression, hardly saying a word and completely red in the face.

'There's someone here to see you,' Mom called from downstairs. I looked through the window and saw my two school friends Kamal and Tamer outside. They had come to talk about the final, probably to cheer me up.

'Tell them I'm not here,' I said, and locked the door to my room. That day all I could think about was the mistake by Oliver Kahn which led to Brazil scoring their first goal.

Many years later I had the opportunity to catch up with Oliver Kahn when he was attending a Doha Goals forum at Aspire Academy. Of course I asked him about that day when the World Cup slipped away from his grasp – and mine.

'My best period as a goalkeeper was from 1999 until the World Cup in Japan and South Korea,' he explained. 'We should not talk about the Champions League final of 1999, because that was one of the worst defeats of my life. In the 2002 World Cup I played six excellent games. Then I made one mistake (in the final). Every goalkeeper is on a fine line between hero and failure.'

The Bayern Munich legend and 2001 Champions League winner also had a few wise words to offer on Qatar's 'controversial' World Cup, as some media outlets liked to call it at the time. 'Generally, I am used to this whole outcry; it happens before any World Cup. It doesn't matter where it is held, there is always a media debate. In South Africa, it was about security; ahead of Brazil there was a lot of talk too. There are also justified topics that are always discussed ahead of World Cup tournaments, but it leads to those problems, like workers' rights here, being improved. In this regard the World Cup in these countries has a certain advantage, because it highlights those areas which are in need of change.'

After passing my A-level exams with good grades, despite the barest of preparations (owing to watching every single game of the 2002 World Cup except the Brazil-England quarterfinal, of which I missed the first half due to an exam), I suddenly had my adult life in front of me. I didn't want to go to university – not just yet, anyway. Instead I took up work. First, as a translator for a swimming pool company at a sports exhibition which culminated in the visit to Doha of AC Milan with all of their superstars in early 2003. Then as a 'leisure officer', renting out sports facilities including an indoor football pitch to people who wanted a kickabout. It was a boring job so I organised a charity football tournament for the community. The 'Charity Cup' turned out to be a hugely successful tournament and I thoroughly enjoyed organising it, not realising that just over a decade later I would be part of the team organising the world's greatest football tournament, in my hometown.

The following February I began working as a trainee sports writer for the very paper I had grown up reading, the *Gulf Times*. And there was a surprising, entirely embarrassing, story on the horizon.

2003. THE GULF TIMES BUILDING
Finding Romario

When I first walked up the heavily set marble staircase into the offices of the *Gulf Times* near the Old Airport area of Doha, I was an 18-year-old trainee who knew he could write but had never done journalism before. Even so, I loved the vintage smell of newsprint all around me as I walked up the beige-coloured stairs towards the office where I'd been told to report. The first thing I did after being assigned to the sports desk was to meet my new boss, a veteran by the name of Anil John whose acquaintance I'd already made when he wrote that feature story about our sporting family many years earlier.

'Great to have you here,' my new boss said from behind his computer in the small office which was the sports desk of the newspaper. 'I still remember writing stories about you and your family in the tennis tournaments. Now, let me get someone to show you how to lay out pages.'

I did a double take: it was my first day, and I was ready to do pretty much anything I was asked, but this was unexpected. Did he mean write pages, or lay out pages?

Over the next few days, I realised that many of those in the office came in, took news from the international news wires which the paper subscribed to, and simply put it into the layout of the pages. They were essentially page designers, rather than journalists as such. It was not what I had come to do, so I talked to my boss.

'Is there any chance I can do some actual…writing?'

'You mean you want to go out and do reporting?'

'Yes,' I said, with a relieved smile, 'that's it, exactly.'

'I suppose we could give you a shot, but you'd better be a good writer.'

I didn't doubt that, so I started going out all over Doha, attending events of every shape and size relating to every sport imaginable, and getting my first bylines in the process. One of the more surprising bylines I landed, just a few weeks into my new job, was a political piece for the opinion pages. The USA was just building up to invade Iraq in the second Gulf War through the infamous and ultimately fabricated 'Weapons of Mass Destruction' media campaign. I argued that the invasion would be a terribly misplaced idea, having seen the effects of the first Gulf War at close quarters. It took me a few days to pull together on one of my first laptops, a massive grey machine which I thought was just fantastic, and then I went to the editor of the newspaper with the piece. The editor was the father of one of my classmates at school. He was an Englishman who always looked busy and shifted nervously at his desk as I approached. What did this youngster want?

'I have written a piece for the opinion pages. I wondered if you'd have a look at it?'

'What, like an op-ed?'

'Yes.'

'Right, let's have a look,' he said with a quick, slightly dismissive gesture. Surely this would only take a few seconds to dismiss and throw in the rubbish bin, which looked ominously full at the side of his desk. He seemed to have more important things to get on with than to read a trainee's random babblings.

With quiet confidence I waited and stood looking at all the other journalists who sat at the surrounding desks, answering their ringing phones and tapping furiously at their keyboards. Some of them gawked my way suspiciously; what could this novice possibly want from the big boss?

'OK,' he said finally, having read it through from start to finish.

'OK, as in you'll take it?'

'Yes,' he said. 'Tomorrow, in the opinion pages.'

'Fantastic, that's great news,' I gushed.

'Is there anything else you need from me?' he asked, and then turned back to his computer. His face gave the impression I imagined it would if he watched a particularly long round of golf on a rainy day. He wasn't the most effusive individual, but I could have hugged him at that moment.

'Thank you very much,' I said and walked quietly away, treasuring the moment the next morning when I opened the paper and found that the piece had indeed been printed in the opinion pages. Surely it would change the world. Maybe not, but at least I had made my point of view very clear for all to read. That day in the office everyone congratulated me, and my boss in the sports section must have taken note, because he soon gave me an opportunity that any trainee would have given a month's salary for in Europe.

'Romario, the Brazilian superstar, is in town,' he said, in his calm, understated way. 'He's playing for Al Sadd now. They signed him for a big fee. Go and cover the game.'

The game was that same evening. I had been to a few local league matches in recent months and the team sheets had always been in Arabic, so I asked my Palestinian friend Tamer, the one I'd left standing outside my house when Germany lost the World Cup final to Brazil, to come along, and he agreed. Maybe I should have suspected something, especially since he was known as the 'prank king' at our school. Ordering twenty pizzas to my house one day was one of his less mischievous pranks. But all I could think about that day was getting a good story. I'd already done my research. My father, although he'd never done journalism in his life, listened eagerly to my plans and said gravely at the end: 'Matthias, always remember: prepare well – research is everything.'

My research was completed long before Tamer and I headed out in my mother's small two-door jeep – my first work car was about to take me to an altogether surprising game of football.

Romario da Souza Faria won just about every prize possible in an illustrious twenty-year career as a football player. After Brazil had gone without a World Cup triumph for twenty-four years, the nimble-footed little forward was charged with bringing home a fourth trophy at the 1994 FIFA World Cup™ in the USA. He did just that, together with his equally skilful striking partner Bebeto. By the time Romario arrived in Qatar in February 2003, he was almost ten years older and coming to the end of his career. It was still an extremely significant moment in the football history of Qatar.

The Brazilian star was the first of a wave of high-profile foreign player signings that helped to put Qatar on the global football map. Cynics might say he was only after the money. A 100-day contract with Al Sadd was reportedly worth quite a handy sum for a giant of the game, a real World Cup legend. Romario countered such suggestions by saying he was after something completely different: breaking the mythical thousand-goal barrier in a remarkable career.

My objective was clear as I headed out to the stadium to see the Brazilian legend play: to get an interview, preferably after he'd just scored the winning goal for his new team.

'The game should be exciting,' I said as we pulled up to the stadium. 'I've never seen a World Cup winner play live in the stadium.'

Tamer just nodded and smiled mischievously; he must have been thinking about his plans already, but I was too excited about my opportunity to see and possibly even interview the great Romario to notice.

As it turned out, Romario didn't actually play that day, and I was disappointed to see him on the bench among the subs. I went over and talked to a few officials and they made it pretty clear that there would be no interviews with him that day. Then they handed me the fateful team sheet – all in Arabic – and I walked back to my seat to sit down next to Tamer. I called in to the office on one of my first mobile phones – a very basic edition which was anything but smart and looked like a blue brick – to explain this to my boss, and he said in his usual succinct way: 'Well, just get me a basic match report then, 400 words will do. And I need it tonight.'

So I went about doing as I had been asked, settling into my plastic chair on the media stand to the reassuring rhythm of a cluster of Al Sadd fans drumming steadily away and chanting their team's name into the warmly melting evening sky. The team sheet was in front of me on the beige media desk. This was precisely why I had brought Tamer along.

'Hey, Tamer, can you translate the names for me?' I asked, keeping track of the movements on the pitch.

'Sure,' he said, taking hold of the sheet with its Arabic letters and numbers. 'You want them all? If you want I can write them down for you alongside the shirt number.'

'Yes,' I said, paying little attention, 'that would be great.'

Al Sadd were doing well on the pitch. The 'Royal Whites', or 'Foxes', as they are known, are Qatar's version of Real Madrid. Not only do the all-white uniforms remind you of the Spanish club, but Al Sadd has a reputation as Qatar's 'royal' and most successful club. At the other end of the scale you have Al Rayyan Club, something of a people's team and generally the one which is acknowledged as having the widest support base in the country. When the two teams meet, it is known as a 'Qatar Clasico', or 'Classico', as they sometimes spell it in the media here, blissfully oblivious of the original Spanish spelling. While Al Rayyan are certainly well followed and loved, you need to understand Al Sadd Sports Club if you want to get an insight into football in Qatar.

Al Sadd Club was founded on 21 October 1969 (so it will be 2069 before it can celebrate its centenary, as Real Madrid did in 2002) and has accumulated an impressive trophy collection for such a short a period (sixty-seven trophies by the time this book was written). All of those different trophies, small and big, normal and completely outrageous in design, are on display in the lobby of the club – some are falcons; there are others in the shape of a basketball net; another one is the twisting and turning Asian Champions League trophy. Little wonder, then, that Raul, the iconic captain of Real Madrid, played for Al Sadd when he chose to come to Qatar before retiring in 2012. Al Sadd was also the club that my dad had competed for in athletics competitions in the shot put and discus. We also lived close to the stadium a number of times, so I had a natural affinity for the 'Foxes'.

On this cool spring evening in 2003, I had to quickly write my article about the appearance – or non-appearance – of the former Barcelona striker Romario. I wrote my match report and included all of the action and the goals and the passes and the through balls, and copied exactly the translated names of the players which Tamer had written down for me.

'You're sure about the spellings, right?' I asked him, sensing perhaps that a journalist's duty was to fact-check everything that was written down, even – or especially – by a friend.

'Yes, of course. You trust me, don't you?'

I nodded distractedly and thanked him for his help. That night I went back to the office and filed the story. There was no internet in the stadium yet and there was still a while to go before Wi-Fi and smartphones connected you to your office minute by minute, so I took my notes back and wrote them up. Then, late at night, I went home with the feeling of a job well done. I hadn't achieved my initial objective of talking to the Brazilian World Cup legend, but then no one had been able to get close to him. At least the basic match report had been done well, I thought, and I had captured the passes and goals and near misses and all the rest of it.

The next day I opened the paper as I always did in the morning. And there it was. There was my story on the almost-Romario appearance, and I re-read it with satisfaction, savouring as always that glowing, ultra-vanity moment of seeing your byline. A few years later I'd gain the nickname 'Mr Front Page' for a different local newspaper, but that was still some way down the road. I was happy just to be featured in the sports pages that day. I was having my breakfast when I got a call from my friend.

'Hey, Tamer,' I said between cornflakes, 'thanks a lot for the help yesterday. I just checked, and they published the story this morning.'

He couldn't stop laughing at the other end. I wondered what was going on.

'Tamer, what is it?' I asked, starting to get a little worried. He'd had a history of some elaborate pranks, as I suddenly remembered. This sounded suspiciously like his pizza prank laughter.

'Listen,' he said, still trying to control his laughter. 'Listen, you have the story in front of you, right? Read it to me. Please, please, just read it to me.'

Tamer also had a reputation for long phone calls. During our last two years at school we'd been close friends, and we talked almost every night to discuss the day's latest school news. But I didn't understand the request from him today. It seemed like a waste of time.

'Listen, I have stories to write today, so I don't have time to read it to you,' I said, on the verge of hanging up.

'No, you won't have any stories to write today unless you read it to me. Trust me.'

I read the story over the phone to him quickly and without much enthusiasm, and each time I said the name of one of the players he had translated for me, he cracked up at the other end again.

Suddenly I began to sense that something was terribly wrong.

'What's wrong with the names?' I asked. 'Have you given me the wrong spellings?'

'Nothing, the names are spelled right,' he said, still laughing. 'They are just not football players.'

I looked in horror at the newspaper in front of me. Only a few minutes earlier it had seemed such a fantastic morning. Now it was turning into a nightmare. My mind began to connect the dots. His propensity for pranks. His complete lack of interest in following the game the previous night. He had given me the wrong names.

'How many?' I asked.

'What do you mean?' he asked. He had this annoying habit of denying everything when he was caught in one of his pranks. I was furious.

'How many?'

'All of them.' He could barely control his laughter now.

'You're kidding. You invented every single name?'

'I didn't invent them. They are all famous people. Some are movie stars.'

Oh no, I thought. This couldn't be happening to me. The job had started so well. Now it was surely time to look for a new profession.

'What about the others?'

There was a moment of silence. You could hear him trying to suppress his laughter again. Then he said: 'There's a really famous Arab singer. And... well, I might as well tell you, because otherwise Kamal will. You know the guy I put down as the striker who scored the winning goal, Shater Abbas? Well, that's the name of the Turkish restaurant I always invite you to, but you never come. It's your own fault – if you'd come out with us just once you would have recognised the name. Anyway, I thought you'd notice yesterday before sending the story to your editor.'

Predictably, I was not amused.

'A restaurant? And it never occurred to you to tell me? Before this made the actual print edition of a freaking newspaper?!'

I could hear him snickering uncontrollably as I hung up the phone. Surely that would be the end of my job at the paper. Would there be a tribunal set up to pass judgment, including my boss and the English editor of the newspaper and perhaps even the Qatari owner? Or would it be a simple call, short and simple, in just three words: 'You are fired.' Or: 'Clear your desk.' Something along those lines.

The whole morning I waited for that dreaded call. Then it was time to go into the office, which was usually early in the afternoon because deadlines were late in the evening. I went in with a terrible feeling. How could I justify my mistake? It was even more difficult to explain my friend's judgment. I slithered up the stairs and into the sports desk to the right, trying to shrink my almost two-metre frame into the smallest space possible so as not to be noticed. Best not to make eye contact with anyone. Should I bring it up first, or would they? I sat down and did the best thing to pass unnoticed – I pretended to lay out some pages, even though I'd never bothered to learn how to do it because I only wanted to write. That day I waited and waited, but the disciplinary meeting never came. Neither did those three dreaded words. Or the enraged letters from readers asking for a correction. In fact, no one said anything about the episode.

'I got fired from the paper for your little joke,' I told my friend for a measure of revenge that evening, and didn't clear it up until the next day. Let him have that on his conscience for a while. No one ever said a word to me about the article; no outraged readers' letters were ever received; and no editor ever noticed and sent this young apprentice packing for his lack of fact-checking. It was certainly a good lesson early on in my writing career.

In Qatar's still-developing sports and football scene, football stars could still metamorphose into movie stars, actors or even restaurants. It was all a bit too magical for me that day, but soon I found my stride again, trusting my friend that little bit less, and writing my daily story with a double or triple check on each fact that I put down on paper. I read voraciously in those months, as the warplanes started flying again overhead towards Iraq, where the second Gulf War had begun. We watched it on TV on CNN, which was putting forward its new brand of 'embedded war journalism'.

'What's happening on the news?' Mom would ask, knowing that I was always aware of what was going on.

When not watching the news I would be lying in the hammock outside in the beautiful garden with white jasmine flowers blossoming on the trees, and their sweet smell floating about me as I read another novel. In that garden I was mesmerised by the magical realism of Gabriel Garcia Marquez, the great Colombian writer, and his *One Hundred Years of Solitude*, about a family and their eternal home which survived many generations and catastrophes. We too were developing into something of an eternal family in Doha, never leaving the place where I had been born, even though we still regularly moved house like the Bedouins who had lived here long ago. While all the other foreigners left after a year or two, or even three, we just kept staying longer and longer.

However, in books as in life, nothing is forever, and change was once more just around the corner.

2004. FROM DOHA TO NOTTINGHAM
Football animals

A transition was happening in our family, one that's completely normal anywhere: the kids were being gently nudged out of the parental home and into the professional world. The tallest of our family of giant kids was Hans, who had grown to 2.05 metres and returned to Doha after finishing school in Germany. We were all reaching the decisive years of our 'development', as Dad liked to call it in the regular sit-down chats he'd have with us about 'how our future was looking'. We all sat solemnly and nodded, and then we'd go upstairs and play the football game on the PlayStation again. The future sounded interesting enough, but just now we had another season on the go on the PlayStation which could win us a Champions League trophy if we just beat the next three teams.

While we dithered about our futures, the country we were living in was starting to study intently the art of international football. Much as with the early visits of Pele and Muhammad Ali in the 1970s, a number of top European teams were now coming to play friendly matches in Qatar on a regular basis. The first one, in the 2002-03 season, was AC Milan. They came to play at Al Gharafa Stadium, and there was a real buzz around the country about the game. Having finished another important game on the PlayStation, we drove to the match and found a parking spot somewhere in the overflowing car park, and then watched as the stars we'd just been manipulating on the console game wove their magic in real life at the sold-out stadium.

The next team to come out was my own team from Germany – record Bundesliga champions Bayern Munich – and we went along to their training session with the neighbours' kid, who was also a big Bayern fan. He got an autograph from Michael Ballack, and left the facility with an enormous smile etched on his face. A trophy was presented to the winning team, which captain Oliver Kahn lifted with almost as much enthusiasm as if it were the career-changing trophy he had almost won in Japan and South Korea a few years earlier.

That year I made a big decision. At the age of 20 I decided that I wanted to expand my horizons. While in the two years since leaving school I'd gathered plenty of interesting work experience, and written for a whole host of publications including the cosy little *Marhaba* magazine, a country guide ('marhaba' literally translates as 'welcome'), I needed a new challenge. That winter I applied to a number of universities in the UK, and got accepted at the University of Nottingham for an undergraduate degree in history and politics. I was about to embark on another unpredictable new adventure – this time in rainy, God-Save-the-Queen England with its eccentric brand of rush-and-grab football.

In my first weeks at Nottingham I joined the university's tennis club and got selected for the first men's tennis team. We were in the Universities Premier League, but I also wanted to try my hand at football, so I played in a few pickup games and even went to some training sessions at the residence hall where I lived. I quickly grasped the English university culture, which was basically to go out every night if possible and drink as much beer as possible, as well as the English football culture, which was basically to punt forward as many long balls as possible and hope for a lucky knock-down and perhaps a scrambled goal. The two cultures seemed equally pointless to me. Combination football, or even the thought of passing the ball around too much – as I liked to do – was dismissed as a 'waste of time' which would not get you anywhere.

University was of course a life-changing experience: my first time of really falling desperately in love, my first taste of living in a country and culture completely different from everything I'd experienced before, my first time tasting the blandness of English food, and the first time I saw a lot of rain. *Lots* of it. Rain and more rain. One of the curiosities of life: I never owned an umbrella in three years in rainy England, but I did in supposedly sunny Spain five years later.

While I was getting used to life in cold and rainy Europe, a whole host of famous football players were making the journey in the other direction to experience Qatar's marvellous sunshine and warmth for the first time. They were brought to Doha to lift the level of local football and, perhaps equally importantly, to tell the world about their experiences. In 2000, Qatar had won the rights to host the 2006 Asian Games, the continental equivalent of the Olympics. And in the ensuing years, as the country prepared the necessary sporting infrastructure and built the impressive, sprawling Aspire Academy on the site where we'd once kicked a ball around next to the athletics training ground, it also continued to project itself onto the world football map. One method used was high-profile player signings – not just one, but a whole handful at once, like a bunch of grapes for Qatar's football enthusiasts to pick at. These weren't just any players, but some of the finest the game had known, real superstars who knew how to handle the ball.

One of the first to arrive was Pep Guardiola. The former Barcelona star played for Al Ahli, Qatar's oldest football club, for two seasons. A desire to go into coaching became evident in the Catalan tactician during his time in Doha. He was as obsessive as ever about football during his time with the club, as his teammates later fondly recalled.

'When we were in training we played a game called "rondos", which they do in Barcelona, consisting of passing the ball to each other with a player in the middle of the circle who must try to get the ball. He rarely ever lost the ball and was furious when he did,' remembered Ali Mahmoud, a junior player with Al Ahli at the time who trained with the senior team. 'One day after training he walked past the car of our striker, who was a Real Madrid fan and had a club flag on his windscreen. When Guardiola saw that he kept hitting the bonnet of the car, telling him to take down the flag. I don't think he was joking, either.'

Shortly after his two years in Qatar, Guardiola went to Mexico for a brief stint, and then moved back to Barcelona to coach the B team. The rest is football history, as he became their first team coach and laid down the most successful four-year stint in the history of any club, let alone Barcelona, leaving their arch-rivals from the Spanish capital blinking in sheer despair. Voilà – a coaching philosopher was born, but the first steps on that journey, the formative moments of his coaching incubation, happened in Qatar. In his second season with Al Ahli, it is said, he was already acting as a player-coach, orchestrating happenings on the pitch with the same authority as he would later show in Barcelona, Munich and Manchester.

For good measure, and to avoid any suspicion of favouritism in the eternal rivalry between Spain's top two teams, a Real Madrid legend was brought into the Qatari league around this time as well. Former Merengues captain Fernando Hierro spent the 2003-04 season at Al Rayyan Club, one of the most popular teams in the country and the one Khattab Al Daffa played for all those years ago at Doha Stadium. Meanwhile, a dose of Total Football inspiration was also desired, so a sprinkling of Dutch flavour was added to the mix. The De Boer twins, Ronald and Frank, ended up at Al Shamal Club in the north of Qatar – the name literally means 'North' in Arabic.

Like the university application system I'd gone through to end up at the University of Nottingham, the signing system in Qatar at the time was centralised, with one body bringing in all the players and allocating them to the different clubs. In effect this meant that not all the big-name signings went to the big clubs, which was why the De Boer brothers played for the historically rather modest Al Shamal team. This structure reflected the fact that the decision to sign big-name players was a strategic one, in line with the policy of winning Qatar international recognition through football and making a name as a sports nation. As a consequence, the level of professionalism in the Qatari league grew rapidly, and across the board.

Or at least that was the intention. Did it really work that way? I put the question to Ronald de Boer in an interview at the time he was playing in Qatar. Having failed so miserably with my Romario piece and the resulting translation imbroglio, I was now becoming rather better at getting exclusive interviews. I looked forward to meeting this talented midfielder who had played in some of Holland's most important World Cup matches, including the legendary 1998 semi-final against Brazil, and was known for his honest answers.

'Do you think you are helping to raise the standard of the Qatari league, or just the public profile of the country's football?' I asked, sitting with him in the lobby of the elegant Four Seasons hotel, where he'd just finished his gym session.

He was typically direct in his response. 'The level of the local players is much better now than it was before we came. It was good to bring in stars such as Gabriel Batistuta and Stefan Effenberg to raise publicity for the Qatari league. I can see that it is getting better – guys like my brother, me or Guardiola really tried to help those boys. I think in our hearts we are really football animals. We want to win every game. We love the game so much that we try to help the boys, and you can really see in the stadiums now that it's working.'

But did these 'football animals' like Ronald de Boer, Gabriel Batistuta, Fernando Hierro or Pep Guardiola really make a long-term difference for Qatari football, or was their impact really more in putting Qatar on the map? The level of football in the Q-League, which was soon to be fittingly renamed the 'Qatar Stars League', did visibly improve. And there were later signs of a shift in signing policy toward bringing in younger players rather than ageing legends who were playing their last days of professional football. Weighing international publicity against local football improvement, the scale was probably evenly balanced.

At around the same time, a significant development was taking place next to Khalifa International Stadium – the building of the futuristic and state-of-the-art Aspire Academy, which hosts some of the most advanced indoor and outdoors sports facilities in the world. The objective of this mega development was to find and foster the best sporting talents in the country and turn them into well-trained and educated sporting champions. In its first season of operation, 2003-04, thirty-one young football players aged 12 to 18 became the academy's first cohort of students.

By 2015, the total number of full-time student-athletes enrolled had risen to 230, with another eighty athletes attending the academy part-time in any given year. On average, Aspire Academy now works with over 6,000 kids through sport and football skill development and talent identification programmes across the country, with a view to them joining the academy on future scholarships. Each year up to thirty-five elite young athletes move onto the professional pathway and into sporting careers or further education. In order to give these graduates further experience playing in European football, Aspire Academy has also invested in clubs – KAS Eupen in Belgium and Cultural Leonesa in Spain – as well as collaborations with several elite clubs and football associations around the world. In short, the development opportunities for young footballers in the country were rising exponentially.

Meanwhile, in the rainy English Midlands I was getting to know the local football culture and the 'football animals' there. In the training games where I tried my luck at university football there were flying tackles which sent players sprawling onto the pitch, as well as a whole collection of long balls hoofed over the defence for a speedy winger to run onto.

'Foul, foul,' I would shout, along with a Nigerian defender who obviously had the same concept as I did of what constitutes a foul.

'Get up, mate, that was a brilliant tackle,' our team-mates would shout angrily. 'And stop playing all those short passes. The ball needs to go in that direction, hit it as hard as you can!'

In three years in England, I never once made it to a live football game, although there was plenty of football on television. What I did make an unwanted acquaintance with was English fans. A whole train carriage full of them. It was on one of my return trips from Doha after the semester holidays when I was sitting peacefully in the train, reading a book as usual. The carriage I was sitting in was not particularly modern. It must have had quite a few journeys behind it, but I was not expecting it to take me so far back in time. Every time we stopped, more people got into this carriage I was sitting in. It was already getting quite claustrophobic when they started singing. I later wondered what had set them off, because I had not said a word. I just sat there reading my book.

'One World Cup, two World Wars,' they started singing, loudly and drunkenly in unison. 'We beat you in one World Cup and two World Wars.'

It was something along those lines, anyway. Then they went on to sing about Nazi warplanes they'd shot down, supposedly these very men in the train by means of some magical time machine, judging by their hearty intonation. It was a long ride back to the university campus in Nottingham that day. A severe bout of flu and a general sense of disillusionment with England joined hands that winter, and I came within a whisker of leaving university to become an unsuccessful writer in a small attic somewhere in Spain or South America. In the end it was the girl I'd fallen in love with in England who convinced me, during a long conversation over coffee one rainy day, to stay and stick it out.

So that's just what I did, and by spring 2006 I was already in much better spirits, because there was a World Cup just around the corner, and it was to be played in Germany. The first World Cup I ever attended in person turned out to be a real game changer for me, as I covered the tournament for renowned football website ESPN FC and had some unforgettable experiences along the way. Germany excelled with their organisation that summer, and the weather goddess even played along by providing a blank-cheque month of uninterrupted sunshine. People took note of a new Germany and a new generation of Germans – people who were surprisingly friendly and welcoming, who even knew how to laugh and joke and have fun. For the first time massive Fan Fests were staged where spectators watched the games together, and the home team even did well, though losing agonisingly to the Italians in extra time in the semi-finals. Back home in Qatar, they took note of the impact a successful World Cup could have in shattering negative perceptions.

Qatar was already preparing for a major sporting celebration of its own later that year, one which would transform the country almost as thoroughly as the World Cup tournament in Germany. Doha was readying itself to welcome Asia on 1 December; over 10,000 athletes, thousands of journalists and officials, and many more spectators were due to descend on Qatar for the continent's biggest sporting occasion. Nothing on this scale had ever been done before in Doha, and all eyes were on this little country in the Arabian Gulf to see whether it could indeed pull it off. I was one of those thousands of accredited reporters, on my way on a flight from Manchester to cover it. During a meeting with my tutor, I'd explained that I needed two weeks' leave from university.

'And what exactly would this be for?' the bespectacled academic asked, peeking out from behind mounds of piling paperwork and half-marked exams. It seemed this historian had just come from writing a paper on the socioeconomic impact of mid-16th-century bridge-building techniques in Wales, and I had taken him rather by surprise with this sudden request.

'I've been asked to cover the Asian Games, the greatest sporting event my country has ever hosted,' I explained. 'I'll be writing for *Marhaba* magazine, a charming little publication run by a nice British lady called Hilary.'

'Well, all right then, just make sure to inform your professors,' he said with typical English reserve. The mention of the British editor must have swung it. At least on this occasion, the English had been most helpful. As it turned out, they also sent along a dramatic opening gift, something quite traditional and unexpected.

On the opening day of the Doha Asian Games, 1 December 2006, it was raining in torrents, or cats and dogs as they say in England, when I landed back in Doha.

Al Najah club members, forerunners of the modern-day Al Ahli, Qatar's oldest football club, 1956–57

Unity Sports Club, which later became Al Arabi Club, lines up before a game in the 1960s

Ahmed Ali Al Ansari welcomes the Santos team from Brazil, including football superstar Pele, at Doha International Airport in 1973

Pele playing at Doha Stadium with his Santos team in 1973

Al Jaish team lines up at Doha Stadium, the first grass pitch stadium in the region

Khalifa International Stadium in Doha was built in time for the 1976 Gulf Cup

Early football team in Qatar including Khattab Al Daffa, one of the first football stars in the country

1976 Gulf Cup in Qatar

My father with his athletes in the early 1980s

Qatari football legend Obaid Juma

The Qatar team who reached the FIFA U-20 World Cup final against West Germany, 1981

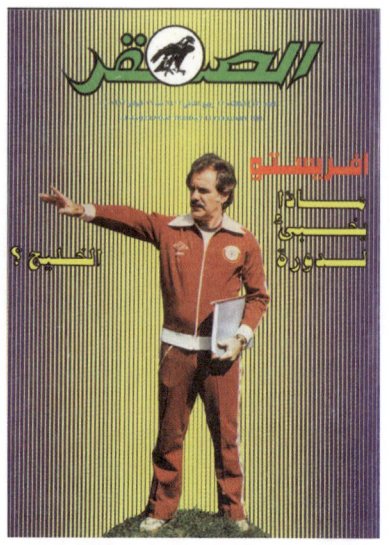

Coach Evaristo on the cover of Al Saqr magazine number 65, 16 February 1982

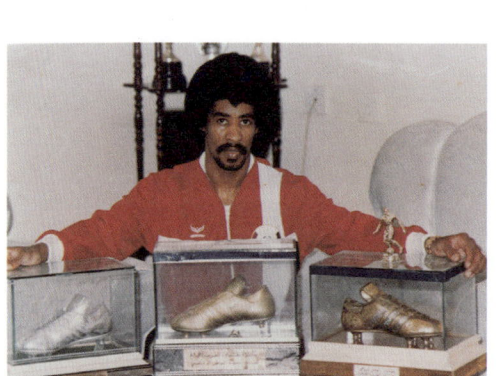

Qatari football legend Mansour Muftah

Qatar's 1984 Olympic squad

1992 Gulf Cup in Qatar, won by the home team

Mohamed Suleiman wins the first Olympic bronze medal for Qatar in Barcelona, 1992

Argentina wins the FIFA World Youth Championship in Qatar, 1995

Sprinter Talal Mansour

2004 Gulf Cup victory in Qatar

The 1981 FIFA World Youth Championship team become bid ambassadors for FIFA World Cup Qatar 2022™

Qatar's team wins the Asian Games football gold medal, 2006

My father with Qatari high jumper Mutaz Barshim (left), who would go on to become a multiple World Champion and multiple Olympic medallist

Team Qatar celebrate their Asian Games win at Al Sadd Stadium, 2006

H.E. Hassan Al Thawadi, Supreme Committee for Delivery and Legacy Secretary-General, with Xavi Hernandez

Flying Qatar's flag at the World Championships in Athletics, Osaka 2007

Coach Evaristo's visit to Qatar, 2018

His Highness Sheikh Hamad bin Khalifa Al Thani, Father Amir of Qatar, proudly hoists the FIFA World Cup™ upon the announcement in Zurich in 2010 of Qatar's successful bid to host the FIFA World Cup Qatar 2022™

The opening ceremony at Al Janoub Stadium, the first newly built venue for FIFA World Cup Qatar 2022™, 2019

His Highness the Amir Sheikh Tamim bin Hamad Al Thani welcomes the Asian Cup winning team back to Doha, 2019

All photos courtesy of the Qatar Olympic Committee (QOC), Supreme Committee for Delivery and Legacy, Mohammed Dabbous, and Joachim and Matthias Krug.

2006. DOHA ASIAN GAMES
The sheikh who rode to the top of the stadium

That winter I returned to Doha with just six months remaining of my university degree in Nottingham. As I landed, it was clear to see that Qatar had already graduated onto the main stage of hosting mega sporting events. The entire city was dressed for the occasion, Asian Games flags and logos visible all the way from the airport to the massive athletes' village which had been constructed in the heart of the city, and all the way up to the centrepiece of the competition at Khalifa Stadium.

It was at Qatar's historic stadium, where I had seen the under-20 teams of Argentina and Brazil go head to head in my first World Cup final, and where my father had met his athletes on his first day in Qatar back in 1982, that the games were set to begin.

Qatar had progressed in many ways since my father first set foot on the tarmac at Doha Airport all those years ago. Back then women's sport had been unthinkable for cultural reasons. It simply did not exist. All of the national team athletes were men. Now women were to be an integral part of the competition, with even Qatari athletes represented in the women's events. I talked to the most famous of them that year. Her name was Nada Zeidan.

We arranged for the interview to take place at her workplace when she had a moment free from her job as Head Nurse at the national dental clinic, not far from the Asian Games village. We sat in the buzzing waiting room area and conducted the impromptu interview against a backdrop of patients coming and going for their appointments, some of them visibly in pain with aching teeth. I hoped my questions would not cause any such pain. It was one of the most interesting settings for an interview I had conducted until then, and probably ever since, but also one of the most fascinating interviews.

'Year on year you will see the number of girls in sports increasing,' the Qatari archer and rally driver told me that day. While in neighbouring countries women's rights had yet to develop as rapidly, Qatar's progressive approach was also visible in the field of sport – instead of women being banned from driving or attending sporting venues, here was a female rally driver breaking stereotypes, one race, one arrow, at a time. Instead of being inspirational in just one sport, she had chosen to do two at the same time. Nada Zeidan was also one of the many Qatari torch-bearers who helped carry the flame all the way into the stadium after a trek of some 50,000 kilometres across the Asian continent.

'In 2002 we were just nine or ten girls in the Asian Games, but if you see in 2006 how many girls participated in different sports and also on the administration side, that means we are developing in the right way. When I started it was very difficult for women in sport, but now I feel especially with the Asian Games there is a big change in mentality.'

Just as my father had started work with a new generation of Qatari athletes in the shot put and discus, so Nada was working to bring forward the best sportswomen the country had to offer, often fighting against long-held stereotypes.

'For the new generation I opened the door; now they accept that women too can participate well in sports. For example, if you see the parents at the Asian Games who came to me during the competition and told me "we wish our daughter will be like you one day", this really gives you a feeling of how much change has taken place.'

The entire city seemed changed that day, the day of the opening ceremony of the Asian Games, as I arrived back in my hometown. I came straight off the plane from Manchester, dropped my suitcase at home, hugged all of my assembled family, and then rushed off, computer bag on shoulder, to pick up my media accreditation. There was no time to lose. I didn't want to miss the opening ceremony, even if it meant having to leave catching up with the family until afterwards. The media centre was at the then newly constructed Convention Centre in the heart of West Bay. It was a marvellous setup, a real dream for journalists. Hundreds of television screens were installed in the main press area, showing all of the different competitions as they got under way. To one side there were interview rooms, rows and rows of computer stations and desks, cupboards with fact sheets, the whole works – even a large dining area where we were served free food. There were thousands of journalists from all corners of Asia and the world. I'd been asked by my editor to write a full-length feature on the entire Asian Games, so I soaked up every moment and filled entire notebooks with impressions. Here was Qatari sports history in the making, and I didn't want to miss a minute.

'Sit down here, sir,' a volunteer said, and my picture was taken for the accreditation badge. I still have that badge to this day; I look sleepy from the long flight over from England and have a tired smile on my face. There was no time to rest, though – I couldn't let my English professor down. The accreditation badge was printed. Matthias Krug. Journalist. *Marhaba* magazine. A number 4 in the box in the corner, whatever that meant. It must have been the code for media access. I didn't care if I sat in the toilet, I just wanted to be in that stadium for the opening ceremony. It was one of my first major accreditation badges, and one I never wanted to throw away. The Doha Asian Games would be officially starting in just over an hour at Khalifa Stadium, at the other end of the city. I had to be quick, but I figured I had just about enough time to get there. I knew all the shortcuts.

'You don't happen to have any tickets left for the opening ceremony?' I asked. As so often in the years that followed, I just decided to try my luck and be pesky. That attitude got me in to a lot of important matches: a Champions League semi-final in Madrid to see a stunning Messi solo goal at the Bernabeu; the opening game of Euro 2008 in Vienna, and quarter-finals of the same tournament in Basel; a Copa del Rey final in Valencia between Barcelona and Madrid – the list of my audacious and successful requests would be long.

The tactic worked: 'Here you are – you're very lucky, you just got the last media ticket. Enjoy the show.'

I had escaped rainy England, yet now it was raining buckets in Doha as I drove just within the speed limit up the road from the Corniche to Khalifa Stadium. What my father had once seen as a winding, pot-holed road in his first days in the country was now the central avenue of the Asian Games, branded flags fluttering in the wind and plenty of cars heading like mine at the last minute to the stadium. In the rush of people trying to get to their seats in time, I dumped the car in one of the huge car parks created specially for the tournament around the venue. There was a feeling of expectancy in the air as I headed over to the stadium, helicopters buzzing overhead and last-minute spectators making their personal hundred-metre dashes to their seats. By the time I reached the gate where the media entered the stadium I was completely drenched, but it didn't matter. I still hadn't had a minute's sleep after an exhausting flight, but as I came up into the stadium it was well worth it; this was a magnificent and energising sight.

The whole city had its eyes locked onto the coordinates of the stadium, just a stone's throw from the place where we first went to play sports with my father at the old throwers' training area. A whole continent was getting ready to tune in to the competitions about to get under way in my hometown. For the next two weeks they would see a city decked out in sporting colours. Ten thousand athletes had checked into the athletes' village in the heart of the city, and now they were all about to parade into the opening ceremony. The very smell of sport hung in the rainy streets surrounding the stadium. The whole country held its collective breath for the opening ceremony. The rain poured down inside the stadium as the hour approached.

Would rain mean good luck, as was traditionally thought in Qatar, or the opposite, as was the case in the 1981 FIFA World Youth Championship in Australia, when the waterlogged pitch swept away the team's title hopes under Coach Evaristo? What was this deluge of water from above to signify ahead of the opening ceremony?

The lights went out. And then the countdown began: ten seconds until the live connection with global TV stations. By the end of the countdown, Doha 2006 was being streamed live across the world's most populous continent. The Qatar edition also marked the first time that the Asian Games could be seen in Europe, with Eurosport beaming it across that continent. But it was more than the global television exposure (nine, eight, seven, six...); this was also the countdown to a new sporting dimension (five, four, three...); Qatar was about to become the capital of Asian sports for the next two weeks (two, one...)

Zero. A goose bump-inducing cheer rippled through the crowd. We were about to get under way. International Olympic Committee President Jacques Rogge was there in the stadium to witness a sporting nation making a definitive step onto the global hosting stage.

Two moments in particular stand out from that rainy opening ceremony. The first was when the national anthem of Qatar was played. The stadium collectively stood and I found myself humming along with the entire crowd, even though I did not know the exact words. My arms were entirely covered in goose bumps. It was a proud moment in the country of my birth. And then, at the end of a remarkable opening ceremony which told the magical tale of Arabian traditions and culture through children weaving a Qatari 'sadu' carpet and other beautiful touches, the torch made its way into the stadium. This same torch had travelled across the Asian continent, visiting thirteen countries and twenty-three cities. Now it was set to make the final few metres, and they were to be spectacular. Numerous Qatari sports stars, including the famous footballers Mansour Muftah and Mubarak Mustafa, were among those who relayed the torch within the stadium.

Then came the defining moment of the day. A black Arabian stallion emerged from the ground underneath the pitch of the stadium. Years later someone confirmed to me that there was actually a small room underneath the pitch which was used to suddenly bring the rider up into the public spotlight. He was a beautiful horse, with intricate Arabian decorations on his forehead and the Amir's son His Excellency Sheikh Mohammed bin Hamad Al Thani riding on his back. Sheikh Mohammed would later become the man to lead Qatar's World Cup bid, addressing the audience in perfect French during the bid presentation, and giving Qatar's acceptance speech upon being awarded hosting rights in Zurich on 2 December 2010.

But on this first day of December 2006, all that was still far in the future. Even a minor misstep could change the course of Qatar's long-term hosting ambitions. The country held its breath as it became apparent that the son of Qatar's Amir would ride with the torch up a steep ramp to the top of the stadium, where the Asian Games flame would be lit. The ramp was wet from the rain, and as he spurred his horse on up the first part of the ramp, the spectators followed his progress seemingly spellbound. It was of course a brilliant script. Barcelona had famously used an archer in 1992 to light the Olympic flame, and this was probably even more audacious and creative. The last part of the ascent had come. The crowd roared in appreciation.

Near the very top of the ramp the horse struggled, slipping visibly on the rain-hit surface. The audience gasped. The rider again spurred the horse on, and in a last-gasp effort reached the top. The flame was lit. The crowd was immediately won over. I frantically scribbled my notes down in the little notebook I carried with me everywhere during those weeks.

Looking back at those notes, it was clearly a symbolic moment. Along with the proud young rider, who later also captained the country's equestrian team at the event, Qatar had reached the highest level of sports hosting, the top plateau of successfully putting on a mega sports event. It was widely seen as the greatest Asian Games ever held. And I was in the thick of things, watching almost every sport imaginable. A total of 424 events in thirty-nine sports and disciplines meant there was never a moment for a true sports lover to rest.

Operationally, Qatar excelled. Thousands of friendly and helpful volunteers graced the events with their smiles. Journalists crisscrossed the city to cover their favourite sports. Together with colleagues from across the Asian continent we covered countless events, and I even managed to expand my writing repertoire to exotic sports like 'sepak takraw' – a spectacular mixture of volleyball and football which included plenty of bicycle kicks – which I had not even heard of before. Apparently the sport is hugely popular in Southeast Asia.

Qatar had come full circle since those early days in 1982 when my father first landed in Doha, when there was a single winding road which led to a faraway sports stadium. Now it was Doha the sports city. The water bottles had Asian Games logos on them. Every television you turned on had some competition or other running. Kids sat on their parents' shoulders waving little Indian flags as they walked up to the tennis complex to see Indian star player Sania Mirza attempt to win a medal for her country. As journalists we were able to follow all of these many competitions either on site or in the outstanding media centre. And Qatar's athletes were also playing their part.

The athletics competition took place at Khalifa Stadium a few days after that spectacular opening ceremony, and I stood in the pitch-side mixed zone press area as one of the runners in my father's team entered the final lap of his race. The bell rang to signal his last round of 400 metres. The crowd got to their feet. A runner in the maroon strip of Qatar was in the lead. The stadium roared him on. I found myself screaming, louder and louder, willing him over the finish line. Qatar won the gold medal that day, adding to a final tally of nine gold medals, twelve silver and eleven bronze. That impressive haul would see the country finish in ninth position in the medals table, completing a successful tournament both on the field and off it.

What I remember most fondly, though, from all of Qatar's medal collection during those weeks was the football competition. If the hosts could win that, it would send the country into collective ecstasy.

Together with a few friends and my brothers and sister I went to Al Sadd Stadium for Qatar's second group match, against Uzbekistan. The talk of the town was Qatar's young new striker, Uruguayan-born Sebastian Soria, who had scored in the sixth minute of our opening 3-0 win over Jordan.

Like my own story, here was another example of a youngster who had come to call Qatar his home thanks to the transformative power of sport. It had been a long and unlikely road to Doha for the determined youngster, who had had his shins kicked by brutish players in the Uruguayan amateur leagues before playing two seasons with Liverpool de Montevideo and then flying thousands of miles to play football in the Middle East. Soria's early progress through the junior ranks in Uruguay was fraught with difficulties and rough tackles, producing the strong physique that made him a defender's nightmare.

At a time when opportunities to leave Uruguay for the European leagues were scarce, Soria jumped at the chance to discover Qatar, despite a little geographical uncertainty.

'When they told me I have a chance to play in Qatar I said, Qatar, where is that? They said it was in the Gulf. I said OK. I went to look at a map because I only knew that (ex-Argentina striker) Gabriel Batistuta played here before,' he told me during an interview, the first of many as I followed his career over the years.

We watched him closely as he searched for his second goal of the competition against Uzbekistan.

'Soria will score, I've heard he's the next Ronaldo,' our Russian friend Alex said confidently. We played tennis every day with Alex in our compound, but on this day all our attention was focused on the football pitch.

'I've heard he's the next Alan Shearer,' said Peter, our English school friend who had grown up alongside our family in Doha. We were a multicultural group, as cosmopolitan as Qatar had become, and even down on the pitch the arrival of Soria signified the start of the country's attempts (which would encounter some criticism) to broaden its horizons in looking for football talent.

That day, though, Soria was unable to help the team as they lost 1-0 to the central Asian side. We jumped at every chance the home team created, but the last pass always went astray. Qatar now needed a win in their next game, against their neighbours from the UAE, to progress to the quarter-finals. This time Soria scored twice, as the hosts rounded off a convincing 4-1 win. A 3-0 triumph over Thailand followed in the last eight at Al Gharafa Stadium, before the team returned to the stadium of Al Sadd for what looked a tricky semi-final on 12 December against Iran. A place in the final on the closing day of the Asian Games was up for grabs. It had the potential to be a dream finale, but then I had had many painful experiences that dream finales don't always turn out well.

The country was awash with Qatari flags that day. And again it was Soria who struck a crucial early goal at 28 minutes, as the team won 2-0 and booked a place in the final. The powerful forward had contributed four vital goals for his adopted nation. And he had struck three of them early on, highlighting his importance to the team. The final on 15 December – the day of the closing ceremony of the Asian Games – was a special occasion for Qatar. Everyone in the media centre wanted tickets that day to the football final and the closing ceremony; luckily I was able to secure both again. Qatar faced Iraq in a thrilling match-up starting at 15:00, with the Asian Games to be officially closed later that evening at Khalifa Stadium.

Al Sadd Stadium was packed, as it always was for such special occasions. The vendors outside sold Qatari flags and scarves and 'haeb' nuts and little cartons of orange juice. People rushed to the stadium minutes before the national anthems began, because it was fashionable to arrive just in time rather than come early. An electric atmosphere could be felt all around the stadium from the start. A whole country was willing this team to win the gold medal in football. In a closely fought match it was defender Bilal Mohammed who headed home Qatar's hugely celebrated winner from a corner in the 63rd minute. And the celebrations began across the country, even more ecstatically than two years earlier when Qatar won the 2004 Gulf Cup on home soil. We'd been granted a Qatari fairy-tale ending to the Asian Games, and again I was in Khalifa Stadium to see the tournament conclude with plenty of style and a spectacular display of fireworks. After the closing ceremony there followed a long night of celebrations and car-honking along the Corniche.

The flags were slowly removed from lamp posts and venues in the following weeks, and the country eventually returned to normal. But now that the Games were over, and Qatar had reached new heights in successfully hosting a multisports mega event, what would be next for this emerging sports nation? I also thought hard about my own future. There were now only six months left to finish my degree, and then I would finally be done in England.

That summer, with a degree under my belt, I felt on top of the world as I walked through the enchanting alleyways of Granada in southern Spain. Soon I headed on to Valencia, where earlier that year I had met the love of my life, my future wife Luisa. She still laughs to this day at the way I remember the exact date we first met because of a Champions League match between Barcelona and Liverpool two days earlier. Such is the fate of us football nutters. After that summer of love in Valencia I ran out of money and, perhaps more crucially, ideas to make more money, so I returned home to Qatar and quickly got back into writing about football. The year was 2007. After three years of returning only intermittently for holidays, I found the country had completely changed once more. There were more top sporting events. More adventurous buildings popping up. More people from all corners of the globe, in search of their future in a country which seemed to have plenty of promise. More cars on the streets. And I joined the *Qatar Tribune*, the newest addition to Qatar's English-language daily press, as a senior reporter.

The office of the editor-in-chief was right at the end of the place, and you had to walk through all the different newspaper sections, from economy to local to business to sport, to reach it. The editor was a well-rounded man in every sense of the word, who sat me down the day I came in and asked: 'Well, what can you do, then?'

'I can write,' I said, sitting in the large swivelling chair across from him. 'I love football, and I know this country inside out, because I was born here.'

He did the usual 'you were born here?' double take, and then composed himself, because he didn't want to pay any more than necessary for my salary.

'What else can you do? Have you ever laid out a page?'

'No, never, and I don't intend to learn. I'm a writer through and through,' I said. He smiled at that. He always liked to drop in to conversations that he had studied in the USA and loved everything American. Maybe he liked something about my gutsy, honest approach.

'OK, then, let's give this a shot. Show me what you've got. Go and work with Rajiv on the sports desk. But write about other things too. I want you to cover the whole country. Good luck.'

'You won't regret it,' I told him as we shook hands, and I think he never did, except when I left the newspaper.

Soon I would become known as 'Mr Front Page' in the office. And one of the first of the many front-page stories I found was something really remarkable. While my own future was starting to take shape in journalism, Qatar's sporting strategists were also about to take a monumental decision. And I was to be the first journalist in the world to report on it.

2007. QATAR OLYMPIC COMMITTEE TOWER
Mr Front Page

As with most offices I've worked in, we were a funny and somewhat dysfunctional bunch on the sports desk that life would never otherwise have thrown together. There was a big, bald, middle-aged American editor with a booming voice and enormous bushy eyebrows which desperately needed a trim. He didn't say much unless he really had to, and just got on with his daily duties of laying out pages. He was in charge of the American sports page, which usually contained a toxically boring (at least to me, as it wasn't about football) mix of ice hockey, basketball and baseball that put me directly to sleep. When he read my stories he would occasionally say 'that's a really good story', and then get on with laying out pages again. He didn't do much writing himself except for his weekly column on the NBA, and his weekly trips to cover the Qatari ice-hockey league.

'Wait, Qatar has an ice-hockey league?' I asked, the first time he announced that he was heading off to cover it.

'Yes, and there are four very good teams competing in it. Mainly Canadians and Americans. Now, I must go before I'm late,' he said, slinging a black satchel over one shoulder.

'OK, then, be sure not to get hit by any flying pucks,' I said, but he was already gone with his trademark long strides.

He was what I imagined the Big Friendly Giant from Roald Dahl's famous novel would have looked like in real life. On days when he felt a bit more talkative he would lean over, raise his enormous eyebrows, and talk to me about his dream of opening a church in the Philippines. After a few years he left the office to do just that.

The second unlikely character on the sports desk was a slightly younger Englishman who was constantly complaining about his job and the other people in the office, and perpetually on the lookout for a new challenge. A while later he got an offer from England and left the paper. At the time I came onto the team he gave me some good tips on office politics, and suggested that I should at least make an attempt at learning how to do page layouts, which he seemed to do most of the day.

'Listen, I'm going to give you some good advice,' Joe said. 'You'd better learn to lay out pages if you want to be a success in this office.'

'OK, Joe,' I said. 'Thanks for the advice.'

In line with my previous policy, I consistently ignored his good advice and made up regular excuses for why I couldn't make the tutorial sessions he so kindly offered me.

Then there was the small, balding sports editor from India, who always just nodded when I brought in another story and said 'very good, very good, we'll use it, we'll use it', as if everything he said needed double confirmation to make it into the newspaper.

'OK, OK, boss,' I said as I headed out of the office door to find another story. 'Thanks a lot, thanks a lot.'

We all sat together at the cluster of desks near the window overlooking Salwa Road, the central and always bustling Doha highway which takes you to the Ramada hotel where my father had stayed for his first three months in Doha. Each day I would come in early when no one was around, to plan my exclusive stories for the day. I had been given a desk, but I was hardly ever there more than a couple of hours in a row. All I wanted was to get out, to write reports and tell the fascinating stories I knew how to find in this country which just would not stand still. We had a group of photographers sitting at the desk at the far end, near the reception area. They were a colourful bunch. One was a big, hearty man with a constant smile and a few spare words of English, and another was the curly-haired sports photographer called Hanson who I took with me most days when I went out to cover a sports story.

It was a warm late summer day in 2007 when I asked Hanson to come with me to an interview I'd arranged at short notice.

'Where are we headed?' Hanson asked, strapping the camera bag over his shoulder.

'The QFA offices, near the Corniche, in the Olympic tower,' I said, heading out to one of my favourite hunting grounds for sports stories. 'I think it could be a good story.'

I didn't yet know that it would be the story which would change the country's sporting history. The previous evening I'd been sitting in a coffee shop with Tamer, chatting about this and that and nothing in particular. He was a fount of ideas for me, because he just loved to talk.

'Anything you've heard that could be interesting?' I asked, sipping a late evening coffee.

'Have you heard this rumour?'

'I won't know until you tell me,' I said.

'Well, they are saying Qatar might bid for the football World Cup. You know, the Asian Games went so well. So they must be thinking, what next? Incredible, isn't it? I don't think it can be true, because they wouldn't stand a chance.'

The next day I'd arranged an interview with a leading official in Qatari football. I'd already learnt that in Arab culture it was best not to be too direct about making inquiries, so I found an interesting way in. Qatar was bidding at the time to host the 2011 Asian Cup tournament – the Asian equivalent of the Euros. And so I went along to the offices of the Qatar Football Association to interview a Greek football official with whom I had been in contact for a while now. Dr Sakis Batsilas welcomed me into his office with all his usual friendliness, his desk filled as always with detailed technical volumes for the bidding process. We sat down, and after a few pleasantries I started the interview. It was all about the Asian Cup which Qatar was hoping to host. Then I decided somewhere near the end to throw in the long-shot question: Would Qatar also like to make the jump from continental to global, and host the World Cup one day in the future? It was unlikely that he would say anything much. I had expected a direct negation, an incredulous laugh, perhaps even a 'maybe one day in the future'.

Instead, what I got was a very clear, structured and concise reply: 'The World Cup is for sure something that Qatar would like to host. As you know, Qatar is bidding for the Olympic Games as part of a strategy to bid for big events over the next eight years. We have the capabilities to go for a World Cup.'

I did a quick double take. Had he really just said that? He had, and it was on my trusty grey recording device. There was no room for doubt. A bid was on the horizon. It was a sensational story. We chatted some more about this and that, and then I wished him good luck for the Asian Cup bid. He seemed eager to return to his bidding files, and I left his room in a hurry. The photographer Hanson was already long gone by this stage because all he got were a few shots behind the desk, but his photos would be on the front page the next day.

The editor at the paper loved the story, having heard from the angry Englishman and the preaching American that this was indeed a big one, and decided to make it the lead story on the front page.

'Are you serious?' the angry Englishman said as he read my story. 'Is this really going to happen? A football World Cup here?'

'Not sure if it's going to happen,' I said, 'but that is definitely what he told me. You want to hear the recording?'

'No, no, I believe you, but it should be made a big headline story on the front page.'

'Are you serious?' the preaching American asked me when he read the story later. 'Not that I know much about soccer, but how can they host the World Cup here? Doesn't it get way too hot for football fans in the summer? I like how you've written it, though. You've got great style, kid.'

That was all that mattered to the big balding American. As if he were some kind of direct descendant of Ernest Hemingway, a writer I was reading voraciously at the time, the preaching American cared only about the quality and clarity of the writing. He was probably one of the only people there who did, because some of the other editors took it upon themselves to hack my stories into unreadable, ungrammatical monsters with way too many apostrophes and commas in places they should never, ever, be. I sometimes woke up in fright at the prospect of seeing those unreadable things they'd turned my stories into when I opened the paper in the morning.

With this story it was different. No one hacked it into anything unreadable because all eyes were on this story. Not a single word was changed. Everyone in the office was aware that this might be something big. The fact that Qatar was even considering a bid was sensational news at the time. And it was the *Qatar Tribune* which had the world exclusive.

'OK, OK,' said the small, balding sports editor. 'We'll use it, we'll use it. That is big news, big news. Big news.'

If he said something three times it really must be big news. There it was the next day in the papers. Not hacked, but word for word the lead story on the front page:

'Qatar considering bid for 2018 FIFA World Cup™'.

At the time, the thinking was still that they would bid for the next World Cup on offer, with Brazil having already been announced as hosts of the 2014 edition. Only much later did the possibility emerge that the Asian nations would bid for 2022, with the Europeans going for the 2018 FIFA World Cup™.

'Have a look at the story in the newspaper today,' I proudly told Tamer on the phone that day.

'Sports pages?' he asked with a laugh. 'Is it another one of your Romario specials?'

'No, front page,' I said, with an unmistakable undertone. 'This time, the information I was given is all correct.'

That was how I became the first journalist in Qatar, and the world for that matter, to report about Qatar's bid for the World Cup. It was still a long shot at the time, a story that might fit better into the bracket of sporting curiosities or quirky side stories than as a real possibility. But I kept tenaciously following up on the story, writing a series of pieces talking to different sports officials in the country, and posing them all at one stage or another the question I knew would get me the biggest story:

'Is Qatar about to bid for a World Cup?'

It was all about getting an official confirmation now that it looked like it was indeed happening. Some officials preferred to keep quiet. Some said they could neither confirm nor deny the rumours, which only got me more interested. When something couldn't be confirmed or denied, there was definitely something being prepared. Others still, like the Director of Aspire Academy at the time, an efficient German sports administrator named Thomas Flock, confirmed that there was something imminent. Qatar had the fantastic facilities and knowhow from the successful Asian Games to go for the next big step up, he said. That gave me another front-page byline in the *Qatar Tribune*, and contributed to my growing reputation as 'Mr Front Page', as the other reporters started calling me, with a healthy mixture of jealousy and respect.

As I walked through the office every morning now, past the photographers' desk where Hanson stood with his camera at the ready, and the business desk with the paper's ambitious deputy editor who didn't like me much, there were some envious whispers and a few openly admiring exclamations: 'Nicely done yesterday, I liked that story.'

The editor-in-chief was also pleased with my work. He'd come up with a new red tagline to go with my stories: 'QT Exclusive'. There were a lot of stories with that tag coming his way. In just over two years at the paper, I revolutionised reporting standards in the country's English-language press. After a short time a rival newspaper tried to poach me, but after some long discussions with their English editor I decided to stay on at the paper where I had established a name for myself. I was given a free hand to decide what I wanted to cover.

Each day I came to the office first thing in the morning, and by the time I walked out the front door and waved goodbye to the receptionist there was another story waiting to be printed in the paper the next day. My father was immensely proud. Even though he'd been a loyal reader of the *Gulf Times* for decades, he started buying the *Qatar Tribune* as well on a daily basis.

'Make sure you cut out all your clippings and keep them in a carefully marked folder,' he reminded me every now and then. 'You never know when they'll come in handy.'

They did come in handy in the end, when I started writing this book and looking back over old stories like that first hint of a Qatari World Cup bid being on the horizon. Dad was quite right with his advice to file and collect everything possible. He was always a keen collector, of everything from our old photo albums, tennis trophies and school reports to the weird and wonderful artefacts and statues he brought home from his many travels, and most famously his travel videos.

It was a family ritual to ridicule him for his incredibly boring travel videos. They were shot with his retro 1980s shoulder-mount camera, which was about the size of a standard suitcase, and usually included extensive filming of a single animal from numerous angles and for several hours. A giraffe munching on leaves could go on interminably.

'Seriously, Dad?' Anna would ask, bored out of her mind. 'You filmed this elephant for so long? We've all seen it now from every angle imaginable.'

'You could at least have filmed a monkey for me,' Tomi added. 'Or brought me one.'

He was still searching in vain for an elusive monkey as a pet.

'This is one of his specials,' Mom would chip in, laughing her happy, airy laugh, 'made with the sole purpose of boring you to death.'

We didn't really have much choice but to watch them, at a time way before the internet age set in with its assortment of different screens to watch. They might have come in very useful back then. We watched the elephant for what seemed like hours, and listened to Dad explaining its significance in the local culture and traditions of the country he'd just visited, Sri Lanka.

'Listen, Dad, we're really happy that you're back. But can we go now?' Tomi asked with the cheek and impatience which only he could get away with as the youngest member of the family. 'I want to go and play tennis.'

That one always worked. So everyone, including Mom, scattered away in different directions, leaving Dad explaining to himself how the mother elephant was protecting the little one that had just emerged from the adjacent bushes.

Maybe I got my instinctive smell for stories from my father's extensive shoulder-mount camera attempts to document life as it happened. As if like some journalistic version of the legendary German striker Gerd Muller, or his Qatari equivalent Mubarak Mustafa, I had developed an instinctive feeling for being in the right place to find my exclusives and smash them quickly into the net of the next morning's print edition. I did stories that year on everything imaginable, except perhaps elephants. Looking back through the archives my dad had advised me to put together, there were pieces on Iraqi students who had won scholarships to study at Education City in Qatar because their university had been damaged during the Iraq War; a column I wrote about the European Champions League;

a trip to London where I wrote about the latest on the price of oil and interviewed the Qatari Oil Minister; the opening of the new Museum of Islamic Art – the list was endless. Every day was a new opportunity to highlight a fascinating story in this country that I knew like no one else in that office.

During those years I made my name as the foremost English-language football writer in the country. Football players talked to me first, sometimes within the catacombs of the stadiums directly after games. Coaches like Qatar's new national team coach Jorge Fossati gave me exclusive first sit-down interviews. And whenever there was any new development in the World Cup story, like a visit from FIFA President Sepp Blatter to say that Qatar had the potential to host a World Cup in the future, I was there to write the story.

'So you think this is really going to happen, they're going to bid for the soccer World Series?' the preaching American asked me in the office the next morning. The angry Englishman had since left the office, heading back to a job with a bank in England, where that country's football officials were in the process of putting together their own bid for the 2018 World Cup. Football was coming home, they were to suggest.

'Who knows,' I said. 'But it is looking increasingly likely. I just need someone to confirm to me that the bid is officially going ahead.'

A few weeks later, in early 2008, I got the long-awaited confirmation. It was out on the balcony of our family villa, after I'd come back from a tennis practice session with Tomi and got through on my brick-phone to a top-ranking Qatari official from the QFA who confirmed that Qatar was indeed about to officially announce its intention to bid for the World Cup. The country had come a long way since first hosting the world's tennis stars, and since I was a ball boy for Boris Becker on Centre Court. If they pulled this off they'd be the sporting epicentre of the world. But that was still a long way off. The next morning I simply shrugged at the American, who smiled knowingly, and got on with writing my big story for that day.

While Qatar prepared to enter the bidding race, I was beginning to broaden my writing horizons. It was all well and good getting hundreds of red 'QT Exclusive' clippings, but there was something bigger that I wanted. My dream of becoming a famous writer, employing the grandiose simplicity of Hemingway or the audacious magical realism of Gabriel Garcia Marquez, pushed me on. Would international outlets be interested in the stories I wrote? So many top writers had previously been respected journalists, and I too saw journalism as the perfect school to craft my fiction. I started building my writing CV, and contacted different news outlets around the world to see if they would take anything from me. It was tough going. Rejections were more frequent than sunny days in Doha. Ignored emails even more so. But now and then I landed a writing job for an international publication. The first one was as far away as Australia. My byline appeared on the other side of the globe, where Badr Bilal and Qatar's youngsters had first made their name in 1981. *Art Monthly Australia* agreed to take a long-form feature piece on the opening of the new Museum of Islamic Art in Qatar. 'The art of building bridges in Doha' I called the piece, or something of the sort, which epitomised pretty much the job I'd be doing a decade later for FIFA World Cup Qatar 2022™.

That year, Euro 2008 was hosted by Austria and Switzerland, and once more, thinking there was nothing much to lose, I decided to try my luck and get accreditation as a journalist. Perhaps helped by the quota system which ensured that countries from each part of the world were accepted, I made the cut as a journalist from Qatar. Now I only had to mention to my editors the small matter of a month-long trip to the heart of Europe.

'OK, OK, just get me something good, good, every day, you hear, every day we'll need something good,' the sports editor said. It was, after all, a major sporting competition that they would get exclusive insights into. The editor-in-chief was another matter altogether.

'You mean you want to go to Europe for a month?' he asked,

leaning back in his large swivelling chair behind his oak desk. His bushy eyebrows twitched nervously.

'Exactly, what I'll do for you is write daily exclusive stories, which will set you apart from the other newspapers in Qatar,' I said, seeing that he was far from convinced.

'What about all the exclusives that you won't be able to find for me here, in Doha?' he asked, annoyed.

'You'll have to do without those for a while. I'm definitely going to the Euros,' I said, driven on by the conviction of my football passion. I certainly wasn't going to accept not going to the first major championship I'd been granted accreditation to, even if it meant losing my job. 'And besides, you'll have loads of exclusives from one of the world's most widely followed football tournaments.'

'Well, everyone has access to the wires anyway – Reuters, AFP, they'll all have lots of stories,' he said.

'Mine will be better,' I said. That bit of youthful arrogance sealed it.

I felt pure excitement pumping through my white-and-black German football veins as I landed in Vienna to cover my first-ever major tournament at the age of just 24. I soaked up the football atmosphere and the colourful Euro 2008 signage at the airport and all over the city. Looking back now at the photo on my accreditation badge, I had an awful mullet haircut at the time, but it must have seemed fashionable in 2008, and anyway I didn't care about anything but the football which was about to begin. To make matters even better, I was granted a last-minute ticket to the opening match of the tournament.

While I was taking in the atmosphere at my first major football tournament, the country I called home was preparing its sensational bid for something even bigger. But in order to stand any chance, they had to overcome a heated problem.

2008. WOMEN'S SPORTS COMMITTEE BUILDING
The girls who bent it like Beckham

Summer in Qatar is a thing of beauty, especially if you don't succumb to the temptation to head on holiday somewhere much cooler, and instead learn to appreciate it. It is all a matter of perspective. To me, Gulf summers are like European winters, only in reverse. I actually prefer the Qatari summer over the northern European winter. A southern European winter is cold but bearable, but a northern European winter is something I'm not planning on enduring again any time soon, unless physically forced to do so. It may just be the half-Qatari blood which I may or may not have had infused as a newborn baby at Hamad Hospital, but I'd rather sweat buckets than shiver my socks off any day of the year.

'Life goes on, even in summer,' as my father always says matter-of-factly. 'Just carry a bottle of water with you at all times. And there is a reason your home and car have air conditioning.'

Over the years here in Doha he's acquired the very local habit of cranking up the air conditioning to deliver around 18 degrees, effectively turning him into a species of Eskimo in the desert. But even if you constantly sip from a bottle of water or freeze yourself indoors most of the day, there comes a point where you have to step outside. You can never quite get used to the sheer heat and the humidity which envelops you, and on really bad days drenches your shirt, from the moment you open the door. Having experienced a good thirty-five summers in the desert, my family has adapted and learned how to get used to them, appreciate them, even enjoy them. For a few summers, when we still dreamed of a professional tennis career, Tomi and I even practised in the heat on many a summer afternoon and left sweaty footprints on the court, as he shouted over the net at me to keep running, and I shuffled around at snail's pace after each rally.

'Come on, why are you moving so slowly?' my brother called from the other side of the net. He continually pushed himself to the limit, even in the hottest conditions, and expected everyone else to do the same. He was in the gym most days and had a six-pack which easily outdid those on most fitness magazine covers. The only six-pack I could boast was the collection of six Hemingway volumes which I'd devoured that summer.

'I need a break again,' I said. 'Have you checked the temperature?'

'No, and I'm sure none of the players we meet on the tour have stopped practising yet,' he shouted back. It was a long hour on the tennis court before we packed up the rackets and called it a day.

After that we usually headed straight over to the nearby swimming pool and jumped in for a refreshing dip, except when Mom was giving one of her water aerobics classes in the pool and told us not to get anywhere near her students with that amount of sweat dripping from our shirts.

The heated issue for Qatar at this time was that the world's football mega events had traditionally always been held at the end of a season, in the summer months. Any other country might have given up the thought of putting the two together: a sweltering summer and the potential influx of a million football fans just wouldn't work. You would have to be a nation of dreamers to press on and come up with a way to overcome the seemingly insurmountable hurdle of the country's climatic conditions. What Qatar began developing that year was the idea of cooling the football stadiums. Plans were under way to build a solar-powered mini stadium to put the cooling technology on show for the FIFA inspectors. And that year, in 2008, Al Sadd Club installed cooling technology in their home ground, with nozzles all around the field of play and underneath spectator seats in the stands blowing cold air out even in the hottest of conditions.

It must have been around the summer of 2008, while I was away at Euro 2008 as a wide-eyed young journalist, that the strategists in Qatar decided they would cool entire football stadiums to try and win the bid.

'At the start we just wanted to put Qatar on the map,' Nasser Al Khater, the then marketing and communications chief of the bid, told me of the earliest hours of the bid. 'We had to start everything from scratch, but that also turned into an advantage, because we looked at things in a new way and came up with innovative concepts.'

I didn't know much about the technical bidding process at the time, but it involved a lengthy series of high-level meetings and discussions about whether hosting the World Cup was something Qatar was willing to commit to, and a whole bunch of files like the ones I'd seen on the desk of the QFA official, outlining everything from the International Broadcast Centre to training pitches and potential stadium sites as well as transport infrastructure – and that innovative cooling technology. It all sounded very futuristic, and would also include an entirely new Metro transportation system which formed part of Qatar's 2030 National Vision.

At the time, I was thinking only about the next game at Euro 2008, having my first experience on the ground of actively participating in a major tournament. Wondrous Vienna awaited, asking to be explored. Everywhere there were fans of all nationalities, making their mark on the historic city centre in colourful clusters and chanting groups. The Croatian fans were particularly noisy and cheerful. Everywhere I turned there was a new story just waiting to be written. The opening game was a close affair, with the hosts narrowly losing to the Croatians. Each time I sent a story back to the main office in Doha the sports editor said 'OK, OK, we'll use it, we will use it for sure.' That was enough for me.

I travelled up and down the country. Train connections were entirely free for accreditation holders, so I visited different cities in beautiful, picturesque Austria, passing through the lush green valleys and up to the mountainous landscapes of Innsbruck. Here the luck of the draw offered another opportunity to watch live football. Although I hadn't been given a match ticket through the online allocation system, my newspaper presumably not having enough of an international reputation to secure one, I waited around to see whether any of the other journalists had not shown up and I could take one of their tickets. The match ahead was Spain against Russia. I'd checked into a little mountain chalet which offered cheap accommodation for some days. The drive to the stadium was breathtaking, past the mountainous backdrop and the cow-filled valleys. We arrived at the stadium and walked up the temporary stands which had been added to the top of the stadium to give it additional capacity during the tournament.

In the World Cup bid which Qatar was preparing at the time, temporary seating was being proposed which would see the upper half of stadiums being dismantled and sent to developing nations in need of sports infrastructure. This was to become a key legacy element of the innovative plans which Doha would present to the world. No more 'white elephants', that was the Qatari promise being drawn up on whiteboards in a futuristic high-rise in the West Bay area of the capital.

My own promise to the editor of the *Qatar Tribune* had been equally ambitious – to provide better content than the big news wires. So I headed to the mixed zone ahead of the Spain-Russia encounter, and got exclusive chats with Cesc Fabregas and Fernando Torres. The latter would score the winner which would break my heart in the final against Germany. I also got into the match and witnessed the Spanish fans celebrating their win against Russia. Manolo el del Bombo, the fanatical Spain fan with the giant drum, was at his best, as were his side that day. Four Spanish goals. Just the one in reply. And some outstanding football. It was the start of a Spanish era in world football which would see them win three consecutive major titles and create a new brand of football led by their 'tiki-taka' pass-masters Xavi and Andres Iniesta. Ten years later, that era would end as possession football hit a wall, and I was in the stadium in Moscow to see Russia beat Spain on penalties to reach the quarter-finals at their home World Cup. But that was all still a world away.

A few days later Sweden and their crazy fans visited the city to play Spain, and I wrote a light-hearted piece for the *Qatar Tribune* calling them 'undoubtedly the best fans of the tournament'.

The quarter-finals of Euro 2008 were upon us then and I switched countries, heading by train to Switzerland and the city of the lakes, Zurich, where Qatar would later, in May 2010, hand in their World Cup bid book, and write history for the Arab world the following December. In clean and pretty Switzerland, the atmosphere was less euphoric than in Austria. The co-hosts had been knocked out in the group stages, and the weather was not playing its part, as I arrived to the drizzle of a grey day beside the lake. On to Basel then, where further quarter-finals beckoned. On 19 June I tried my luck at getting a ticket to the Germany-Portugal quarter-final. It was a long shot, but perhaps some journalists would stay away from what for me seemed one of the biggest games of the year.

A further train ride, and I was walking up to the stadium in Basel. In a spectacular match, Germany edged out the Portuguese 3-2. A few days later I walked with thousands of orange-clad Holland supporters toward the same stadium for their match against Russia. It was to be an exhibition from the outsiders, who were inspired by Andrei Arshavin to a 3-1 win. For me these were to be the last days of the tournament. I headed briefly back to Spain to spend some time with my beautiful future wife, and watched with great disappointment as the Spain of Xavi and Iniesta rewrote history and beat Germany 1-0 in the final. My team had once again lost a major final.

After the lost World Cup final in 2002 and now their defeat in the final of the Euros, I began to wonder whether I was jinxing all of my teams by being an active supporter.

Perhaps it was best not to watch at all, although that would be simply impossible with my level of football affliction. I had come to the end of my Euro 2008 experience, and was soon headed back to Doha, where World Cup preparations were intensifying behind the scenes.

'Some lovely pieces from the Euros World Series,' the preaching American said to me upon my return to the office, adjusting his glasses and stroking his chin thoughtfully. 'I especially liked the feature on the best fans of the tournament. What a colourful bunch the Swedes were. You could really feel the atmosphere from your stories.'

'Thanks, I was really trying to capture the essence of a mega event like this…Euros World Series in soccer,' I said with a smile.

As I arrived back in Doha, I went through all the possibilities: could Qatar host a tournament on this scale – and even bigger? Hundreds of thousands of fans 'invading' cities. Seamless transportation linking all of the match cities by train to take fans right up to the stadiums. Accommodation of all star ratings for fans on all budgets. This was even an issue in touristic Switzerland – during my time in Basel I had looked for hours for an available hotel room one matchday, and had had to accept one that was much too expensive and ate into my limited budget. Thousands of volunteers making the tournament a success. Media from all corners of the globe descending on the host country. It was a massive undertaking, and would require a monumental commitment from the country to make it happen.

Little by little, news of the other bidding nations for 2018 and 2022 trickled through. England. Russia. Holland and Belgium in a joint bid. Spain and Portugal in another joint 'Iberian' bid. The USA. And the other Asian nations: South Korea, Japan, this time in separate bids. And Australia. There was a whole selection of nations with fantastic credentials, but Qatar was entering the bidding race with plenty of confidence.

A few international outlets took note of the story I'd first written many months ago. Of course no one really believed in Qatar yet as a serious candidate. At Qatar's first official press conference, at the Sharq hotel overlooking the Doha Corniche, I was present as a journalist. The message from the country's bid officials was clear: Qatar would work to overcome all obstacles, weather included, with an innovative bid which would make the world take note. It sounded adventurous. But there was also plenty of self-belief. There seemed to be a solid plan in place.

'You're Matthias Krug, right?' a tall, blonde and suited Norwegian asked me after the press conference as I was about to leave to file my story.

'Yes, that's me.'

'We've seen some of your work, very interesting.'

'Thanks,' I said. 'And who do you work for?'

'We're the PR agency working for Qatar's bid.'

We exchanged numbers but I thought nothing further of it as I wrote my story that day. It was all crazy enough that my country of birth was bidding for a World Cup, let alone that I should work for it. In the mean time, my own writing exploits advanced as I collected bylines, exclusive stories and important interviews. In one story I broke, Qatar's cycling federation said it was considering hosting a stage of the Tour de France cycling race.

'But Qatar is not next to France, how will that work?' I asked.

'It doesn't matter, we could fly them all in,' was the reply.

'But what about the weather, isn't it too hot during the summer when the Tour usually takes place?'

'We could make it a night race, under the floodlights.'

The story epitomised Qatar's belief that anything was possible if you thought about finding the right solution, with the same approach being taken in the football bid. While the football officials worked out the details of the Qatari bid, it was becoming increasingly evident that the country as a whole was evolving rapidly and showing a certain readiness to welcome the spotlight of the world.

Aside from sports, one of my most important topics was one that the country had progressively been dealing with more openly for a while now: the treatment of migrant workers. When I first started reading the *Gulf Times* it was a taboo topic for the local papers. By the time I was writing daily stories for the *Qatar Tribune*, I began discussing the subject regularly in my articles.

One of my most important sources for stories at the time was quite a surprising one: my mother. She was a constant and creative source of support for my writing career. When I was making decisions about what I wanted to do with my life, she said: 'Do whatever makes you the happiest.' This I did. She lent me her car, the small blue two-door Nissan 4x4, to go to work and do my interviews. She only asked to have it back in time for her daily dog walks, which I always tried to keep in mind. When she saw I was writing stories every single day, she started coming to me with ideas.

'You know, there is a lady in my water aerobics class who works at Qatar Foundation,' Mom said one day. 'She might be interesting for you to meet.'

'Why is that?' I asked.

'She's this lady from Uruguay who teaches at one of the universities,' she said, 'and she does a lot of exciting things for workers with her students. They put on IT and English classes for them for free, so they can build better careers for themselves in the future.'

'Sounds interesting,' I said. 'Can you put me in touch with her?'

It was one of many stories that I did during those *Qatar Tribune* years from 2007 to 2009 on the situation of workers in Qatar, and what was being done to improve it for them. The classes took place in one of the brand new buildings at the massive Education City campus on the outskirts of Doha, which many of these construction workers had themselves helped to build. A host of top American and European universities are housed in the futuristic campus, which is Qatar's long-term investment into turning the nation into a knowledge-based economy. During the World Cup in 2022, the campus will also host matches at the Education City stadium.

The students stood there in front of the workers, teaching them essentials in English and computer skills. I interviewed the workers and the students afterwards, and there was a refreshing willingness to address the evident problems.

'We want to help these workers create better lives for themselves here and for their families back home,' one of the Qatari students told me.

There was a rising awareness in society of the issue that world media would focus on a few years later when the spotlight really turned on Qatar. Another story I wrote at the time was about a gate guard at the compound we lived in; his job entailed letting cars in and out, as well as giving us the keys to the gym in the clubhouse. It was when we went to the gym that we would talk to him and his colleagues from Nepal. My brothers Hans and Tomi eventually befriended him and told me of the tough conditions he faced.

'So how many hours a day do you work?' I asked him one day, as I signed the book for him to hand me the gym key. He always had a broad and genuinely warm smile on his face.

He said: 'Twelve hours a day, sir. No day off. My company doesn't give me the day off. It takes us one hour to get to accommodation, so no time to relax or do anything. Then back to work.'

The company in question was a big, internationally renowned security firm based in Europe. They obviously didn't feel that it was necessary to give their employees from Nepal any rest at all. I turned to the only remedy I could think of and wrote a story for the *Qatar Tribune*. It was not on the front page this time. But it still made it into the paper the next day: 'Opening the gates of injustice' I called it, or something along those lines.

More things began moving on the topic in Qatar at the same time as I wrote those stories. My mother's water aerobics class gave me the tip-off for another great story. It was the same professor from Uruguay. This time her English class had been given a grant by the Qatar National Research Fund to start quantitative research into the lives and conditions of migrant workers living in Qatar. There was an evident willingness to look at these issues, which affected not just this country but millions of migrant workers throughout the Middle East. I went out with the professor and her students to the Souq one warm day, where they had their clipboards ready and were soon surrounded by hundreds of guest workers from India, Bangladesh, Pakistan, Nepal and a whole host of other countries.

'Are your salaries paid on time?'
'Do you have your passports?'
'When was the last time you went on holiday?'
'How many days off do you have every week?'
'Are you satisfied with your work in Qatar?'
'Does your salary help to support your family back home?'

These and many others like them were the questions asked by the Qatari students and their professor that day in the Souq in Doha. It was just another sign that the topic of workers' rights was taking on increasing importance in public perception, long before Qatar won the rights to host the world's greatest football event.

A few months later I got another, bigger, writing opportunity. I had started contributing to the Al Jazeera English website, and there was another interesting, perception-changing story in the making. In 2008, Qatar's first-ever national women's football team was taking shape. I headed over to the women's training facilities, a legacy from the Doha 2006 Asian Games. It was at the same venue that Ahlam Salem Al Mana, then President of the Qatar Women's Sport Committee, saw the desperate need for a women's team at a local futsal tournament.

'On the first day of the event we had huge crowds of female spectators; the venue was sold out,' Al Mana told me that day. 'I could not believe it: women in Qatar are just as crazy about football as men.'

The girls called up to the initial squad of thirty players readily admitted that while they were proud to be in Qatar's first female team, they had a long way to go before the sport became mainstream for the country's women.

'I'm so proud to be in the first women's national team for Qatar,' the team's striker Moza Ali told me, before adding with a laugh: 'But I don't watch much ladies' football. I follow more of the men's game. I like David Beckham.'

Ali, who worked at a local energy company in the morning before coming to training in the afternoon, told me she had found society willing to accept her passion for football.

'I love to play football, and everyone supports me – sometimes my company gives me time off work to practise.'

Her team-mate Moza Maarij, the first-ever Qatar women's team goalkeeper, told me she was ready to train hard every day of the week in order to improve rapidly.

'We are very happy because we can play football. For us this is a dream come true. We'll train two hours every day.'

Qatar's sporting development had reached a crucial stage. It was a time when everything seemed possible, when age-old boundaries were being pushed back by a new and optimistic generation, when it seemed fine to challenge the status quo and work hard to achieve the seemingly impossible.

By the summer of 2009, I was ready to embark on a new adventure myself. Having applied and been accepted to do master's degrees in both Madrid and Barcelona, I had to make a decision between living in one or other of two authentic capitals of world football. Very soon I would also be writing for the team putting together Qatar's bid for the greatest sporting event in the world. Qatar's audacious plan was now being shifted from the drawing board into action.

In an interview conducted in late 2008, QFA's then General Secretary Saud Abdulaziz Al Mohannadi had told me: 'Qatar has a very good chance of hosting the World Cup.'

It was just that no one quite believed in this small sporting nation with the big dreams. Not just yet. But by this time it had become known that European nations would be bidding for 2018, while Asia and North America would compete to secure 2022, and this had opened the door to this sense of optimism among the country's football authorities. The bidding race was about to heat up just as I was readying to leave for Spain.

2010. ZURICH

'And the host nation for 2022 is...'

Most football fans like myself who are well past the 'normal' measurement on the barometer of passion and have reached levels more adequately described as 'unusual', 'overly committed' or even simply 'insane' (although we ourselves always find our football passion to be quite reasonable) will tell you that they can still recall in vivid, almost photographic, detail major football moments in their lifetimes, even if they happened decades ago.

For me this is true for moments of insanity like Bayern Munich winning the Bundesliga title with a last-minute goal in 2001 and me jumping around the living room screaming at the top of my voice together with my younger brother. Or running around our apartment in Madrid with my future wife looking on in surprise as I waved my Germany shirt around over my head when we beat England at the 2010 World Cup in South Africa. She still decided to marry me anyway a couple of years later, so I guess it wasn't all that bad. But also simple moments like the time I got a phone call asking me to work for the FIFA World Cup Qatar 2022™ bid just as I was paying my rent (exactly 550 euros, which I always paid in cash) in a Madrid bank (the elderly lady cashier with the glasses always complimented me on my Spanish, which improved every month).

In the summer of 2009 I packed my bags, having decided to move to Madrid. At the age of 25, I wanted to expand my horizons once more, learn a new language, and follow my heart. There I stood at the check-in counter for my Qatar Airways flight to Spain. This time

Dad just dropped me off and wished me luck. He hadn't even packed my suitcase with his usual precision hand-folding. He knew it was not like the trip to university in England, with its wrong-sided driving and pouring rain. This was different. It was sunny Spain, and my choice to go and live with the woman I'd fallen in love with.

So many times in the past years we'd flown out from Doha International Airport as a big family, only to return a couple of months later. This time it felt like a definitive move, and I was not sure if or when I would be back.

The call of love and finally studying in Spain was too strong to resist, so that summer I made the move to Madrid to study at the Universidad Complutense de Madrid. It was a wonderful choice. The city seethed with culture, arts and football. It was also a city under construction at the time, with the centre near the parliament undergoing a seemingly endless wave of renovations. It reminded me of Doha in that way. In other ways it didn't.

Madrid is a mad beast of a city: pulsating, exasperatingly hot in summer, ice-cold in winter, people always on the move and in a hurry to get some place, others going so slowly through the gorgeous museums that they fall off the scale of time, parks which the locals call the 'lungs' of a polluted city, and enough literature to keep you going for a lifetime. And then there is the football. Luisa and I headed to the Spanish capital with just each other, our suitcases, and plenty of dreams as baggage. We arrived in the centre of Madrid without anywhere to stay, but quickly found a small studio not far from the Estadio Vicente Calderon, where Atletico de Madrid played their football. At the time they had not yet been turned into the effective winning machine they became under Diego Simeone; they were still maddeningly inconsistent, as my friendly local hairdresser, a diehard Atletico fan, explained to me as he gave my hair the classic lawn-mower treatment.

We went to see his team play numerous times in those years, including the big match against Barcelona, who I finally got to see live in the stadium. Going to see La Liga football every other weekend was something else, having watched the Spanish league week in, week out for so many years on television. We had the best players in the world right on our doorstep. And I wrote about football for numerous publications to make a living while I studied. During what turned out to be almost four years in Spain, I wrote for a whole range of outlets where I would never have dreamed of seeing my byline when I first started as a wide-eyed apprentice at the *Gulf Times* sports desk: the BBC, CNN, *The Huffington Post*, *FourFourTwo*, ESPN FC, *El Pais* English, the *Irish Examiner*, and many more articles for Al Jazeera English. But the biggest job, the one which meant the most to me personally, was just a call away.

One day, while I was handing over the monthly rent payment to the friendly old lady in the bank, I got a call from Qatar.

'Matthias, is that you?'

'Yes, this is me,' I said with a smile, happy to hear the familiar sounds of the English language, which not many people in Spain seemed to have mastered. Now it was my command of written English – and my near obsessive knowledge of everything related to football – which was in demand.

'Great, we need you to work for us, starting today.'

'Sure, what is it for?'

'Qatar's World Cup bid. We need you to write for us. Are you interested?'

Was I interested? I would have done it for free.

We talked through a few details, then the Norwegian said he was happy to welcome me to the team and we shook hands virtually through the telephone. Work had begun in earnest on the bid for FIFA World Cup Qatar 2022™, and I was excited to be in the midst of things from my computer in the small studio apartment in Madrid where we had our bed next to the sofa next to the fridge not far from the shower and the door to leave to university.

Each morning I awoke to a new email or phone call from Qatar. It was the Norwegian, who seemed to have taken a liking to my work. Or perhaps it was his Qatari bosses who had. Anyhow, I was delighted. It was certainly the most exciting opportunity imaginable for a 25-year-old football fanatic to be writing for my home country's World Cup bid.

What was I going to be writing?

'Everything,' the Norwegian explained. 'They like your style and your insight, your football knowledge and your intimate knowledge of Qatar. You've become the chief writer for the bid, they want you to write everything.'

I'd never talked to any of the Qatari bosses who were leading the FIFA World Cup Qatar 2022™ project, but I'd written their biographies and the releases for bid ambassadors when they were announced. I put forward ideas to my boss about who might work as an ambassador because of their connections to Qatar, and what I thought would make a compelling bid slogan ('Dare to dream', which was not used in the end). The requests just kept coming in, including speeches, the early narrative and key messages of the bid, and coincidentally the biography of my later boss Nasser Al Khater, as well as the press release announcing that coach Bora Milutinovic was to become the latest bid ambassador. A few years later he would become my good friend, and we'd play chess together on a regular basis.

'Are you writing for Qatar again?' Luisa asked me every morning.

'Yes, and we're going to win this thing,' I said, enjoying a visualisation of her words in my mind: each morning I pulled on the maroon jersey of Qatar and typed away against the illustrious jerseys of all the rival bidding nations. Inspired, I forgot to eat and drink as I tapped away on my laptop, sitting at a tiny desk with bamboo chairs at either end.

'So we won't be able to see much of Madrid today?'

'Afraid not, maybe later,' I said.

It felt inspirational to be part of something as big as a World Cup bid for your home nation. Would writing for a German bid have felt the same? Probably not. My wife still reminds me to this day of the time when 'you used to write for the bid and we stayed in the apartment all day'. I never realised that it took so much time because I simply enjoyed it as I had never enjoyed anything so much before.

Some days I would work on bid assignments during the day, and then head to the Santiago Bernabeu in the afternoon to watch Real Madrid play. Kaka was the big 'galactico' signing at the time, although he never made it as big as his predecessor Zinedine Zidane. The French World Cup legend would become one of the last big ambassador announcements of Qatar's bid. His Arab origins were the connection. With each assignment I got, I let flow the wealth of football knowledge I had acquired almost religiously over the past two decades since Germany last won the World Cup in 1990. The hours upon hours of watching seemingly obscure football matches, ranging from the Argentine league (where the commentators always fascinated me, with their fierce and unparalleled passion) to Italy's Serie A, were now coming in rather handy.

It was a football fanatic's dream job, and all the while I enjoyed going to university again in a setting that emanated incomparably more human warmth and openness than rainy, self-important England ever could.

That next summer, Germany defeated England again in the 2010 World Cup in South Africa, and I watched my first major tournament of the last three from afar, doing my exams and wrapping up a memorable master's degree in Madrid. It was such an enriching experience and enjoyable lifestyle in Spain that I decided to stay on and do a doctorate at the same university. The professors recommended it based on my outstanding results from the master's, and I loved the atmosphere at the university in Madrid. The buildings were ageing compared with the sparkling English campus I had studied on, but the place felt authentic and warm.

That summer I wrote a regular column on Asian football for ESPN FC, and watched in delight as Germany played some of the most exciting football we'd seen in years. The 4-0 quarter-final defeat of Diego Maradona's Argentina was particularly memorable. But in the semi-finals it was the Spanish again who stopped our dream run, and I was in Madrid once more to see the celebrations as the country lifted their historic first World Cup trophy. The fact that South Africa had successfully hosted the event on the African continent for the first time, despite all the pre-event criticism, was an inspiration and a game changer for Qatar's bid. One of the most important key messages I had helped to formulate throughout those bidding months was that Qatar would open the tournament to an entirely new region, the football-crazy Arab world and Middle East.

As the bidding race continued, I got a call from my Norwegian boss saying that a different PR agency had been given the nod for the remainder of Qatar's bid.

'It is nothing to do with your work of course, which has been excellent,' he told me that day.

I was obviously disappointed not to be writing for FIFA World Cup Qatar 2022™ any more, but proud to have played my part in my country's historic effort in its very first World Cup bid. My focus turned back fully to my doctorate and completing it in record time. I'd given myself a year to do it, which only my fantastic thesis advisor Enrique – who spoke about ten languages, including Icelandic and German, and was the most laid-back Spaniard I'd ever seen or believed was possible.

'It's a short time for a thesis, but if you think you can do it, why not?' he said. 'Just send it through to me when it's done, and I'll be fast with the review as well.'

It was a bit like the underdog story of Qatar's bid. No one thought it possible, except those like me who knew the country and its sporting potential well enough. A World Cup in tiny Qatar? What nonsense! thought the Western media and public. As one friend from the university in Nottingham jokingly told me, 'it seems about as likely as the Queen of England being snapped by paparazzi surfing a big wave in Hawaii, wearing a Union Jack bikini: no chance at all'.

It was an inappropriate but interesting choice of metaphor from my English friend. While Her Majesty could perfectly well physically attempt to surf, he explained, our perceptions of English propriety and probably also her age tended to rule out such a scene occurring. In just in the same way, he dismissed the idea of Qatar going into bidding decision day because of certain perceptions. Rather than it being too old, the supposed prejudice was that it was too young a football nation to host such an event. It had too little 'football pedigree', or so the reasoning went.

But Qatar continued to make its case confidently, almost incessantly. Wherever there was a football event 'we were there, making our points, putting across our messages, saying what we had to say,' Nasser Al Khater, the bid's communications and marketing chief, explained. 'We saw this as an opportunity to put Qatar on the map, to make it known across the world, win or lose. The other bidding teams were there too sometimes. But we were there always. It reached the point where at one event someone who didn't see us asked: "Where are the Qataris? They are always here." We were. He just hadn't seen us yet.'

Besides Qatar's aggressive communications approach, which included high-level ambassadors like Pep Guardiola, Sami Al Jaber, Zinedine Zidane, Gabriel Batistuta and Ronald de Boer, as well as the entire Qatar team from 1981 in Australia, there was another clear advantage. The fact that European bidders were going for 2018 meant that Asia and North America were left to fight it out for 2022. And Qatar was one of the earliest to focus exclusively on 2022. Qatari officials were aware that if the highly ambitious bid they were proposing succeeded, they would need the entire twelve years to prepare all of the planned infrastructure.

Just three weeks before decision day in Zurich, I wrote a piece for the website of the renowned English football magazine *FourFourTwo* entitled 'And the host nation for 2022 is…Qatar?!' In the article, I listed reasons why I believed the smallest bidding nation had the biggest chance of becoming host nation of the world's most important sporting event. My main argument was that there was an almost morally binding trend of giving major sporting events to new regions of the globe. The trend had developed in past hosting decisions, as countries and regions had been chosen which had never hosted these events before. A Christopher Columbus-like 'discovery' approach to hosting decisions seemed to be taking over. South Africa that year had been the first African World Cup. And Rio de Janeiro had been awarded the first South American Olympics. My last line in the article was: 'Perhaps the question about Qatar's highly ambitious bid should not be why, but rather why not?'

Why not give the World Cup to the Middle East? What better place to build bridges, inspire young generations through football, really change things in a way that you perhaps could not aspire to any longer in highly developed Western nations, which would not be hugely impacted by such a tournament?

Still, no one really took the article, or the possibility, too seriously. Just a few weeks later, though, I was writing a different article, this time for the BBC. It was about Qatar's 'World Cup miracle'.

A moment everyone from Qatar will always vividly remember is the day Qatar won the right to host the greatest football event on earth. You can ask anyone in Doha what they were doing on that day and they will tell you precisely what it was. On 2 December 2010, I turned on the tiny television set in our small flat in Madrid with an expectant feeling in my stomach. I sat with my future wife on our small orange two-seater sofa and watched the build-up. Spain and Portugal too hoped for their chance. Anyone who watched the presentations of all the bidding nations for 2022 that day could come only to one conclusion: Qatar had prepared the best presentation.

And if the presentation is the culmination and a reflection of the entire bid, then it had presented the most compelling case. Qatar wanted it the most.

Together with Luisa, I watched the entire presentation process on television in Spain. Then, some five years later, I watched the presentation once more on YouTube, where it is readily available for anyone to see. It was not only goose-bump material for me, but also a resounding answer to critics who did not understand why Qatar wanted to host the World Cup. The country had presented the most convincing concepts. Compact. Cooled. Modular stadiums to avoid white elephants. It all made sense. And the emotive argument it presented was that it was time for the first-ever World Cup in the Middle East. But when? That was the question asked by Her Highness Sheikha Moza bint Nasser. Importantly, and very much in line with my earlier interviews with Qatar's pioneering rally driver and the women's football team, Her Highness Sheikha Moza was the only female speaker out of all of the countries presenting in Zurich that day. Her question was simple: When would it be the turn of this football-crazy region?

The time is now, Qatar's bid said. It was a winning concept. To secure the 2012 Olympics some years earlier, London had come up with an equally strong message of focusing on youth, while also flying out Prime Minister Tony Blair for decision day in Singapore. It worked, and swung the voting in London's favour over previous front-runner Paris. But for the 2022 race there had been no big favourites as such. South Korea and Japan were in the running after co-hosting in 2002, but a World Cup there again so soon after that event would not necessarily send the most encouraging message for football development. The USA had quite recently hosted the World Cup, in 1994. The two newcomers who could credibly claim to open the game to a new region were Australia and Qatar. With all due respect to the other bidders, rewatching all the presentations five years later showed it to be a clear-cut affair.

The US bid used the word 'soccer' in their presentation in front of the global football audience; illustrious actor Morgan Freeman came up and spoke but unfortunately forgot some of his lines; and the USA provided a good case for why the World Cup would benefit the USA. Qatar's bid touched hearts and changed mindsets; featured a speech by five-time World Cup coach Bora Milutinovic; and compellingly made a case in multiple languages for how the World Cup coming to Qatar would open a new region to football development. I felt very proud indeed.

I asked Coach Bora about his speech some five years later over lunch, and he said: 'Nasser (Al Khater) told me that I was going to be speaking for Qatar. It was an enormous honour and responsibility, and I was very nervous. So I prepared meticulously.'

When Coach Bora prepares something, it is always meticulous. It is as if everything he does is to prepare one of his minnow teams for a run at unlikely World Cup glory. His classic underdog story, having taken Costa Rica to the second round in Italia 1990 and the USA to the same stage four years later, as well as working his magic in 1998 with Nigeria, is reflected in the story of Qatar.

Of course I am not an 'objective' viewer, as Virginia Woolf would argue, and can never hope to be one, just as the English, Americans or Australians cannot be because they lost that day. While Qatar was presenting to the world in four different languages, I was studying literature and linguistics in Madrid. I began one football article that I wrote for Al Jazeera English at the Santiago Bernabeu Stadium with a line from Woolf. I will quote another here, from *A Room of One's Own*: 'At any rate, when a subject is highly controversial... one cannot hope to tell the truth. One can only show how one came to hold whatever opinion one does hold. One can only give one's audience the chance of drawing their own conclusions as they observe the limitations, the prejudices, the idiosyncrasies of the speaker.'

In the same way I can only show how I came to my conclusion that Qatar's bid won the 'shocking' 2 December decision quite deservedly.

The envelope was opened. FIFA President Sepp Blatter read out the name and held up the card for all to see: it read 'Qatar'. I looked again at the television screen and still it read 'Qatar'. That was my country's name being beamed across the globe, the country where I had been born all those years ago at Hamad Hospital, when my father had smoked a quick cigarette in the car park and taken my mother home two hours later. I hugged Luisa and screamed out my joy across the Madrid rooftops, and then I was jumping around the flat as I did at any of the major goals Germany or Qatar or Bayern Munich or Barcelona scored over the years.

It was the culmination not only of the past two years of bid preparation, where I had played my small part from Madrid, but also of Qatar's entire transformation over some three decades into a sporting capital of the world. I have argued about this at length over coffee with some sceptical journalists. But if you'd like to draw your own conclusions and make up your own mind, all the final bid presentations are there on YouTube for everyone to see.

Qatar celebrated, and the Western media – especially from the countries which had not been granted the hosting rights – soon started to criticise the country. At times it felt like trying to play football on massive sand dunes of doubt. Sand dunes shift gradually over time. But the negative headlines kept coming, especially from the UK media, and I followed them from afar over the next few years.

My own student life in Madrid continued perfectly normally after that decision day. In 2012, I had several of the most special days of my life in quick succession. First, the final presentation of my doctoral thesis, which I had indeed completed in the record time of just a single year – and then waited half a year for all the Spanish paperwork to be completed. I had prepared for it well by practising what I was going to say in front of Luisa. In fact, she encouraged this and prodded me to practise the presentation every day with a stopwatch. It felt like football training. I earned my European PhD with honours just two days before marrying my lovely wife in Aranjuez, a small and picturesque town with a castle on the outskirts of Madrid. We had a memorable wedding meal with our families at a charming restaurant called El Rana Verde ('the green frog') next to the river which runs through the town. On the day of the wedding my father and I both wore the same jacket, each acquired the day before in a frantic search for suitable garments for the special day.

We said 'yes, we do' and kissed, and then suddenly we were a married couple. It was a full five years before I would forget our wedding anniversary for the first time (I pretended that I had of course remembered it, and rushed off to buy some spectacular presents). Our first baby was already on the way and due to be born later that summer of 2012. So while the waves of criticism kept coming Qatar's way after it won the bid, I was learning how to change our beautiful newborn baby's diapers and getting precious little sleep.

It seemed the media coverage was continuing to get worse. A year later, I got another call. This time it was from Nasser Al Khater in person.

'Would you like to join the team?' he asked. 'And how would you propose to counter all the criticism we are facing?'

I told him my thoughts: we needed to be positive and proactive, and regularly communicate all Qatar's strengths to the world. Soon after that, I was on my way back to Doha, having been offered a dream job working on the media team of the FIFA World Cup Qatar 2022™ Supreme Committee. It was an interesting homecoming, because I had not been back for three and a half years. How would the country of my birth have changed since winning the bid? I was about to find out.

2013. NEW DOHA
The football revolutionaries

When you find yourself writing a poem to a player whom you idolise, and go ahead and publish it proudly on your blog instead of secretly burning it or flushing it down the toilet, you should theoretically start to realise you might just be taking this football thing too far. But then, when your wife understands and encourages it, or at least does a good job pretending to like your poem to Lionel Messi, you know you've chosen the right wife. To be fair, I've written many more poems to Luisa than to Lionel.

There were many great games of football which I had the privilege of watching in the stadium in my almost four years in Spain, and one of them was the visit of Barcelona to the Vicente Calderon Stadium to play against the grittiest Atletico Madrid side you could imagine. It would need something truly special to beat this highly organised side. Courtesy of a press ticket, I was in the stands as Messi turned a free kick from an outrageous angle into a stunning lifted shot which dropped in at an angle for a winner. He should have crossed from there. It was even the wrong angle for a left-footed player to imagine taking a shot on goal. But he did. That evening I wrote a poem from the perspective of a ball, aching to be constantly close to Messi's left foot. My wife lovingly shook her head and said it was brilliant. What she really meant was that it would be brilliant if I had my head checked.

The best football players, and those I enjoy watching the most, have the capacity to constantly transform themselves within each game. They change around what has previously worked, and adapt to new circumstances from teammates and opponents, to make something audacious and previously unseen happen. There is no country, I find, that has mastered the art of transforming itself constantly and at such incredible speed as Qatar has done over the past three and a half decades. My father confirmed this when I talked to him recently on the occasion of the thirty-fifth anniversary of his arrival in the country.

'When I landed in Qatar in 1982, I remember writing to my coach in Germany – by postcard at the time – that the entire country was under construction. Everything was in motion,' he said with a laugh, thinking back to the days when postcards were the quickest form of communication.

Over the decades since then, the country has constantly evolved and transformed itself, to such an extent that I didn't recognise it at all when I returned from Spain after just four years away.

I arrived back in Qatar in March 2013 in basically a new capital city. This was the new Doha, home of the football revolutionaries who had shaken up the established order. It was a shock to be back in this completely changed hometown; the city had grown spectacularly skywards. The entire West Bay district was now a jungle of futuristically designed skyscrapers, all fighting for attention and appreciation, and I got lost a few times driving through these new streets because the old landmarks had changed so comprehensively. But the thing which had changed most was something intangible: the mindset of an entire nation.

Football's biggest event had come to my hometown while I was gone, and the country was changing by the day as it prepared to welcome the world. There was an altogether different dynamic in play. A new generation had come to the forefront.

'Welcome to the job,' said the head of the Human Resources department as I signed my contract. To me it felt as important a moment as signing for a big club. There were no photographers with flashlights waiting outside, but it was a proud moment all the same as I became employee number 213 and was shown to my new desk. I was now officially working for the World Cup, the same one I'd read about so religiously as a kid in the Falcon Club library. It seemed beyond belief, but now I had to get down to it and convince my new boss he had made the right decision.

By pure coincidence, I now worked in the same building as my father. He'd been in the Olympic tower before, just a few hundred metres away on the other side of Al Bidda Road. But recently the Qatar Athletics Federation had moved to the same building, Al Bidda Tower, where he now sat in his office on the first floor. My job began that day on the 33rd floor. We drove to work together because I didn't have a car yet.

'So listen, enjoy yourself, and just do what you're good at – getting things done,' Dad said in the car, the smell of his cigarettes ingrained in the grey seats. Now that all the kids were gone he smoked in the car again, something Mom had long forbidden him from doing for the sake of our health, and of his.

'Sure,' I said. 'That should be easy enough. And the job is about football. There's nothing I know better.'

My first day at work in Al Bidda Tower, the spiralling, twisting skyscraper now known as 'the Home of Football in Qatar', was a telling experience. Everyone around me was young, energetic and enthusiastic about the challenges ahead. None more so than my boss Nasser, who was in his early thirties. One of my first memories at work there is of watching a World Cup qualifying match in Nasser's office, and Khalfan Ibrahim scoring a stunning goal for Qatar against South Korea. We celebrated together. Then the hard work began. Wave after wave of criticism from the Western media had washed over Qatar since the bid was won, and as I told Nasser in the telephone interview when he hired me: 'What I think we need to do more of is to highlight the positives, of which there are so many.'

In my first week in the job I went about putting together a strategy paper on how I thought this could be done. I approached it in the same structured way I had my doctoral thesis just a few months before. The plan had three phases, the last covering the period from 2018 to 2022. I called it the 'BARCA' plan, in reference to the revolutionary team around pass-master Xavi and the incredible Messi which was playing total football at the time and dominating the world game with their unique style, seemingly at will. We needed to bring out our own unique style and voice to the media outlets who were otherwise just waiting for more bad news. We needed the confidence and proactive mindset to change negative perceptions about Qatar. We needed to tell our own story.

'I like it, shows that you're thinking long-term,' said my boss.

It was the only approach to take, because the criticism of Qatar and specifically FIFA World Cup Qatar 2022™ had become deeply entrenched over the past three years in four key areas:

1. Workers' rights
2. Corruption allegations
3. The weather in summer
4. (Supposed lack of) football tradition

What I also brought along, aside from long-term thinking and some useful languages and experience in the European market, was a completely different perspective on all the areas of criticism.

On workers' rights, mindsets had already changed in the country. I could see that movement very clearly upon my return, where others did not and were impatient. If ten years earlier it had been taboo to even mention workers' issues in the local press, by the time I became a reporter in 2007 it was a topic I was able to write about in numerous articles. And by the time I returned to Doha in 2013, there seemed to be a universal consciousness in place that things needed to change, and much was already moving in that direction. At exactly the time I arrived back, the Supreme Committee was finalising a Workers' Charter as a guiding set of principles for all our projects.

Shortly thereafter the Workers' Welfare Standards, a fifty-page document of contractually binding standards which everyone working on any World Cup project had to implement, were designed with input from human rights organisations. Over the next five years I witnessed the progress and changes myself, taking journalists out to our various worker accommodation areas as the welfare standards were implemented. They significantly helped to lift the standards of all the contractors we worked with.

Having said that, I am no proponent of blaming 'the media', as a generalised and evil entity that is supposedly out to get us, for taking a lopsided view of Qatar. Certainly there are some outlets which have a clear editorial agenda against us, as well as others who have reported factually incorrect stories over the years. A few years later there would also be a concerted and well-documented smear campaign against Qatar from certain neighbouring countries. I think it is our duty to take things up with each outlet that reports inaccurately. Over the years, talking with many of the world's leading media outlets and journalists in countries ranging from Germany to the UK and the USA to Brazil or Mexico, India or China, I've had plenty of interesting debates in this regard.

I remember vividly one discussion with a German journalist over the telephone late one night in early 2013. They'd just published a story showing pictures of the new, high-quality accommodation where our construction workers were housed, but then added a line near the end saying: 'This comes after thousands have died working on World Cup sites.'

It was simply inaccurate, so I decided to call the journalist at the paper and ask him to correct the story.

'Listen, I appreciate that you showed our new accommodation sites for the construction workers,' I said, tired after a long day in the office. 'But can you please correct the sentence about thousands having died on World Cup sites? It is not correct. To this day there has not been a single fatality on any of our projects.'

'Listen,' the journalist said, 'I'm already pushing it with my editors by writing something which is not in line with the Qatar-bashing the rest of them do. And now you want me to go and tell them to change the story?'

'Yes, essentially. Not everything, just that line.'

'I can't. The line is in there for a reason. To give balance. We can't just report the positive.'

'I know that very well; I was a journalist for a long time,' I said, standing out on the small balcony of the first flat we had rented in Doha, near Hamad Hospital, where I'd been born almost thirty years earlier. There was a new apartment block being built behind our flat, where the tinkering and hammering and welding began early every morning. 'All I'm saying is that it is factually incorrect.'

'Says who?'

'I'm telling you. We know the safety record on our sites, and they are very stringent. We've had zero fatalities to this day.'

'That's what you say,' he said. It was a Catch-22 situation. He would not believe me because he could not believe me because of the editor who did not want to be too positive about Qatar. I knew for a fact that it was untrue but there was no way to convince him. I've had similar arguments and debates with journalists who are convinced there was corruption in play in the bidding process, with those who think that Qatar has no football tradition or passion, and with those who suggest that the Arab world is not ready to host a major tournament like this. Over the years, I've come to enjoy these debates, because they usually provide people with more knowledge and information than they previously had.

There is one major point that stands out to me from these debates: journalists take 2010 as their starting point on Qatar. My starting point is 1984. That of my father is even earlier, 1982. If you take the awarding of the World Cup as your starting point, then you miss everything that happened in Qatar beforehand. For me it is very clear that since winning the rights to host the tournament, an entirely new dynamic has been unleashed. Progress which was taking place before has been accelerated exponentially. In this way the World Cup in Qatar has, in the past eight years (at the point in time when I am writing this), already had an effect which it did not have in any of the previous tournaments; it has changed thousands of lives for the better, years before the tournament even begins. You may call that an unsubstantiated claim, but I always like to go out and take a look for myself at things on the ground, as I did in my reporting days at the *Qatar Tribune*.

Over the course of the first five years in the job, I took hundreds of journalists out to our construction workers' accommodation, because that is the area they were most interested in. It made me personally proud to see how the welfare standards devised on paper by our expert teams were implemented in the living accommodation of those building our stadiums. The general reaction I have had from journalists from around the world whom I have taken to see our workers' accommodation is one of disbelief. At first there was a phase where they thought that these were not the workers' real living quarters, because they were so vastly different from what they'd seen in photos. Then, when they were taken to more and more housing areas that all looked the same, a gradual realisation dawned that good work was being done here.

'This is nothing like what we expected,' journalists told me. Or 'this is how university dorms look back home', or 'they have a swimming pool, gym and even free Wi-Fi!'. I have also taken countless journalists to our construction sites, and the feedback from one journalist, writing for a major German magazine, particularly sticks in my mind: 'Let me tell you that there are some sites in Berlin which do not have these types of safety standards, with a separated walkway for workers away from the heavy machinery.' At a June 2017 conference in Berlin with a variety of trade unions present, I talked to Rita Schiavi, who represented the UNIA trade union from Switzerland.

'We had an inspector visiting your sites, and he was amazed, and said the standards on World Cup sites were as good as on Swiss sites,' Schiavi said.

That is not to say that everything is now perfect. It is a work in progress, but one which can leave a truly important legacy not just in Qatar but for the entire region, which faces similar issues with regard to workers' rights and legislation. Anyone following the Qatari media on a daily basis will see signs of progress almost every other day. I read through all the local papers first thing every morning when I come in to the office. Some days it's news on the Wage Protection System which was written into law to ensure timely payment of salaries; on others it's a half-page advertisement on the front page of *The Peninsula* newspaper stating that the new 'Labour City' accommodation for some 95,000 people is now open for companies to rent, or new regulations stating that all buses for workers must have functioning air-conditioning. Most recently, it has been about the new laws coming into effect to replace the much-criticised 'kafala' sponsorship system. The country has made it clear that it acknowledges there have been problems in the past, that improvements are now being made, and that work is under way in that direction. While change may not be happening fast enough for some critics, most have recognised the country's willingness and its open and transparent approach to workers' welfare. And in 2018 even the fiercest critics, including the International Trade Union Confederation (ITUC), Human Rights Watch, the International Labour Organisation and others, commended Qatar's progress on workers' welfare, and called on others in the region to follow suit.

As Nasser Al Khater said in an interview in 2018: 'If there is one area of progress I am most proud of so far, it is the improvements that have been made on workers' welfare, leaving a true legacy.'

On a hot summer day a few years into the job I went out with our workers' welfare team to have a look at the new accommodation and associated facilities which the country has developed at 'Labour City'. A thirty-minute drive from our offices on the Corniche took us to the Industrial Area, where as youngsters my siblings and I would often accompany our father when he took the blue Toyota Land Cruiser to be fixed after one of its many breakdowns. On the way there we passed the run-down garage where he used to go, and where the owner became his friend. Very near to that area a new part of town has now sprung up, which contains a full-sized cricket pitch, a shopping centre (where we stocked up on water that day), cinemas, a travel agency, and next to that a massive development of apartment blocks and green spaces. We went into 'Labour City' to have a look.

Across the board the facilities were good, with air-conditioning in each unit and no more than four people to a room, and the dining facilities were clean and comfortable. It was clearly a step up from any other facilities I'd seen until then and more such developments were under way, as new accommodation for over 250,000 workers was being built in Qatar at the time of writing this book. Without a doubt there are also still facilities that are not up to these standards, and this is not an attempt to deny that. However, it is equally clear that the kind of progress I have seen both on construction sites and in numerous accommodation buildings has been accelerated – and significantly so – by the World Cup coming to Qatar.

On that occasion we were accompanied on our visit by a contractor who was looking for new accommodation for his workforce. I asked him whether he thought accommodation standards were improving across the board, and not just on our projects. 'We all have to step up and put forward our best side,' he said, adding: 'Any contractor across the country knows that to get work with a major project like the World Cup you need to have good standards for your workers. It is like going to the office in your best suit. You certainly don't want to be going naked.'

After the visit, the company in question decided to move its entire workforce to Labour City. It was just one example of the new dynamic being felt and seen across the country. Other examples occurred closer to home. The Kenyan gate guard I talked to regularly in the apartment block across the street told me one day that he and his colleagues had been moved to better accommodation, with fewer people to a room, hot showers and sports facilities, all of which was a major step up from their previous conditions. The company in question didn't work with the World Cup committee. But contractors and companies across the country were now taking note of their responsibilities.

Slowly but surely, while criticism still kept regularly coming our way, more people were also reporting and speaking out about the improvements Qatar was making. In September 2015, we received a visit from German lawyer and former 800-metre runner Sylvia Schenk, who took part in the 1972 Olympics in Munich and was a board member of Transparency International Germany from 2006 until 2013. At the time of her visit she was leading their working group on sport, as well as coordinating the Sport and Rights Alliance (SRA) with Amnesty International, Human Rights Watch, the ITUC, Terre des Hommes, FIFPro and Football Supporters Europe. On her second visit to Qatar, for a UNESCO conference, Schenk took time out to see Khalifa International Stadium for herself. I was on hand for the visit, as she put on her safety boots and got her safety induction, and we then walked together through the construction site and were briefed on what was done to keep workers safe and hydrated throughout their working day. We stopped in an air-conditioned rest room supplied with cold water along the way, and then went on to the mess hall – an enormous air-conditioned indoor space where different types of food were served. When the whole tour was done, we sat down in the room where we'd had the safety briefing, and I talked with her for twenty minutes.

'Qatar has the right to catapult itself into modernity, and I find it a very exciting development,' Schenk told me. 'The interesting thing to see is how strategically they are going about it. With Qatar

National Vision 2030 in mind they are, for example, also looking at women's rights.'

And then Schenk raised an important point. She said that hosting the World Cup in a country like Qatar had the potential to act as a catalyst in a way that it never could in Germany.

'It is interesting to see how you can keep traditions and still build the future. A World Cup always moves a lot. Because Qatar is doing so much in a short space of time, such a World Cup can be an accelerator for change beyond the infrastructure. I still remember on 2 December, during the bid presentations in Zurich, Qatar's was the only delegation where a woman said something. Everyone else – the Americans, the English, the Australians – had only men presenting. So back then I thought: I would not have expected this; they surprised me in a positive manner.'

Like this visit with the German official, I have been on countless site and accommodation visits over the past years since my return to Doha. These visits have also surprised me in a positive manner, because they show what can be done with sustained effort and continued commitment. The work continues. Ironically, it may be managers or companies from the UK, Germany, or a whole host of other countries who still settle for the status quo because they don't want to cut into profits. I have heard of such cases. They should all be held accountable for making the wrong decision. Putting human beings first is always a good economic choice. And for those who don't have human empathy, in a world driven by capitalism and profit margins there is always the most convincing argument of all: caring for your workers actually increases their productivity significantly. In the end, it is simple maths. All the contractors who worked with us on our projects adopted our standards, and said that as a result the productivity of their workforce had increased significantly.

Much of my work in those first years back in Qatar was a matter of sheer persuasion, debating in the old-school fashion, pointing to the impressive bid which had easily outdone the others, revealing facts that people didn't know – such as successes of the Qatar national team that I researched and even people in Doha hadn't heard of – and generally representing my home country in its true colours. I did so with pride both in Doha and abroad.

Together with Qatar's smart young World Cup officials, I travelled to every corner of the world in those years, from Kuala Lumpur to Berlin and London to Rio de Janeiro for the FIFA Confederations Cup 2013, where I witnessed the unprecedented social unrest associated with the lack of legacy planning for the event. It would be the backdrop for an unforgettable meeting which connected Qatar's sporting past with its future.

2013. RIO DE JANEIRO
The man with the magic touch

We are driving to the stadium for a football match in Brazil, exactly a year before the 2014 FIFA World Cup™. While I am in search of a very important person, who seems to be linked with Qatar's football past like a pattern on an intricately woven carpet, this is a country in search of itself one year before welcoming the world. More than that, perhaps, its population is using the global attention brought about by football's biggest sporting event to highlight things which are going wrong at home. By the looks of the massive protests across the entire country this summer, there are many things which concern the people.

There is a helicopter buzzing overhead. A special police force car has just whizzed by with shotguns drawn and hanging out of the blacked-out windows.

'Don't worry,' a Brazilian guide in the bus with us explains. 'The shotgun is just put out of the window as a warning. They do that all the time, it's nothing serious.'

That is hardly a very reassuring message. It is June 2013 and we are in Brazil to observe operations at the FIFA Confederations Cup, also known as the warm-up event to the World Cup. We find the country engulfed in a massive wave of popular protests against government spending on football and failed promises on education, transport and healthcare. There are tense moments as increasingly frustrated crowds resort to violence to put their point across while the world media's attention is firmly on Brazil.

A few miles later, all traffic comes to a standstill. The protesters have blocked all routes to the stadium, it seems. Our small group of observers from Qatar are whisked into a nearby police station for a reassessment of the situation. It seems there is no safe way to get through the masses of protesters and find a way into the stadium. In the midst of this tense atmosphere Nasser Al Khater, who is leading the Qatari delegation, turns around to us and tries some humour for reassurance: 'Let's keep going to the stadium. Unless they call in the air force too. Then we will turn back.'

Football above all? Must a game like this go ahead at any cost? At what point do they have to prioritise public safety and call it off? Can they find us a way through? I've been to a great many football games but never felt such unease minutes before kick-off. With the turbulent scenes getting no better we are whisked back out of the police station and the car in front of us takes us another way, past low houses and police blockades, until we finally reach the stadium. In the 100 metres immediately around the venue this looks like any normal football game. But evidently it is not a normal match.

Inside, the home nation is about to begin playing. Moments later the entire stadium begins belting out the Brazilian national anthem together with the eleven players out there on the pitch, singing at the top of their voices, continuing even after the music has finished in another minute or so of entirely goose bump-creating madness. Here is everything football can do, encapsulated in a single day: while outside angry crowds protest, fully aware of the heightened media attention, everyone inside the stadium suddenly takes the opportunity to express their love for Brazil, a moment of emotion and national pride which makes this tournament a sporting success for the hosts, even though it will also contribute to the following year's disastrous World Cup semi-final loss against Germany.

It was this which brought me to Brazil in the first place – to study emotions. The emotional pattern that runs through Qatar's football history. It always brings me back to a single name, that of Brazilian coach Evaristo de Macedo, who turned a Qatari team of complete underdogs into a winning side capable of defeating the most celebrated teams in the world.

Is this the essence I am trying to capture? Even if it is just small droplets in a miniature bottle that I can take back with me to Doha, it is this crazy defiance in the face of all the odds, this daring to dream even if you have no right to dream (but who am I to tell you that?), this one-in-a-million chance which makes every sporting contest so enthralling, which defines Qatar's sporting dreams. This is the Q-factor in the country's unique sporting strategy. The belief that with the right approach and the correct mindset absolutely anything is possible.

Just a few months after settling into life with the FIFA World Cup Qatar 2022™ team, I found myself trying to find the man himself, Evaristo – if he was still alive. My father had tried to establish contact with him through some of his former athletics coaches who lived in Brazil, but nothing had materialised yet. A couple of Brazilian journalists I contacted knew he was alive, but didn't have his number.

I kept trying, and eventually came across a journalist who said he might be able to help. A few days later I had his number. It had taken some meticulous research to track down the legendary Brazilian coach in his native Rio de Janeiro, but the effort was certainly worth it. There at the other end of the telephone line was the man I had read and heard so much about, saying into the receiver at the other end in his distinctive Brazilian accent:

'Alo?'

'This is Matthias from Qatar,' I told him, 'and there are some important people from FIFA World Cup Qatar 2022™ who would love to meet you.'

On the day we met Evaristo in Rio de Janeiro, the sun was shining brilliantly outside, the air sang with that unmistakable tune which only Brazil knows how to hum, and I'd just walked the streets of this marvellous city to find a printing shop before the meeting. The light is different in Brazil, and life felt different too that day. It felt like walking backwards into the delightfully untold and uncharted pages of Qatar's football history. As a special souvenir, we had prepared a framed photo of Evaristo on the front cover of the Qatari sports magazine *Al Saqr* (Arabic for 'falcon') from the early '80s. It was a classic Christopher Columbus-style pose, one arm stretched out pointing the direction in which his team was going. There was another photo, the one I was trying to get printed that morning, which had only just been sent to me by the Qatar Sports Museum. It was one of his Qatari under-20 team which had famously reached the final in Australia in 1981. In the picture they were posing as ambassadors for the successful Qatari 2022 bid.

As Nasser and I waited for Evaristo to arrive in the hotel lobby, we wondered whether we would recognise the coaching legend. We only had the photo on the 1980s magazine cover to go on. Over thirty years had passed, and time stops for no one, not even the most successful coach in Qatar's young football history.

'What if he walks straight past us?' I asked Nasser.

'That's your job, to identify him. I thought you were good at all this historical stuff,' he joked.

Shortly thereafter, though, Evaristo arrived, and we did recognise him immediately. He walked in through the revolving doors with a surprising spring in his step, wearing beige trousers and a simple blue short-sleeved shirt. He walked with great elegance and poise. Across his face spread an enormous smile, as naturally warm and welcoming as this magnificent city all around us. He carried his age gracefully, joyfully, as seemed to be the case with many people strolling up and down the Copacabana walkway next to the iconic beach where the hotel was situated.

'It's a pleasure to finally meet you,' Nasser said, shaking the hand of the man who had successfully shaped Qatar's early football history.

As we all sat down together with our Secretary-General, Hassan Al Thawadi, the excitement on all sides was clearly visible. We had all been transformed back into kids, looking forward to meeting a sporting hero. A television camera from Qatar's Al Kass sports channel documented the moment for viewers back home. It didn't take the Rio-born striker long to remember what Doha had been like when he first reached the shores of the Arabian Gulf – some two years before my father had made the same journey from Germany. In fact, his initial reaction upon arriving in Qatar seemed similar to that of my mother.

'When I first arrived in Doha in 1980, it was very small and there was nothing much there, so I said to myself – shall I go back to Brazil? But I stayed, and it was good that I did,' Evaristo remembered with a fond smile, as he sipped a Diet Coke with ice. 'We played in Doha Stadium, where Pele had come for a friendly match with Santos in 1973. When I arrived in Qatar everyone kicked the ball far up the field. I asked: Why do you do that, don't you like the ball?'

For Evaristo there was one key to success for his young and inexperienced side – belief in the seemingly impossible.

'When I first arrived in Qatar there was an old team. I thought, with this team we won't go anywhere. So we made a new team, the team that went to Australia. Before going we had a lengthy training camp in Brazil, where we played friendly matches and formed the team spirit that was needed to do something great.'

At the end of a memorable morning chatting about the initial days of football in Qatar, Evaristo put on his glasses and looked at the photo of his former charges which our Secretary-General had just presented to him. He laughed heartily at how they too had been transformed by the unstoppable forces of time, and smiled with the warmth of a Rio morning. We all felt the positive energy of this man who had helped transform football in Qatar. It was clear to me then how he had done it. He had believed that miracles were possible if you had a dream and worked incredibly hard to achieve it, and through his infectious energy he had caused all those who played under him to believe the same. But now he had grown a little tired and bade us farewell, inviting us to visit him in his home on another occasion. And before he left, he had one more gem of a story to share with us.

'Keep this one between us. There was one defender, I won't say his name now, who came to me before we left for Australia,' he recounted, before heading back out through the revolving doors. 'He said: "Coach, I won't go with you, because I know we will lose in the first round and that would be too embarrassing." So I left him in Doha. And when we returned, every one of the players who had reached the 1981 final got a house from the country's ruler as a present for our achievement. So he came to me again and asked: "Can I have a house too?" I told him he should have believed in us in the first place.'

We all laughed heartily at the anecdote, but the lesson Evaristo de Macedo taught us all that day was a simple one: if you don't believe in yourself, you won't get a new house. He'd also given me a whole lot of new insights into the history of football in the country I called home. Then he was gone, walking back along Copacabana beach towards his own home and another unforgettable Rio day.

The 2013 tournament in Brazil also confirmed a vital lesson for Qatar: a World Cup without adequate legacy outcomes for the population has the potential to quickly turn negative. Qatar's consistent focus on legacy outcomes was clearly based on the lessons learned from past major events. There were now just two FIFA World Cup™ tournaments remaining before Qatar became the next host of the greatest football event on the planet.

Exactly five years later, in the early summer of 2018, it was time for Evaristo to be reunited with his former Qatar players. The stage was set for a memorable return to Doha. Much had changed. A whole skyline had popped up out of the sand behind the Corniche. Qatar was now a World Cup host nation. The first morning I saw Evaristo and his son and grandson after they landed in Doha, we met in the lobby of the Sheraton hotel. It had been decades since the former Barcelona striker was in Doha, but everywhere he walked, Qataris stopped him to share memories of his teams and to take photos that they promised to send to numerous relatives. He smiled as brightly as a Rio morning as these memories were shared, and then he turned to me and asked: 'So what are we doing today?'

As we took Evaristo around Doha, he saw a city and a country completely changed from what he had witnessed all those decades ago. The highlight of the visit was the Amir Cup final at Khalifa International Stadium, where he met old players and colleagues, and then he visited Al Bidda Tower to see our plans for FIFA World Cup Qatar 2022™.

'I feel very happy when I am here in Qatar, because I have made very good friends – the people have recognised all that we achieved with the national team,' Evaristo told me that day. 'In just a little over ten years with the national team we were able to do things no one imagined we could do.'

Nasser Al Khater, now our Assistant Secretary-General for Tournament Affairs, showed Evaristo round the Legacy Pavilion, our floor dedicated to Qatar's hosting plans and legacy programmes for the World Cup.

'It gives us great pleasure to welcome you back to Qatar, your home,' said Al Khater, presenting the legendary coach with a customised portrait as a souvenir of his visit to Doha.

Another special moment awaited as Evaristo's visit to Doha neared its end. We had invited a number of his former players to surprise him live on the Al Kass TV show Al Majlis, in the traditional colourful sitting room setting which has become a part of Qatari sports folklore. There were incredulous hugs and jokes all round, and you could see tears in some eyes that May evening. Time had not stood still for any of those present, but their friendship still seemed as strong as ever.

'We were able to use the result in 1981 as a springboard to build new football stadiums and clubs,' said Evaristo. 'Now you can see that while we started to put Qatar on the map, today the country has arrived on the world stage.'

Concluding with a look back at his own exploits with the surprise U-20 side from Qatar, Evaristo smiled wistfully as he said: '1981 is a date which a lot of people here remember. Sport has grown as a result, and football in the end is a means of friendship which unites people and cultures. Football has grown a lot here. Today Qatar is known around the world. This is a dream which has been transformed into reality.'

2014. AL GHARAFA SPORTS CLUB
The Nepalese defender who lifted the Cup

The sun was setting as I headed with Wilfried Lemke to watch the Workers Cup. He worked for the United Nations, directly advising the then Secretary-General of the organisation, Ban Ki-moon, on the significant topic of sport for development and peace. Now he was sitting next to me in his car, asking how the World Cup preparations were going and what progress had been made on the issue of migrant workers in Qatar.

We pulled up in front of several busy-looking football pitches at the Al Gharafa Sports Club fields that evening in March and got out of the car. I didn't know how the UN Special Adviser would react to what he was about to see. He had small round glasses and a significant, well-groomed moustache above his upper lip, and he broke into a broad smile when he saw the ball rolling.

On the pitch in front of us, two teams were playing football with a great deal of passion and a fair sprinkling of skill thrown in for good measure. They had their kit in fine order, and wore boots which were shiny and new. The studs dug into the green grass of the pitch as they raced after the ball. There were plenty of spectators standing around the pitch, shouting their teams on. The standard of the football was quite high, and a few players were dribbling their way through the opposition defence with the ease more usually associated with their illustrious idols.

'That one, he is our Cristiano Ronaldo,' one fan told us amid a noisy array of chants and shouts. 'He trains every evening after work.'

Lemke stood by the side of the pitch and watched the game with great interest.

'Impressive,' he said, more to himself than anyone else. 'That player, he could try out in the Bundesliga. He's fast and skilful. He might make it in my team, Bremen.'

All the players in question were from companies working in Qatar. They were part of the 'Workers Cup', a direct result of the social inclusion and 'sports for all' projects promised in Qatar's bid for 2022. Wilfried Lemke went over to talk to some of the players who were taking goes at a 'hardest shot' competition while they waited for their turn to play.

The doctoral dissertation I had written a year earlier at university had one major hypothesis: everything you think can be deduced from the words you put on paper and the linguistic choices you make. When I looked at the language choices made in Qatar after my return, I saw that everything which was changing and improving on the topic of workers' welfare could be read and deduced from the words describing it. Just a few months after I'd returned to Doha, I heard excited talk in the office of a new football competition.

'A tournament for workers,' someone explained. 'It's going to be called the Workers Cup.'

From the name itself you could see the importance the country was attaching to the topic. The tournament was still in the conceptual stages at the time, but from the moment I heard of it I thought it would be something big. In other areas, too, language was changing. For too long the living quarters of construction workers had been described as 'labour camps' or similar things with equally negative connotations. But now, through the work done by the workers' welfare team to improve standards, the names were changing to 'accommodation', 'villages', or simply 'living areas'.

Shortly after that office conversation, the first edition of the tournament opened for registration, and there was big demand. Teams from all over the country who were involved in the construction sector wanted to take part. And when the football got under way, the true importance of the tournament became evident. It was more successful than anyone could have imagined.

Wilfried Lemke was talking to some of the players with the precision of a carpenter taking the measurements for a kitchen table. He asked them everything in a very neutral and calm manner – how their work was going, what conditions they lived in, how much they got paid, whether they had their passports, if they were happy working in Qatar. Then the action turned again to the field. Goals were scored. The fans had turned out in big numbers and made themselves heard whenever the scoreline changed. I stood by the field of play with Mr Lemke and together we watched as the fans of one side went absolutely crazy when their team scored the winning goal.

'I think this is a fantastic initiative,' Lemke said. 'And I think it should be shown to the world.'

Directly after visiting that match I also took the German sports official to one of the accommodation sites where men working on our stadiums were living.

It was an unannounced visit, because he just asked me there in the car on the way back. He wanted to see it for himself, as so many others would over the years. It was an advantage that he asked to go at night, because many of the visitors and journalists we'd taken there during the day, when the workers were out on site, didn't believe us: 'Is this a real living area? Do people actually live here? It looks like a model accommodation block.'

When Wilfried Lemke arrived at the accommodation in question, he saw it full of people. Some were watching television after dinner; others were sitting about, Skyping their families back home; still others were relaxing in the games room. We walked around for a good while.

'Can I see some of your bedrooms?' he asked.

They let him in to have a look. He saw the laundry rooms and the bathrooms and then he took a few pictures 'to show the people I meet on my travels what the conditions are like'. Go ahead, I said. We had nothing to hide. Finally he nodded and said he'd seen enough.

We headed back in his black car through the streets of the city at night. A few weeks later I got an official letter from Mr Lemke on the United Nations letterhead. He thanked me for showing him the Workers Cup and the accommodation our workers lived in, and encouraged us to keep doing such a positive job on workers' welfare.

In the following years, the Workers Cup tournament grew bigger and better. More teams entered, and they all took it extremely seriously. It was about more than the prize money on offer, the equivalent of a month's salary for some of the participants. Subsequent editions of the tournament kicked off and the crowds just kept increasing in size. A whole colourful array of fans turned up to attend the opening ceremony of the next tournament, which took place at Al Sadd Stadium.

I decided to take along my wife and daughter to the match – one of a whole host of sporting events we'd attend together over the years in Doha. My daughter basically had to grow up a sports fan with all these events she had seen in her first five years. On that day she really enjoyed herself, watching the players parade in with the flags of their companies, and the fireworks go off, before two of the teams played the opening match. There was a mascot too, with whom she wanted a photo at any price. A few weeks later, the final took place at Aspire Academy's indoor football pitch.

The third-place match took place just before the final in the enormous indoor arena, where inspirational quotes from Pele adorn the far wall. The teams came out onto the field to a smattering of warm applause, with the stands on both sides of the pitch completely packed. It was a goose-bumps atmosphere. One of our contractors for the Al Wakrah Stadium won third place, edging the match 1-0. Each time the teams got close to the goal a roar went through the crowd. You could sense the passion; you could feel it in the shouts and the dancing fans and the flags waved wildly in celebration.

The construction workers were the protagonists in this tournament, and they were clearly enjoying the limelight. It turned out to be a memorable final. In front of 3,500 fans at the Aspire Dome, workers from cleaning services company Tanzifco celebrated a nail-biting penalty shoot-out victory over opponents Outlook Trading and Contracting Company. After a tense 2-2 draw in ordinary time, Tanzifco held their nerve to win 4-2 on penalties.

After the match I walked down onto the pitch and joined the teams as they celebrated. I talked to one of the heroes of the match, the man who had just converted the winning penalty and celebrated it as enthusiastically as if it had been in a World Cup final for his national team.

'It was a great moment for me to win a tournament like this with my team,' said Nepalese defender Til Badur. He looked with excitement at the winners' trophies and the medals which were about to be presented. 'I have never witnessed anything like it before. The venue and the support we received today and throughout the whole tournament was really great, because it encourages people to take part in sports.'

That year twenty-four teams took part in the tournament. The teams we had seen today were the last four remaining after weeks of intense competition. Nearby stood Hassan Al Thawadi, our Secretary-General. You could see on his face how much this tournament meant to him.

'This is what it is all about,' he told me as he watched the match. 'This tournament, this passion and these fans and players. What the game of football means to them. This epitomises why we bid for the World Cup in the first place.'

Meanwhile Nasser Al Khater was being asked for a continual stream of selfies which would end up on the social media accounts of players from both teams. He was visibly enjoying the final, shaking hands with the players who had just received their medals and trophies. Slowly, the crowds headed back home, and only the players remained behind, taking pictures with their medals from every imaginable angle. Another edition of the tournament had concluded, and again things had shifted imperceptibly in my hometown. The Workers Cup was fast becoming an integral part of Qatar's sporting calendar.

The following year, I went along to the opening match again. As the ball bounced off a defender in the penalty box and almost found its way to the back of the net, the 5,500-strong crowd at Al Gharafa Sports Club in Doha roared as if the first goal had already been scored. Watching from the stands as Gulf Contracting Company beat ETA Star 3-0 was John, a 28-year-old defensive midfielder from Kenya who had just minutes earlier paraded in with his team at the opening ceremony. I went over and joined John and his group of friends.

'I like challenges and I like the competition,' John told me of his team's first participation in the event. 'Next year I will know where to improve. This is my first tournament, and the first time I will play in this big stadium. This year we have a great team and we are aiming to reach the final; since we have good players I hope we can make it.'

John's team had big hopes for the tournament that year, but it was about more than winning or losing to him and his team-mates.

'We selected our players in training according to their talent. We want to win as one family. We work on different sites, and we come together three or four times a week to train so that we can get ready to put on our best performance in this tournament. God willing, I will also be here to watch the World Cup in Qatar in 2022, to see the whole tournament and attend my first World Cup.'

His side lost their opening game 3-0 against Amana Contracting, but that could not diminish his excitement about being on such a grand stage, in a stadium where professional players played their football on a weekly basis.

The opening match that year took place after a Qatar Stars League (QSL) match between Al Gharafa and Al Khor. Also on hand to have a look, after his side's 3-1 victory over Al Khor, was former Australia international and World Cup veteran Mark Bresciano. What did this player with multiple World Cup experiences for his country think of the initiative? I walked over to ask him.

'I think it's a very good idea,' Bresciano said, still dripping with sweat from his own game at the venue minutes earlier. 'It's good to see that the construction companies have thought about their workers, because playing any sport is healthy and something to look forward to at the weekend. To see that it's happening for the third successive year shows it has been successful, and I'm happy to be part of a club that supports it. It's something worthwhile, and something that other companies should consider also. It has big potential to grow.'

The Australian midfielder had won the Asian Cup with his nation on home soil that January. Now he looked on and clapped as players from many different countries in Asia represented their companies in the Qatar Workers Cup.

Another year later, and the stands of the Qatar Sports Club stadium were packed full of spectators. They had come to watch the opening match of the 2016 edition, this time a match between Nakheel and Aalco. The atmosphere was electric.

After the match I eagerly awaited the opportunity to talk to the coach of one of the winning teams. His antics on the sidelines had been worthy of the best Jose Mourinho nights with Porto in the UEFA Champions League. He wore a red tracksuit, and each time his side scored, which they did four times that evening, he sprinted up the side of the pitch and jumped into the arms of his players. It was such an emotional outburst that you just had to get off your seat and jump up too. I did. I started shouting and celebrating. I had no immediate connection to this team. But there I was, shouting it on, jumping at every goal and screaming like an ecstatic Icelandic football commentator. That's what football does to you sometimes. For no apparent reason at all. It was just some casual Workers Cup magic in front of a cheering crowd on a Friday night at Qatar Sports Club, with Doha's skyline shimmering in the background. Nothing else.

For the semi-finals that year, the new President of FIFA came to watch. The tournament had come full circle from the early days, when I had taken the UN Special Advisor to have a look. Now it was the FIFA President himself, Gianni Infantino, who came to personally shake hands with the two semi-finalists he happened to see play that day. All around there were journalists from across the world, who had come to watch the president watch the tournament, and to attend his press conference half an hour later. One journalist would make it a front-page story for the New York Times. Another was filming it all for Globo TV from Brazil. I'd taken journalists from Germany to the tournament too. The Workers Cup was fast becoming a symbol of Qatar's efforts to use the World Cup to accelerate progress on workers' rights in the country.

The final that year was held at Al Ahli Club, where Pep Guardiola once played club football for two seasons. This time CNN was there with a crew. Many others too. A whole host of diplomats had made it to the final, including the American and British ambassadors. The German ambassador was also there, and I greeted him with a handshake. He smiled at the fantastic atmosphere and told me to send him the footage of the tournament. He wanted to make sure everyone in Germany saw this contagious passion for football.

Down there on the pitch to help hand over the trophies that year was Bora Milutinovic. The legendary Serbian coach had wanted to be there too.

'The Workers Cup final, can you make it?' I asked. 'We'd like you to help present the trophies to the winning teams.'

'I have an important five-a-side match,' he said, 'but I'll cancel it. They will understand. Count me in.'

The tournament had become something that you couldn't miss. Looking back now, I think of those matches as some of the most important I have been to over the years in Qatar. I have nothing against those friendly matches with all the star names – I've seen Zlatan Ibrahimovic, Cristiano Ronaldo, Ronaldinho, Kaka and even David Beckham at various times out on the pitch in Doha. But these Workers Cup matches where you see amateurs playing with such passion and commitment are something different altogether. They symbolise everything good about football, and everything positive that this nation I call home can achieve by embracing the beautiful game.

By the 2017 edition of the tournament, the Workers Cup counted a record-breaking thirty-two teams. It had reached the size of a World Cup tournament.

SPRING 2014. THE NEWSROOM
A chat with the World Cup-winning captain

'Ey, Mati,' Gianfranco Zola, generally seen as one of the greatest Chelsea players ever, called my way. 'Come over here, I need to climb up on your shoulders.'

'Sure,' I said, chuffed at my new nickname coined by an authentic football legend. 'Which colour do you want to sign with, red or blue?'

It was obviously blue. The little Italian genius on the ball was trying to make use of some additional height to sign our 'Wall of Fame' in the newsroom at Al Bidda Tower. The wall was filling up nicely with autographs. Next to him stood another Chelsea legend, former France defender and 1998 FIFA World Cup™ winner Marcel Desailly. The two had just completed a rather dull 0-0 draw on the PlayStation in the newsroom, because neither knew how to play, in stark contrast to their skills on the pitch in their professional careers.

In early 2014, about a year after I had first joined the team preparing Qatar for the World Cup, I was writing another strategy paper for my boss. This time it was about setting up a newsroom, which would be tasked with proactively telling our story of the first-ever FIFA World Cup™ in the Middle East.

'We're going to be starting up a newsroom, and I want you to lead it,' Nasser told me that day.

If we were not always given a fair voice in some parts of the media, so our reasoning went, we'd take to telling our story ourselves. The topics had shifted around but the general tenor remained the same:

how could you give the World Cup to a country like Qatar? We'd reached breaking point. It was time to fight back. In April 2014, a few months before the start of the World Cup in Brazil, we started the World Cup newsroom. My boss signed off the strategy and then had a long chat with me.

'Listen,' he said in his familiar no-messing-about tone, 'this is your opportunity. I know you can do a good job on this. You take your swing, and knock it out of the park. Hit a home run on this project. And if you ever need advice from me on anything, don't hesitate to ask.'

So we started taking swings at the balls coming our way. It was not my opportunity alone, but by extension that of the whole team, and perhaps beyond that a whole country which was tired of waiting to be understood. Here was an opportunity to speak out in a fresh and direct way about what this World Cup, and this small country with the big ambitions, was really all about.

When we started the newsroom we were just a bunch of youngsters looking to do something important. The first thing was to design the floor plan and organise the team into different topic areas to cover, and then I called an initial meeting to explain to the whole team what the idea was.

'We will be producing stories every day, each day anew, without fail, about what it is that makes this first-ever World Cup in the Middle East so exciting and unique,' I told the gathered group, and saw a lot of blank faces blinking at me in response. They had never been asked something of this nature before.

Then came the fun part, moving desks with everyone into the new space we'd been given, in the former 'brainstorming room' overlooking the entire Corniche and the city of Doha from a beautiful vantage point. We were an excited bunch. It was a moment to begin something new. A new approach. A new adventure. Would we succeed, though?

We were just a couple of former journalists and a few other youngsters with energy and enthusiasm. There was a football-crazy Mexican who had taken a real liking to Qatar; he was an Arsenal supporter with an encyclopaedic knowledge of everything you'd ever want to know about the world of football, which made me give him the nickname 'The Machine' – and he also made phenomenal guacamole. The oldest of us all was a Moroccan lady who had been there since the FIFA World Cup Qatar 2022™ bid and took care of the younger members of the team like a mother. There was a thin American who liked to put post-it notes all over his desk and did not have any experience in journalism. We also had a Spaniard from the Canary Islands who had a quiet determination and a good eye for stories, since she too had been a journalist, for the Spanish news agency in Doha. And that was basically it. Then we were under way, swinging at stories like there was no tomorrow.

I suppose no one believed much in our ability to change things, but we had one very important backer. The boss who believed that this could work. We faced a world that seemed to be hostile toward anything positive coming from Qatar. As a first step, I brought in guest speakers to inspire the team. The first of them was an American professor of journalism at Northwestern University in Qatar. He reminded me of my former colleague at the *Qatar Tribune*, and he gave it to us straight and hard about how to be a great reporter: no frills, and no punches pulled.

'Go out there and find your stories,' he said. 'Don't care about anyone else. Make your beat yours.'

And so we started, small steps first. Baby steps in a world which seemed set on the idea that a World Cup in my hometown was a bad idea. Every morning we held a newsroom meeting to discuss story ideas and the things happening that day. The first story ever written by our very own newsroom was by no means earth-shaking, but it was the one with which everything took off. Fittingly, it was about the new Hamad International Airport which had just opened in

Doha at the time, and where most fans will be arriving in 2022.

The title of the story after it came past my desk was 'Eleven things football fans should know about Qatar's new airport'. I thought it was a good read. I made a few changes, had it translated into Arabic as well, and then pressed 'publish'. Would the world start turning differently now? Would people begin to change their minds about Qatar? Not really.

Nothing much happened. The story didn't take off much further than the local papers. But we'd made a start. Slowly, people started to take notice, both internally in the building and outside in media outlets in Qatar. Looking back, that was the most important effect the newsroom had. It changed the mindset and the mentality of the people in the building and the country at large. From constantly reacting to bad news, we were now starting to create our own news. And slowly, journalists from other parts of the world started looking at our stories too.

'So what's our next story?' I said the next morning in the meeting. I needed to instil in the team the mindset that the end of one story was the start of the next. There was no time for rest.

From there things started moving along nicely. After the initial stage of setting up the newsroom and organising the team into different 'beats' to cover their topic areas, the next step was to bring in star players to visit us. My thinking was simple: show people what we were doing, interview them, and then use the multiplier effect to get their thoughts out to the world. It was also a simple way to guarantee media coverage in football publications across the world.

After watching all these players over the years on television due to that football obsession which had my whole family baffled, I now saw them walking into the office in person. Michael Laudrup, Roberto Carlos, Xavi Hernandez, Bora Milutinovic, Patrick Kluivert – the man who had made me a Barca fan all those years ago – all of them came into the building, and I would meet them in the lobby with a handshake. A handshake! Sometimes we'd have a quick coffee downstairs first. A coffee! Then we'd whizz up in the lift to the upper floors of the building, where they met with our management, marvelled at the views and the plans and stadium designs we showed them, and the programmes we explained to them, as well as the important progress taking shape on workers' welfare. At the end of each visit I sat down with our guest for an interview. Then we'd put out the interview the same day on our channels and send it on to media outlets in Qatar, the region and internationally. The newsroom was starting to fly, and my boss could see that the ball was heading either for the stands or, even better, for the water behind the stadium. There was no way back now.

We spoke to a veritable dream team of football legends past and present, and one of my personal favourites was an interview I conducted with the captain of Germany's 2014 World Cup-winning squad. The interview had been arranged at short notice during the annual Bayern Munich training camp in Doha, and took place in the area where the players were due to have their lunch in the hotel overlooking Aspire Academy's pristine pitches.

It was around the same area of Doha where I had heard on the radio, a good quarter of a century earlier, the news that West Germany had just won the 1990 World Cup, defeating Argentina 1-0 in the final. The interview also had a special significance because not for nothing was Philipp Lahm one of Pep Guardiola's favourite players – he was as intelligent off the pitch as he was on it.

'When we train here in Doha there is always a lot of interest from the fans, which is nice. Football lives from the fans and from people coming together, and that is the most important thing – football unites the whole world. This is the positive power that the sport has, and I hope it will be the same at the World Cup in Qatar in 2022.'

With Bayern Munich facing questions every year about the situation of workers in Qatar, Lahm took a very clear position on the issue. 'I always believe it is best to come to a place and talk about things. What we experience in our own countries, what it is like in other places, the most important thing is that you talk about things. You will not be able to change anything by staying at home and not talking about it.'

Those four years that I was in charge of our newsroom also marked a significant change in our overall communications with the world: for the first time, we really entered the conversation in a sustained and confident manner. We hit not just one but a whole series of home runs, which made the boss (and would have made the preaching American editor) proud. We unearthed a jewel of a story about a thirty-million-year-old rock found under a stadium site, which went across the world. We had great global success with the story of 3D-printed World Cup stadium models being created at Qatar University for value engineering and to optimise the cooling technology. We reported extensively on workers' welfare improvements, and on Qatar's first stadium for 2022 being opened, and explained the 40 per cent more efficient cooling technology installed there. We covered countless events and visited all of the stadiums being built on a regular basis. We started producing short, fun videos for social media audiences, and moved our focus into digital and video content.

Every day of those four years was exciting and challenging, and I was extremely proud of the team. We had dignitaries of the highest level pass by the newsroom, including even, very briefly, His Highness Sheikh Tamim bin Hamad Al Thani, the Amir of Qatar, as he toured the offices one day. It indicates both how well we were doing and how important it was to tell our story proactively. No one would tell the story of Qatar for us if we didn't tell it ourselves. So we did. Every day of the year. We had the weight of the world, and the expectations of the country, on our shoulders. But still, there was nothing quite like this job. And some days it included unannounced visits from the man who would probably coach the United Nations football team, if ever there was such a thing.

2015. DOHA, SPORTS CAPITAL OF THE WORLD
The football nomad

Working for the organisers of a World Cup for over seven years is the most incredible experience. Some days, if you come into my office you will find me playing chess. Across my desk from me will be a formidable foe – Bora Milutinovic.

In the office I'm usually distracted when I play against him, because I'm thinking of the million and one other things that need my immediate attention. The best matches I've played against Coach Bora have been in the fish restaurant that he likes to visit near the waterfront at Katara, or at his home in The Pearl.

Coach Bora doesn't like you taking too long with a move. That's because he's already thinking five moves ahead, and bored out of his mind.

'Come on, for goodness sake,' he says.

'What, is it my move?' I ask with feigned innocence.

I know it's my move. I'm just trying to win time.

He knows I know it's my move, and he's just trying to hurry me up in order for me to make the mistake from which he can win the match faster.

Bora has a clear advantage. He has all the moves automatically stored in his mind, like a plane on autopilot. He can fly through a match without even breaking mental sweat, taking selfies in the sky while we toil away below. Over on the small table next to where we play there is a picture of him and his daughter playing football. I love the picture, because it reminds me of playing football with my own daughter in the park in Doha near the flat where we first lived. Bora's got plenty of other pictures. There's one with his daughter and Pele, the greatest footballer in the world. There's one of his time in China, when he took the world's most populous nation to the World Cup for the first time in 2002 and became a Chinese national hero.

Coach Bora has just moved and now it's my turn again.

Just behind where Bora is sitting is a magazine cover with the headline 'Fifty foreigners who changed China'. I haven't checked yet to see if his name is on the list, but I'm guessing that it is, and that's why he has it in his apartment.

It is still my turn to move, and I decide to do something before this great brain of world football completely loses patience. There's a couple of moves I'm torn between, but if years of playing chess against my dad have taught me anything, it is to listen to my intuition and be daring. To be attacking. Above all, I need to keep the momentum going. The minute I lose momentum against someone like Bora, I've lost the game. In that way it is very much like preparing to host a World Cup. The minute you lose momentum, the minute you stop being proactive and reaching out to people and building bridges and telling your story, you're getting yourself into trouble.

I've moved now. It's Bora's turn to move.

'That's "Coach Bora" to you,' as he jokingly likes to correct me. He says it with an entirely serious expression so that one doesn't know whether he's joking or deadly serious. His expression is serious now as I watch his face closely. I've played the right move. It has put him in a spot of trouble.

At moments like these he moves with incredible precision and speed, knowing that I know that he knows he is in trouble. He wants to keep up the appearance of invincibility, you see. It is the same appearance he kept up at World Cup finals for over two decades. First in Mexico in 1986, when he took the hosts to the last eight, losing only on penalties to West Germany. Then at Italia 1990, where he helped dark horses Costa Rica to stun Scotland and reach the second round. It is the kind of mental strength that helped his USA side – made up of little more than a motley bunch of college students, as he always likes to point out – reach the Round of 16 in 1994 and push eventual champions Brazil to the limit in a 1-0 loss.

Coach Bora doesn't like losing. You can see that every time I push him to the limit in a chess match. I like to reach over a hand to him when it's going well for me, and say 'OK, I guess I win this one?' He will laugh and bat my hand away, knowing full well that he will soon turn things around.

In the first four World Cup tournaments he coached teams at, they always went further than the first round. Mexico – quarter-finals. Costa Rica – second round. USA – second round. Nigeria – second round. Only with his fifth team, China, in 2002, did he miss making the second round. But by then he was already a national hero, and still is, for taking them to the World Cup at all for the first time. He's a bit of a 'miracle maker', as his boss in the USA once famously called him.

He's also an excellent coffee maker. One day he just calls me after work and asks, in his unmistakable manner, 'Matheus (because he pronounces my name like Lothar Matthaus, the German World Cup-winning captain from 1990), Matheus, what are you doing?'

'Nothing,' I say.

'Where are you, Matheus?' he asks, in Spanish of course. He's adopted the language as much as he has the Mexican people, so it feels only natural to talk to him in that language.

'I'm at home.'

'Let's go, come for a coffee and three games of chess.'

'Sure,' I say. 'Where?'

'At my house, of course.'

'I'll see you in a minute.'

It is not a long walk, because he lives right across the street from me. The views from his apartment are beautiful, looking right over across the Doha skyline. The game of chess is already set up on the table. There's loud, loud Mexican music playing. Something romantic.

Out of the kitchen comes this great genius of world football, wearing his trademark beige scarf and pink polo shirt. He's carrying two coffee cups and two lemonades on a tray.

Then the game begins. The previous day I'd taken a single win off him. 2-1 to Bora. Clearly, he liked that. It challenged him. Today he will not let me win a game. Before the game I ask him whether he'd ever coached at an Olympic Games.

'Every day you surprise me,' he says, with one of his enigmatic smiles. 'Of course, of course. Atlanta 1996. Italy, we beat Italy, you remember…'

He goes into further detail with the familiarity of someone who can still replay exactly every moment of that match, and every other match in that tournament, in his mind.

The game starts, as always, with a handshake and a quick but brilliantly effusive smile. An opening sequence of moves is played which is always startlingly similar. In a flash the first ten moves have been made. It must be like the initial minutes of a football match at a major tournament. There is a definite tension in the air. He looks at the chess board with deep concentration and his game face on, showing no emotion, and doesn't take long over any move. It reminds me of the way my dad plays against me. And the opposite of the way my grandfather used to play.

My opening position is quite strong. I have made good starts in many of the recent games against my friend Coach Bora.

When we were young, Dad taught us all the basics of chess. He sat us down in the evening at the big wooden table in the bungalow across the street from the Falcon Club, and took out the chess board and pieces. He showed us where to place the pieces first. I can't have been much older than 10 at the time. Then he explained how each of the pieces is allowed to move. The next thing Dad taught us was the basics of a good opening.

'Get all your officers out first,' he would say, 'because they are the ones who will dictate the game.'

I'm trying to do just that against Bora right now. And to be nice and positive, to take the initiative. I learned that when we played more with Dad, and when I got a win or a draw from the games now and again.

'Dictate the pace of the game,' he'd say, 'otherwise you have no chance of winning.'

One summer in Germany, in my grandparents' house, I graduated to playing against my uncle, the crazy one who went to South America to start a new life in Bolivia and was tragically murdered in the jungle a few years later. It was never quite clear why he was killed, on his property in the middle of the Bolivian jungle. He was a good chess player in his day, and a great uncle. He would sit outside in the garden in the long summer evenings in Germany when seemingly it never got dark, and play chess with my father. Then one summer I started playing against him too, and they both agreed that 'he's got potential', meaning me. Maybe I had. I enjoyed playing. Not the mathematical part, of calculating God knows how many moves in advance, as the grandmasters did, but the silent eloquence and elegance of the game. And, of course, sitting with my dad and having something in common with him. I was never good at maths at school, so I decided to play by intuition, a mix of experience accumulated from chess games already played and a gut feeling for the next move.

I think that is also how Coach Bora plays.

'Did you ever play chess at the World Cup finals you coached at?' I ask him, partly curious and partly trying to distract him a little from his next move.

'Yes, sometimes,' he says distractedly (it's working!), as if the World Cup games themselves were his chess matches.

He moves so quickly, pausing only briefly to calculate future moves, that it must be his wealth of experience that makes him so good. I've only beaten him a handful of times. Today is not one of them. I start well in both games, but even though they are exciting he wins them both. 2-0 to Bora. Coach Bora.

In the lift on the way down from his apartment, Coach Bora has a thoughtful expression on his face, which is very normal for him. He seems to have enjoyed the clean sweep.

'Maybe I was taking too many risks today, playing with too much attacking,' I say to him.

'Chess is like football,' he says. 'You need to find the right balance between defence and attack. But the important thing isn't winning; the important thing is playing.'

There is his great piece of football wisdom for the day. Like the country he has chosen to call home, which is also constantly striving to find the right balance between tradition and modernity, East and West, between the culture it has nurtured for thousands of years and the influence of the thousands of foreigners who have passed through Qatar and will continue to do so over the coming years. In a few years they will all come, thousands upon thousands of fans, from every corner of the globe. They'll bring their flags and their chants and their way of celebrating football which they have known for decades. It will work if Qatar finds the right balance.

Coach Bora leaves the lift now to go to his car. He turns and waves goodbye, then he is gone. Later that night I wonder what it was that brought this football nomad – who has wandered numerous times around the world and made so many different people happy by getting their football teams to win matches – to Doha? To the building opposite mine, on this man-made island reclaimed from the sea where we used to swim with the family on Fridays? When there was nothing here but a simple pier going out to sea where a few people put out their fishing rods, and we always swam out to the small barren rock where you could see the long-beaked fish swimming along beside us. What was it, and how did it bring him all the way here, to play chess with me in the evenings when he's in need of a win, whether 2-1 or 2-0?

It must be the same thing that brought me into my job: the love of football. Coach Bora is one of the smartest men I've known. He has an innate football intelligence, and he'll only stay in a country where he can be surrounded and completely immersed in the game. And this football nomad has decided to make Qatar his home.

There is a new generation of young Qataris growing up who have only ever known this country as an epicentre of global sports. This Generation Q has grown up with Qatar's beIN Media Group beaming the world's top leagues and tournaments into their living rooms from its futuristic studios as it has done since 2013, when it was rebranded and spun away from Al Jazeera Sports. The CEO and Chairman of beIN Sports, Nasser Al Khelaifi, is also the President of Paris Saint-Germain FC, which regularly brings some of the world's best football players, like Neymar, Kylian Mbappe, Edinson Cavani and others, to Doha in December for their winter training camps. I still remember playing in a Futures tennis tournament at Khalifa Tennis Complex against Al Khelaifi – who represented Qatar as part of its Davis Cup team and was one of the best tennis players in the country – and losing with a resounding 6-2, 6-1 scoreline. Much has changed at an incredibly fast pace in Qatar's sporting scene since we played together on Court 1.

Those were the days when the country was finding its sporting feet and beginning to formulate its ambitious visions. Nowadays youngsters grow up in a Qatar awash with sports events and sporting stars. For young footballers, the country's football leadership has procured the best coaches and facilities and even built the impressive Aspetar Sports Hospital next to Aspire Academy for the treatment of injuries and rehabilitation. As a result, Qatar has started producing a young generation of sporting champions of its own, Olympians and football players and boxers who are breaking down barriers and perceptions with their own careers. Many of these young athletes have graduated from or passed through Aspire Academy, the elite sports development centre founded in 2004 which has become an epicentre of talent development for the country.

One evening in the spring of 2016, on a walk out with my daughter and wife, we stopped in the ice cream shop where we like to have a single scoop of chocolate ice cream, and we bumped into Qatar's London 2012 Olympic bronze medallist Mutaz Barshim. Qatar's high jump star is one of the most easy-going athletes you will ever encounter. He shook my hand that day as I wished him well for the Olympic Games that summer in Rio de Janeiro, signing off with some greetings from my dad, whom he knew well from the athletics federation. A few months later Mutaz won the silver medal for Qatar in the high jump at Rio 2016, adding to his already impressive list of accolades. Another year later, in the summer of 2017, he became a world champion for Qatar in the high jump, claiming gold in London at the IAAF Athletics World Championships and succeeding Usain Bolt as the best athlete in the world that year, after a stunning season with no real rival in sight.

The first time I met Mutaz was a few years before that, when a German journalist came over and wanted to meet him. We sat down on a wooden bench near the sports field looking out over Aspire Academy, where Mutaz had spent his formative years and been put through his paces as a youngster by his Polish coach. To his disappointment, training did not consist of an hour of run-ups and magical jumps over heights approaching 2.43 metres (his personal best, and the second highest jump ever recorded in the world). Instead, it was a series of two-legged jumps over hurdles and stretches which prepared the super-athlete for the types of jumps which have made him a social media sensation. A series of images with the hashtag

#ThingsBarshimCouldJumpOver, showing the young Qatari jumping over Photoshopped elephants, double-decker buses and so on, went viral. Mutaz wears a hat with his motto on it: 'WHAT GRAVITY HUH ?!!'

Like Mutaz, Akram Afif also has a cool hat, which he likes to wear back to front, and plenty of self-belief as he walks into the room. He too graduated from the Aspire Academy in Doha. I met Akram at the National Team Centre in Qatar in November 2016, just a few months after he became the first Qatari footballer to play in Spain's La Liga, for Sporting Gijon. Just 19 years of age, the youngster walked in with a spring in his step and a cheeky smile on his face. Akram comes from a sporting family, with his brother Ali also having played for Qatar, while his father starred for Al Gharafa Club a generation before his two sons came to prominence. After helping the Aspire-owned Belgian side Eupen gain promotion to the top flight with some stunning goals, Akram was signed by La Liga side Villarreal and then loaned out to Sporting Gijon to gain top-level playing experience.

When I talked to him in Doha, he was refreshingly different in his approach to what he wanted to achieve in his career. 'By the time of 2022 I will be 25 years old and hope to be in the best phase of my career. With the young generation of Qatari players playing in Europe, in Belgium, Scotland, Spain, I believe we will be able to challenge the top teams to win the World Cup.'

It was a completely different tone from what I'd heard from anyone previously: not just to put up a good showing in the group phase, not even to qualify for the second round – Akram Afif said that night that he wanted to challenge the best teams and lift the trophy. It might have sounded overly ambitious to some people, given that Qatar had not as yet qualified for any World Cup, but it was also symbolic of a new way of thinking among this generation of Qatari athletes who had grown up as part of a sporting nation.

That same day I met with Qatar's national team captain Hassan

Al Haydous, a skilful striker who said he grew up in the Al Sadd neighbourhood of Doha, playing football on the streets with his friends.

'As kids and Barca fans we grew up watching Xavi play on television every weekend. Now I can't believe that I have him with me in training sessions and playing passes to me during matches,' Haydous told me, exemplifying how Qatari athletes were benefiting from close contact with the world's best players. Just a few years later, Haydous would lead his country to their greatest-ever sporting achievement, lifting the 2019 AFC Asian Cup in some style.

Sporting events of the highest calibre were making their way to Qatar on a yearly basis. In 2015, Qatar hosted the World Men's Handball Championship, including matches at a spectacular new stadium in Lusail, where the final of the 2022 FIFA World Cup™ will also be held. The trophy was presented to the victorious French side by His Highness the Amir of Qatar. It was just the latest in a long series of major events the country had hosted smoothly and with plenty of innate charm. The World Boxing Championships were held later that year in one of the three new arenas constructed for the handball event. It was there that I met one of the greatest heavyweight boxers in the history of the sport, Wladimir Klitschko, who is also one of the most refined and reflective speakers outside of the ring. His philosophical responses and strategic approach to boxing have earned him the nickname 'Dr Steelhammer', and he was the reigning World Champion of four sanctioning bodies when I spoke to him on the concluding day of the boxing event in Doha.

'I repeat the words of Nelson Mandela,' the Ukrainian champion told me. 'Sport has the possibility to change the world. You see that it is not always the easy way – if you look at the World Cup in Russia and in Qatar, there are occasions where sport has become politicised. I believe that through sport you can win more tolerance, more mutual understanding between cultures. Here they see it as a positive sign because you have international media, the international presence of sports fans and tourists, and that makes people more open.'

Hosting so many sporting events and champions is having a knock-on effect for young Qatari athletes too. Qatar's first professional boxer, Fahad Al Thani, got his inspiration from watching videos of the great Muhammad Ali boxing at Doha Stadium in the early 1970s. When I met Fahad in Doha, he'd just come off winning his second pro fight in Spain. We did a photo shoot with him in front of the skyline next to the Corniche esplanade, with a boxing glove in one hand and a football in the other. It was a lovely contrast with his flowing white robes and the palm trees swaying softly in the breeze behind him. Later, when our story was published, he got a message from the daughter of Muhammad Ali wishing him good luck and saying that her father had greatly enjoyed his visit to Doha in the 1970s.

In the summer of 2015, an authentic legend of the world game made his way to Doha, following in the footsteps of other greats before him. Like Coach Bora on the chess board, here was a player who thought five or six steps ahead from where the ball currently was. In that way he was much like the country he was arriving in, which also had to stay ahead of the game in order to hold on to its most prized possession.

SUMMER OF 2015. AL SADD STADIUM
Xavi's survival instinct

It is a hot and humid summer day in August 2015 in Doha, and Qatar is playing a friendly game against Singapore. The air-conditioning is switched on inside the stadium, which has an illustrious guest within the cooled stands – Xavi Hernandez. Just two months earlier the Catalan midfield maestro was busy lifting the twenty-fifth title of an unparalleled career, none more fitting than the UEFA Champions League trophy, with his beloved FC Barcelona. Now he looks out over the Qatari players as they score a series of second-half goals and win the friendly match 4-0.

On this hot summer evening I have the privilege of sitting next to a player who, until very recently, I could admire only on television as an integral part of Barcelona's revolutionary short passing style. We are sitting comfortably in an open-air, cooled stadium in the middle of Qatar's hot summer. This is the country's first generation of cooling technology, which certainly feels as refreshing as it is futuristic. From the early days of football in Qatar, when Khattab Al Daffa played with his friends using a socks ball, it has come all the way to this in the span of a single lifetime. Xavi, possibly the world's greatest midfielder, is sitting next to me in a cooled stadium in Qatar and leans over to ask: 'Who is your favourite player for Qatar?'

Xavi is soaking up knowledge about the local football. He has already, in the space of the month that he has been here, attended countless matches of different age groups, and says that he has 'made the best decision of my life by coming to Qatar'. There is something about his questions and his way of talking and thinking which feels very much like the way it must feel to receive a pass from him on the pitch: they come fast and furious, full of intensity and quality. He is having a good time, and has an easy laugh and an entirely positive energy about him, even as he is interrupted numerous times for photo requests from fans.

'Ali,' I tell Xavi, pointing down at his young Al Sadd team-mate who plays as an attacking midfielder. 'I really like him. I think he's like Messi…' Then I reconsider the comparison, which I've made many times before with other people. But this is Xavi. He has trained and played with Messi, given him decisive passes in finals and shared the dressing room with him for so long that it must seem an insult to compare anyone to Messi. So I quickly add: 'Well, to you he can't be exactly like Messi. But he has great quality in his left foot and dribbles very well.'

Xavi, though, is a very humble man and agrees, probably partly out of courtesy: 'Yes, he is very talented and still very young, and you're right, the way he can dribble past people is impressive. There is also Hassan, he is very good.'

The amount a 19- or 22-year-old can learn from being around, listening to and playing with someone like Xavi must be truly incredible. Between now and the 2022 FIFA World Cup™ in Qatar, these players will spend their most important formative years alongside someone who has helped to shape the modern game. This is the man who institutionalised the tiki-taka style of play, and asserted through his game that central midfielders don't need height but rather speed of thinking, passing, and anticipating the game three or four steps ahead. He's like a chess grandmaster on the football pitch. It would be like having Ernest Hemingway, Virginia Woolf, Gabriel Garcia Marquez or Scott Fitzgerald chatting with me about my writing. What would I give! So how good are the next generation of Qatari players, who could be representing their country at a home World Cup by the time 2022 comes around?

'I have been surprised by how good the quality is,' says Xavi. 'They have very good technical qualities. What they need to improve is their concentration and intensity. Sometimes they will be in a match and lose concentration.'

Xavi knows better than anyone that you cannot afford to lose even a second of concentration if you want to win a World Cup trophy. And so many others.

The first time I met Xavi he was about to set out for the first press conference of his life, at Al Sadd Sports Club, the same club my father represented as a shot putter a few decades earlier. Having started out as an 11-year-old cadet at Barcelona's famed La Masia youth academy, he became the very epitome of a player loyal to his club, and helped define the spectacular playing philosophy of a club and a nation.

On that day Xavi was standing in front of The Torch hotel near Aspire Academy, a few guests walking quietly in and out of the hotel on what was already quite a hot day at the start of the summer. But there was a smile on his face, conjuring up the excitement of a kid about to sign his first major contract. His entire family had come along too, and were heading now for the signing ceremony where Xavi pulled on the white shirt of Al Sadd Club for the first time. The press conference room on the first floor of the club was so packed that journalists had to watch it on television screens in the lobby area below.

What had made him decide to come to Qatar?

'It is an ideal project for me,' Xavi told me that day, with his mother looking on. She had been the one to convince him to stay another year in Barcelona, the year that ended with the treble-winning side lifting the Champions League title. 'Three different components came together perfectly for my family and me. For one, there is the possibility here at Al Sadd to continue winning trophies, to try and do our best to win the league and the cup and compete well in the Asian Champions League. Then there is the fantastic project at Aspire, where my professional formation will continue; and finally, to be an ambassador for the FIFA World Cup Qatar 2022™ is something that is very interesting.'

For Xavi's first game in Qatar we drove over to Al Ahli Club, where Pep Guardiola had regularly laced his illustrious boots. It was an evening kick-off after work and there was some traffic, but we made it on time, and a few minutes into the game something spectacular yet ordinary happened. Xavi provided his first assist, one of many to his team-mates that year. It was a free kick from the left-hand side, and he curled it in magnificently for an easy nod into goal by one of his new teammates. I saw him play many times that season. It was always a pleasure to watch the rhythmic simplicity of his passes as they were zipped across the pitch.

It is clear, though, that Xavi's biggest impact on Qatari football has transcended the action on the pitch. He has changed the football philosophy not only of his club, Al Sadd, but perhaps also of the country at large. If Qatar arrives at the 2022 FIFA World Cup™ on home soil as a team playing attractive, tiki-taka-type football, it will no doubt be partly thanks to this philosopher of the modern game.

Over the four years Xavi spent playing in Qatar, I was privileged to build a friendship with the Catalan midfielder, and to be there alongside him for some of the most important moments. One of those for me was a simple interview with a French journalist which he asked me to sit in on. It was truly spectacular to hear him speaking, explaining with such great simplicity his football philosophy. That day it suddenly became very clear to me how he had done it all, what his secret ingredient was, the X factor.

We sat in a plain room on the 29th floor of Al Bidda Tower, with three glasses of water, and Xavi spoke for over an hour about his way of understanding football. A couple of lines for me epitomised the whole importance of this player.

'Intelligence is the ability to adapt to a medium that you have never encountered before. I have always had to think to play football. Since I was 11 years old, I have had to understand the game, to understand what happens on the pitch. Football is thinking. Thinking is my survival.'

Football for Xavi was, if you simplified it down to its most basic element, a form of survival. His most basic commodity in that undertaking was the passes he played and saw so much earlier than everyone else, because he was constantly processing information, checking on which side of the pitch his team had a numerical superiority, on which side they could play their way out of trouble, and what was the right pass to play next. As events in the region would show, he had come to a country where football and sports were also essentially a means of national survival, a way to keep your country on the map in a neighbourhood where alliances were constantly shifting.

Sometimes football is a wondrous and simple game which brings people from all walks of life together. I witnessed this inspirational effect one evening in December 2016, when I met Xavi one evening for a drive out to Labour City in his car.

'Just tell me where to go, and I'll head in that direction,' he said in his easy-going way.

In my hand as I pointed out which roads to take were a bunch of tickets for a friendly match between FC Barcelona and Al Ahli of Saudi Arabia, which was to take place a few days later in Qatar. The idea was for Xavi to visit some of the construction workers who took part in our Generation Amazing 'football for development' programme in Qatar, and give them free tickets to attend the match and see Barcelona's stars and their incredible attacking trio of Lionel Messi, Neymar and Luis Suarez in action.

After a short drive we pulled up to the gate of Labour City, where Xavi let down the window and was instantly recognised.

'Welcome, Mr Xavi, this way please.'

He parked the car, and we walked through the corridors of the new accommodation building into a room brimming full of football fans. A spontaneous round of applause rang through the room as Xavi entered. He looked over at me and asked me to stay by his side as he was given a microphone: 'Can you translate this for me?'

It would have been a more fitting role for my wife, perhaps, who is a qualified translator and interpreter among other things, but I readily agreed, and Xavi started talking.

'It's a pleasure to be here with you and meet you all today,' Xavi said in Spanish. That much I could still remember, but then he kept going and going and talking and talking until finally he turned to give me the microphone. The expectant crowd cheered loudly at his Spanish speech, then looked over in my direction. With a whole room of expectant fans looking my way, all of them eager to find out what the Spanish World Cup winner had just said, I tried to make up something vaguely resembling all of the things he'd just said and I had already forgotten. To be fair, I think I managed to remember most of it. After being asked a lot of follow-up questions from the crowd, with a predictable focus on who was the best player in the world, Messi or Ronaldo (and an equally predictable answer from the Barcelona great), Xavi then took the time to pose for a photo with each and every one of the (over 100) people present in the room, as he handed out their tickets for the match.

One of those there that memorable evening at Labour City was Justin Santiago, a 36-year-old FC Barcelona fan from Chennai in India, who couldn't quite believe he was standing next to his idol.

'I love football, and I'm a huge fan of Barcelona because they have the best players, like Lionel Messi. I've seen so many matches of Xavi on TV, winning the World Cup, the Spanish league and the Champions League, so it was an incredible surprise to see him in person,' Santiago said after the Al Sadd captain warmly shook his hand.

'Everybody in the room was extremely excited, and it was very impressive to meet a player who is also such a nice person. He was very cool and easy to speak to, and had a smile for everyone. On top of that, we were all personally invited by him to watch the match, which is a fantastic opportunity.'

For Xavi, the visit to Labour City that December evening also brought back memories of the first time he was given a ticket to watch a live football match, at his beloved Nou Camp in Barcelona.

'I remember the first time I was given tickets to go to a match, I was five or six years old and it was to attend a Barcelona game. We all love football in our family, and we went to a Joan Gamper Trophy match with my father and grandfather. It was a great excitement that I felt before the game. So it was a pleasure to give tickets to the workers involved in the Generation Amazing programme for the Barcelona game. This Generation Amazing project is about reaching out to people in Qatar who are helping to build this country.'

2016. RAS ABU ABOUD
The Qataris shaping the most futuristic World Cup ever

On a spot of land overlooking the entire Doha skyline from the other side of the Corniche, I stood looking one warm day in 2016 at reminders of my childhood in Qatar. In front of me were the two tennis courts of Al Gazal Club, where many years ago we played in the local tennis tournaments and took home an assortment of trophies in the different age categories.

I can still remember the purple tennis shirt I wore as I stepped onto the court. The memories were so vivid that I could still hear the tennis balls being knocked back and forth, where now the construction machines were moving around with their mechanical beeping and buzzing. The site of the leisure club where my father had once worked and the tennis court I still remembered from my youth were soon to make way for one of our stadiums for 2022. It was not sadness that I felt in that moment, because the club had long been abandoned and the facility lay unused. It just felt as if a piece of Doha's architecture, and my personal history, was changing in front of my eyes, slowly but surely transforming from a local sports facility of the past into a World Cup stadium of the future.

In a few years' time this very place will see the world's first-ever completely moveable stadium welcome the first fans. The venue features a unique 'shipping container' design which can be dismantled in its entirety, packed into shipping containers and reused in another location or country. The design for the 'Lego stadium', launched at the end of 2017, made headlines around the world as an example of how legacy planning is being taken to the next level by Qatar in an effort to avoid the 'white elephants' which have plagued mega events in recent years. The winning concepts from the bid were rapidly coming to life, and changing the skyline of the country I have seen constantly evolving since my childhood.

'When you remove the tennis courts, can you keep the net for me, as a souvenir?' I asked someone from the site team with a laugh. My wife would surely be happy to have more 'junk' lying about the house. Luckily for her they didn't give me the net in the end.

A few decades earlier, my father had split his time between five different sports clubs owned by the state petroleum company, including this one, and even a gym on an oil rig out at sea, where he was transported by helicopter once a month.

'I used to pray that the helicopter pilot knew what he was doing, because the platform he was descending on looked tiny in the enormous sea,' he remembered.

I can already hear the television helicopters buzzing overhead in 2022, in what will be one of the most visually stunning sites of the World Cup in Qatar, overlooking as it does the entire Doha skyline just across the water. The stadium at Ras Abu Aboud, which has a Metro station popping up on the other side of the road and is just a two-minute drive from Hamad International Airport, will have been built on the place where I used to play tennis and hit winners as a youngster in my purple shirt. But not many of the thousands of fans walking into the world's first moveable stadium will know that.

There are two giant Germans walking through the lobby of the waterfront Museum of Islamic Art, just a few minutes further down the road from the Ras Abu Aboud stadium site. On either side of the museum hundreds of dhows, the traditional wooden boats of the

Gulf, bob romantically at anchor in their mellow hues of brown, maroon and purple, with Qatari flags on their masts shifting slightly in the breeze.

One of the fans is covered in scarves of his football team, Bayern Munich. Literally covered in them. They cover his arms, his chest, even his trousers, in fact his whole body. He wears a giant red hat too, which looks like a mushroom or an enormous Mexican hat and is covered in Bayern Munich badges as well. He wears football boots all the time, and they make a clicking sound – click, clock, click, clock, as he walks through the museum. Michael Zeman has the build of a potentially dangerous football hooligan, but in fact he's the friendliest and most softly-spoken guy you will ever likely meet in a football stadium. The only fight you are likely to have with him is if you don't let him watch his team every weekend.

Next to him is an equally towering figure. Thorsten is wearing a jacket covered in pin badges – thousands upon thousands of them, too many to count. Each pin represents one of the Bayern Munich matches he has attended, with all the details written on the little badge: competition, opponent, date – all there for anyone who wants to see. If I had not met my beautiful wife and had two wonderful children, maybe I'd have ended up like this as well, I think. In a good way. You have to admire their passion for their team.

'You want to try the jacket?' Thorsten asks. 'It weighs five kilograms.' I hold it in my hands and it seems to weigh twenty-five.

The two walk through the museum, breaking with some long-held stereotypes that football fans and a thousand-year-old culture don't go together, and at every second step they are stopped by a Qatari family.

We've been showing these German fans around Qatar for the past few days. So far they've had a terrific time, racking up more selfie requests than the Bayern Munich stars they are here to follow. But will this meeting of cultures go well in the museum? Will Qatari families appreciate the entirely crazy football passion which these two giant Germans have displayed so blatantly all over their bodies?

It goes more than well. The local families can't get enough of the two fans.

'Can my kids get a picture with you two?' the Qatari dad asks with a sheepish smile, as if it were too much to ask.

'Yes, of course, we'd love to,' Michael answers with his usual happy-go-lucky smile.

'One more, please,' says the Qatari dad, having snapped a few already with his smartphone. He pushes his younger son, who is obviously slightly intimidated by the two towering Germans, into the picture as well. There's now a whole family posing with the two superfans. A queue is forming behind them to take more selfies. Over the course of the few days that we invited the fans to spend experiencing Qatar, they must have posed for thousands of selfies.

It was the third successive winter that we'd met with visiting football fans. In January 2014, we'd seen the potential to do something with the fans of Schalke 04, a German club from the traditionally working-class mining area of Gelsenkirchen. A considerable group of around fifty fans had made the journey over to Qatar to follow their team's training, so we wanted to find a way of interacting with them and getting their feedback. We booked a traditional Qatari dhow, and asked the fans if they'd like to come on a boat trip with us to see Doha from a different perspective.

'You want me to go and talk to a group of German fans on a dhow?' Nasser asked, sitting in his office overlooking the entire stretch of the turquoise Corniche waterfront where we would be chugging up and down with the fans.

'Essentially that's it. They're Schalke fans, who are known as some of the most diehard and loyal fans you will get anywhere in the whole of Germany.'

Nasser thought about it for a second. Then he nodded.

'Count me in,' he said. 'I like the idea.'

Nasser had spent a few years living in Germany during his youth. He played as goalkeeper for a club near Bonn when he was young, and was there when Germany won the 1990 World Cup in Italy, while I was still a young boy growing up in Qatar. Now he was about to join a boatload of German fans on a dhow cruise. There were no guarantees. It had been my idea, so if anything went wrong then it would probably be on my head. My thinking, though, was that without calculated risks we would get nowhere, fast.

Everything was ready, and the Schalke fans arrived in orderly fashion, walking up to the boat anchored near Souq Waqif on the waterfront overlooking the Doha skyline, in their football shirts and shorts and flip flops. Then Nasser came and we were ready to push off, after an initial round of greetings and an introduction from the man they were all here to meet.

'I'm Nasser Al Khater,' he said into the microphone on the boat, 'and I'd like to welcome you all to Qatar and on board and tell you a little more about our plans for FIFA World Cup Qatar 2022™. We're also open to all kinds of questions, so don't be afraid to ask me anything at all which is of interest.'

They all listened with rapt attention. A loyal Schalke fan who had not missed a single game for some forty years was the first to ask a question. He put up his hand as if they were at school and then said, through a thick, well-groomed moustache: 'It is a pleasure to meet you, Nasser, and thanks for inviting us onto the ship. I have one pressing question, though: will we be able to drink alcohol in 2022?'

It was one of the most frequent questions we faced. It was not asked with any malice this time, just with the curiosity of an old German fan who was used to going to the pub before and after every match and wanted to know whether he could have a pint if he came to Qatar in 2022.

'Alcohol will be available in certain designated areas for fans who want to watch football while having a beer,' Nasser told the group, to what sounded like a collective sigh of relief from those gathered on the boat. 'And there will be areas where it is not available for those who wish to celebrate football without alcohol.'

'That sounds like a good approach,' said the moustachioed football fan. 'I'm happy with that.'

It was a very balanced answer and approach, and the fans on board the boat nodded in agreement. A few years later, at Euro 2016, fan violence between groups of English and Russian supporters, among others, led to a partial alcohol ban around some venues ahead of certain games. Nasser was on hand at the tournament, shadowing the CEO of the event, to bring back lessons that could be learned for FIFA World Cup Qatar 2022™. He must have thought back to all those questions we'd had about alcohol, and suddenly this approach seemed the most sensible of all.

The fans that day asked other questions, too: when would the Metro be completed, what about the new airport, would there be more immigration officials at the airport, did Nasser know what kind of hotels and fan packages might be on offer? There were answers from Nasser to all of these questions, but the thing that struck me most that day, apart from the fresh breeze which had even some of those weather-hardened Germans shivering a little in their habitual flip flops and shorts, was the incredibly positive meeting of cultures. It was for me a small preview of what the World Cup in 2022 would feel like. In the space of only an hour, fans and organisers had been brought closer together, questions were openly answered and concerns addressed, and we'd offered our guests some tastes of the local cuisine and an opportunity to get their names written in Arabic by an on-board calligrapher. The fans loved it. When they left the boat that year, we'd gained a whole group of diehard Schalke 04 fans as our supporters, who all wanted to take selfies with Nasser before they headed back to their hotel. We also had a few journalists on board who told the story to their audiences back in Germany.

'Alcohol will be available in Qatar,' was the headline one major

German tabloid chose to run with. But for me the whole success of the boat ride had been to bring two cultures – the two I knew the best – just a little bit closer together.

The next year, when German teams visited Qatar for their winter training camps we tried to keep improving. And we took an even bigger calculated risk. It was to be another boat ride for Schalke fans, with all the same ingredients: discussions, Arab food and calligraphy. But this time we were bringing another set of fans on board. We'd invited some Bayern Munich followers to join us too.

For those not acquainted with the rivalry, Schalke 04 and Bayern Munich fans are not exactly the friendliest towards each other. In fact, the opposite can safely be said. So when I told some people in the office of the latest plan, they joked: 'What, this year you're going to cause a big fight on a dhow between rival German fans, and we'll be in the thick of it? Just what we need!'

Regardless of the irony, I thought it would be more inclusive if we had different fan groups on board. So when I bumped into big Michael Zeman and his friend at a Bayern Munich training session and told them about it, they were extremely excited.

'A boat ride, with the organisers of FIFA World Cup Qatar 2022™? Of course we'll come,' big Michael said that January 2015, handing me his autographed business card with his contact details. 'How much do we have to pay?'

'Nothing, it's free, we're trying to put on a fan forum to inform you guys about what we're planning for 2022,' I said.

'OK, we're in,' he said with a huge smile.

We'd also invited the German ambassador to Qatar, and she duly accepted the invitation. This time more journalists came along, including one from the leading daily *Frankfurter Algemeine Zeitung*. If anything went wrong this year, we'd get even more publicity for it. Anything negative on Qatar was all the rage at the time anyway, so it wouldn't take much to get some more criticism. The stage was set. The dhow was booked. The Arab food was cooked, dished up and smelt deliciously of fresh herbs and rice. I'd been on board the boat that morning with our team to check that everything was in order. Even the weather was good: while we'd been worried about heavy rain the previous day, it turned out to be warm and sunny.

The Schalke fans started arriving in large numbers, as they had the previous year. Many of the previous year's guests had returned and told their friends about it. Would the rival Bayern fans show up?

There they came now, marching down the gangway with steely resolve and determination. Big Michael had his usual scarf decoration and big Mexican hat, along with the obligatory football boots. His friend chose to come that year in typical Munich Lederhosen with a few Bayern Munich badges stitched onto them. The Schalke 04 fans squinted into the wintry sun and frowned, and I wasn't sure what would happen next. We had told the Schalke 04 fan leader that Bayern Munich supporters were also going to be invited, but all he had done was mumble a gruff response which I took as a 'fine, then' or something of the sort.

We welcomed them all on board, and the big Bayern Munich fan walked precariously across the small swaying gangplank onto the boat. The official car of the German ambassador pulled up a few seconds later, with the little flag of Germany on the bonnet swaying in the wind. This really was something serious. Her Excellency got out and smiled at the gathered group of fans. Nasser had also arrived, persuaded to come for another year and present our plans and progress to the visiting German fans. Everyone was on board and the boat was ready to pull away.

'We did have insurance included in the rental price, right?' I whispered to my Qatari colleague.

'Yes,' she answered. 'Everything will be fine.'

Then I turned round, and there was the big surprise that no one had expected. The Bayern and Schalke fans were sitting directly across from each other. They seemed to be laughing. I looked again. It was a little miracle out there in the water as we chugged slowly into Doha Bay, past the cuboid blocks of the Museum of Islamic Art and the hundreds of little and big dhows moored at anchor. Two rival German fan groups, brought together by a World Cup in Qatar. It was still a good few years away, but I got another glimpse that day of what it would look like in 2022. They didn't even have any alcohol. But they were having a fantastic time, learning about a culture different from their own.

We didn't need any insurance that day. The fans didn't have a fight. They took pictures together. They didn't scream insults at each other. They asked about the best places in the city to eat Arab food. There was a fantastic group photo where everyone seemed to be in each other's arms. Madam Ambassador disembarked safely and the official car with the German flag on the bonnet pulled away, after she had thanked us for a pleasant hour. Nasser was left with the fans.

'Mr Nasser,' Michael, the big German, asked, 'please can you sign this ball for me?'

Nasser was smoking a cigarette at the time, but he nodded happily. 'Sure.'

I stayed in touch with the fans, and especially with big Michael, the scarf-covered fan of Bayern Munich who had spent some of his pension money to come out to Doha and follow his team.

'My mother gave me a bit of extra cash for my birthday as well, to make up the numbers,' he said with a sheepish smile.

As the next winter approached, Bayern Munich announced that they were again headed for Doha. I got in touch with big Michael, but he was unable to come this time: 'No money. It's a big shame, but I won't be able to join the team this time around. I used up all my savings last winter.'

We were thinking about how to make the fan initiative even better that year, and for some reason I didn't think a hat-trick of dhow trips along the Corniche would do it justice. What could be bigger, and better, than before?

The team got together and we came up with something new: we'd invite fans from all corners of the globe to Qatar on a dream trip to see their teams in Doha. There were fans coming from France, from Italy, Kuwait, even as far away as China and India. They all wanted to see their teams in action during the winter training camps at Aspire Academy. It was a taste of the incoming flights to come in 2022. Together with the Qatar Tourism Authority, we arranged a programme for them, including sightseeing and training and autograph sessions with the stars. It would be the kind of coming together of fans from all corners of the world that we expected in 2022. Only two spaces were left, and we wanted to bring some German fans to watch Bayern Munich.

Nasser had taken a real liking to the big Bayern fan, who regularly sent us home-made cookies in the post, and from the moment we presented the idea of inviting two more fans over he said: 'One of them has to be Michael.'

I called Michael that day from the office. The newsroom could be quite bustling and busy at times so I went into an adjacent room which was empty at the time.

'Hey, Michael, it's me, Matthias from Qatar,' I said.

'Hey, what a surprise!'

The real surprise was still in store for him.

'Are you doing anything in January?'

'I'll be here spending time with my wife,' he said.

'Well, we'd like to invite you to come to Qatar for the Bayern Munich training camp. You'll have a programme that we've put together with the Qatar Tourism Authority, and you'll probably get some special access to the players as well. What do you think? Will your wife let you go?'

There was silence at the other end.

'I don't know what to say. I can't describe what this means to me,' he said, his voice starting to break up. Then he started crying. 'It was my birthday yesterday; this is the best present I've ever received.'

'Well, then, I should have called yesterday,' I joked.

That's how Michael and his big friend Thorsten became selfie magnets that winter. It was an incredible run they had going. It started in the hotel lobby, continued at the training pitches where everyone wanted to get a photo with them, and went on to the museums they visited.

'Unbelievable,' Thorsten kept saying with a dazed look on his face. 'All of this is just unbelievable.'

We'd made the year for two regular German football fans, and made a big 50-year-old covered in scarves cry like a five-year-old, and it felt fantastic. We received an invitation from the new German ambassador to a reception at his residence. The fans couldn't quite believe anything that was happening to them. They were interviewed live on TV after a football match of Qatar's under-23 team, the journalist calling them a 'lucky omen for Qatar' and asking them to come back soon. One day we took them down to Souq Waqif for a meal, and they became an instant attraction. Everyone wanted a photo. We lost count of the selfies.

At Souq Waqif we also took the fans to see the falcons. We walked past the Falcon Hospital and they turned in at the falcon shop.

'Take a picture, sir,' the falcon salesman said to one of them, 'with the falcon on your hand.'

'How much does that cost?' Michael asked.

'It's free. Though if you want to buy a falcon, that can be expensive. Hundreds of thousands.'

They didn't want to buy any falcons, but the colour and unique feel of the whole experience clearly impressed them. It was the first time these fans had come into contact with Qatari traditions, and it was obviously something special for them.

'And you, sir,' the falcon salesman said, pointing to me. 'Now your turn!'

'Well, actually I live here, but why not,' I said, realising that in all those years I had never actually held a falcon on my hand.

Sometimes you need a group of incredibly crazy fans from all corners of the world to appreciate what you have so close to home.

2017. LUSAIL STADIUM
The man who wrote about Mandela

The day before finishing the first draft of this book, I visited the site of Lusail Stadium, where machines were crushing rocks and works were under way to build the 80,000-seater venue which will host the opening game and final of the 2022 FIFA World Cup™ in Qatar. We drove through the new city which was springing up rapidly at Lusail. A brand-new area of town was coming together here in a historic location for the country, where the home of Qatar's founder had been located. Eventually we found our way to the construction site, where a sign outside said simply 'Lusail Stadium'. A cone had been placed right at the spot where the centre circle will be, where the World Cup opening game and final will kick off in 2022.

We stopped there, and it was a proud moment to feel we had been there from the start. This very place would be the centre of the universe for one month in 2022. We had taken a football along and now passed it to each other, just as the players on the final two teams would do when the World Cup in Qatar reached its climax. I picked up a small rock and put it in my trouser pocket, intending to keep hold of it until well after the world's attention had once again moved away from the country of my birth. On a plot of land overlooking the Doha skyline in the distance, the outline of a football pitch was becoming evident in the sand.

When I am old and decrepit, and have a long grey beard and long hair tied back in an attention-seeking pony-tail, moving slower than a snail and hunched over to half my previous height, I'll try to impress my great-grandchildren by telling them to search for the video of the Germany team that lifted the 2014 FIFA World Cup™ in Brazil.

'Look behind the players celebrating, and you'll see me in the first row of spectators,' I will tell them. 'That's right, there in the Germany shirt with the three stars, on the day we won the fourth star. I even waved to Germany team manager Oliver Bierhoff just before they were handed the trophy, and he winked back at me because he remembered me from our previous meeting. There I was, live on TV, can you believe it?'

'What is TV?' they will probably ask me. 'Was that what you had before our latest super-cool invention?'

It will sound somewhat random to them, busy as they will be with their five different screens all demanding attention. But that is the life of a football fanatic for you, encapsulated in a single image. Sometimes football can be cruel and gut-wrenching and blatantly unfair. But sometimes it is wonderful and indescribable and everything, absolutely everything, comes together for you.

Like the girl that got away, football always seemed to have a last-minute rejection in store for me, whether in a World Cup, Champions League or European Championship final. My yearning to celebrate a major title for my team always remained the same, and yet that triumph never seemed to materialise. Why did I keep watching, then? Why did I stay in love with the beautiful game?

Probably because I knew that one day, with enough persistence and the sheer stupidity of wanting it enough, even though that could never influence the outcome on the pitch, my luck would change.

Coincidentally, things started to change when I returned to Doha in 2013. A few months into my new job, I was chosen to go to the all-German Champions League final in London. It was Dortmund against Bayern, my team since the long-gone playing days of Jurgen Klinsmann. We travelled over the day before the match, and I met many German journalists to brief them on what we were doing in Qatar. An attempted meeting with my former idol Boris Becker, the player I had once ball-boyed for in Doha, did not work out. But I also met with a writer who had marked an era in sports writing with his magnificent book on the South African rugby miracle of 1995.

'Sport can change society for good and for bad,' John Carlin, author of the book made into the Hollywood film 'Invictus', told me in a London coffee shop one rainy spring morning in 2013. Did he see any parallels between Qatar and South Africa in their respective sporting miracles?

'Hitler abused sport at the 1934 Olympics. Mandela in 1995 was the anti-Hitler. If the purpose of leaders is good then sport can take on the force of the emotional current. Mandela once told me that sport has more power than politicians to change the world.'

I thanked him for the coffee and said that I too was writing a story about a miracle, the story of my quiet hometown which had metamorphosed into a sporting capital of the world in the space of a few short decades.

'I too think it can change the world,' I said. He wished me good luck as we went our separate ways that rainy London morning.

Later that day my team made its way to the final. It was a richly historic venue, at the renovated Wembley Stadium, and it was full of German fans. They were everywhere you looked, invading London in their Lederhosen. Bayern Munich trailed early on but pulled two goals back for a late win. I had seen the club of my life win the Champions League in one of the most famous football stadiums in the world. It felt in London as if I were on top of the world. But little did I know that an even bigger occasion was in store for me just a year later.

My boss called me into the office some time in June 2014. The World Cup was already under way in Brazil, and I'd watched Germany win their opening game at home with my brother and father in Doha.

Nasser talked to me a little about the newsroom, and told me he thought it had been a fantastic success. We exchanged opinions for a while about the stories we had coming out of the newsroom – and there were many good ones coming up – and then he looked at me and said in his usual disarming way: 'How would you like to go to Brazil, for the World Cup?'

Did I want to go to the World Cup?! I did a quick double take, and then tried to sound as calm as possible in the circumstances. 'Yes, of course.'

There were a number of media interviews to arrange in Brazil, and a whole selection of players we could interview for the newsroom. It was my second time going to South America, having seen the Confederations Cup the previous year, when we met the legendary coach Evaristo and almost got held up in the wave of protests on the way to the stadium. This time the whole of Brazil was talking about the national team and their dream of a sixth title on home soil. I was on my way to the World Cup in the spiritual home of football.

On the flight over, the closer we got to Brazil the more the excitement grew, as the pilot kept us informed us of the latest score in the Brazil-Chile second-round clash. At Sao Paulo airport when we arrived there was a large screen set up where Colombia supporters were going wild celebrating their team's 2-0 win over Uruguay. I called my wife to congratulate her. Then it was off to Rio de Janeiro, on the aptly named Gol (Portuguese for 'goal') Airlines.

There is nothing quite like arriving in Rio to attend a World Cup. The Marvellous City ensnares you from the moment you land, capturing your imagination and overwhelming you with sights, sounds and smells all of its own. It smelt of football. The streets were filled with fans and coconut trees, with ruggedly beautiful hills in the distance. I checked into my hotel and then headed directly for the giant Fan Fest on Copacabana beach to immerse myself in the atmosphere of a World Cup in the home of football. The entrance was on the sand. A game was being shown on the giant screens, and the fans danced and sang and met up and had a giant party on the beach.

I talked to fans from all over the world that first day in Brazil for the World Cup. I asked them what they thought of a World Cup in Qatar. The opinions were split pretty much straight down the middle. Half of the fans seemed to think it was an interesting idea, and that they'd like to check it out. The other half said it was an outrageous idea. I smiled and realised how much work we had left to do, showing the world what Qatar was really all about. No one really understood the place where I was born; there were still too many stereotypes, presumptions and half-truths flying about.

In the first few days I arranged interviews for Coach Bora with media outlets from around the world, and we bumped into his friends from the world of football as he went for morning walks on the famous black-and-white wavy-tiled walkways of Copacabana beach. The first match we attended at that World Cup was the quarter-final between France and Germany at the legendary Maracana Stadium in Rio. The last live Germany game I'd seen was six years earlier, in a Basel quarter-final at Euro 2008 against Portugal. Although it was the same round of the tournament, this time the stage was even bigger, as was the stadium. Rather than hoping for a German win, I tried to keep my nerves in check by telling myself that it was already an incredible experience simply to be there in that stadium, on a hot and sticky Rio de Janeiro day.

Germany won that day with a single goal by Mats Hummels, who headed home a free kick, sparking massive celebrations from myself and the thousands of other German fans in the historic venue. I thought that day alone was pretty awesome. But then work also took me to the quarter-final between Argentina and Belgium in Brasilia. To the Argentina v. Holland semi-final in Sao Paulo. And then to the famous semi-final in Belo Horizonte – Brazil against Germany. The hosts with a whole football-crazy country behind them. Looking to make it to their final. It was quite an occasion. From the bus on the way to the match we saw Brazilians milling hopefully around the stadium, and my colleagues joked about my shirt (a black t-shirt with a German flag on the chest) and the likelihood of Germany going out. The streets were seething with Brazil fans in their famous yellow jerseys, already dreaming of a place in the final.

'You'd better hide that shirt, pull over your jacket,' Coach Bora told me earnestly that day. He wasn't joking this time.

Before the game the Brazilian national anthem sounded, and the entire stadium sang like one giant lung, and then kept singing and singing even after the music had stopped. Maybe there was too much emotion at stake for the home side. The German team began playing football, and started scoring goals. At the first two goals, I jumped up and celebrated. Coach Bora, who sat nearby, gave me a warning look. Then the goals kept coming, three, four, five, and I couldn't quite believe it. Neither could the crowd in the stadium. Some just stood shaking their heads. Others were crying. Others started booing. Still others started applauding the incredible football being played by this exciting German team. I stopped jumping up after the third goal went in. Miroslav Klose got on the scoresheet too, reaching his all-time World Cup goal-scoring record: sixteen goals. The first ones I'd seen on television as an 18-year-old studying for my final school exams in Doha. The last one I watched live in the stadium with my colleagues from Qatar. Rather tactfully, and at Coach Bora's insistence, I stopped celebrating the goals as they kept coming, and put a neutral jacket over my Germany t-shirt. It was of course 7-1 at the end, and Germany were in the World Cup final. In the bus on the way back from the match, I was not being teased by my colleagues any more. Instead, it was me who kept going on about how good Germany had been, and that there was no denying it now.

Then came the World Cup final. I suppose any supporter of any team in any sport dreams up their perfect match, and that is what keeps them going through some of the tougher moments in a supporter's lifetime.

It is all a dream. The one where you know you are dreaming but it is a fantastic one, the way you always wanted it to be, so you savour it and enjoy the moment before you have to get up and go to work and drink your usual cup of coffee with too much sugar.

But actually, this is my work. There is a moment before the start of the 2014 FIFA World Cup™ final in which I look up, observe the leaders of Germany, Russia and FIFA engaging in small talk, and then glance down in childish disbelief at the most famous golden trophy in the world. It's the same trophy I used to admire in the book on World Cup history in the Falcon Club library in Doha. One of the two teams on display today will be recording their name in football folklore. The players of Germany and Argentina are warming up on the pitch. You can see the tension etched on their faces as they force themselves to have fun ahead of the most important game of their lives.

At this very moment, on 13 July 2014, this is the centre of the universe. This precise point, the coordinates on a world map of the legendary Maracana Stadium in Rio de Janeiro, is where around one quarter of the world's eyes are turned on this warm Sunday. Within the stadium, you can physically feel this intensity. It is as if every step you take is slower and more eternal, every movement documented by a million little cameras and the countless helicopters buzzing overhead, every gorgeous-looking celebrity on earth crammed into the vast confines of an 80,000-seater stadium which looks stunning inside and out and just might be the most perfect place imaginable for such a spectacle. Looking to my right, I can actually see the statue of Christ the Redeemer, for Christ's sake.

Nothing could be more exciting than sitting in this stadium and watching, in jittery agony, as Argentina squander a series of perfectly makeable chances. Leo Messi, of all people, to whom I once wrote that poem, misses one of those sitters which he usually slots home while looking the other way and slurping a Barcelona cappuccino. Maybe even this superhuman player feels the pressure sometimes.

The Germany fan in me clearly overrides the FC Barcelona fan and thanks the football god that he did not score.

For as long as I can remember, I have been fascinated by the World Cup. Now I find myself sitting in the stadium for a World Cup final. What started for me as a six-year-old boy in 1990, as my dad pulled up to the dusty athletics training pitch in Doha and the radio news bulletin said 'West Germany has just won the World Cup in Italy, beating Argentina 1-0 in the final', has brought me here to Brazil. Now I try not to blink so that I won't miss a second of this repeated final match-up twenty-four years later.

The first half features chances on both sides, and my colleagues from Qatar look over at me every time Germany comes close to the goal and I jump up frantically. There is our Secretary-General, His Excellency Hassan Al Thawadi, and my boss, Nasser Al Khater. In the past days I've arranged numerous interviews for them with a variety of Qatari, Spanish, German, English and Brazilian media outlets, and they have skilfully explained how Qatar will handle hosting this very same competition. At half-time I take a picture with Nasser and tell him: 'Thank you for bringing me here, it is the experience of a lifetime.'

He nods in his casual way and tells me to enjoy the match. In a way it does not matter any more whether Germany wins or loses. But as the second half gets under way, I feel the tension rising again. Argentina come close again, as do Germany. The game goes to extra time. It turns into an incredible fight, with German midfielder Bastian Schweinsteiger famously bloodied from his many scuffles with the Argentina midfielders. I try to enjoy the game without hoping for a winner.

Then Germany coach Joachim Loew makes two inspired substitutions. Right below where we are sitting, Loew gives his final instructions and then Andre Schurrle and Mario Gotze come on. Miroslav Klose is off the pitch at this stage. So the two substitutes combine. I watch the move build up early on the left side of midfield, and then Schurrle goes down the left wing and I'm up on my feet again, and he's crossed it over to Gotze, who still has it all to do, but he's chested it down perfectly and instead of letting it drop he's falling into a volley already, and my hands are going up, and then a split-second later the ball is in, so beautifully in, the net is moving and surely, yes, it must be in, and it is – double-check that there's no offside flag going up, there isn't, and it's the moment I've been waiting for all of my life – the goalkeeper is picking the ball from the net because he had no chance, the ball is really in and really not offside, the ball is in, and half the stadium is erupting, and I'm jumping, just jumping high and higher and higher yet into the beautiful, perfect Rio de Janeiro night, I'm screaming and jumping, and everyone from Qatar is leaning over to congratulate me or to slap me over the head because I'm so excited and clearly overdoing it. But wouldn't you overdo it too?

Then I notice that there are still seven minutes to go. Agony. They are the longest seven minutes ever. Will there be late goals like in the 1999 Champions League final? Argentina are pushing every man forward. But then there is the final whistle, and we've done it, Germany are World Champions and I can't quite believe it – that we've won, and that I'm actually standing in the stadium just a few metres away from where the trophy will be handed over in just a few minutes.

The celebrations begin, off the pitch and on it. The players are coming up to collect their medals, and then the trophy. That trophy. It is right there in front of us.

'Hey, Matthias, come down here,' says our Secretary-General, and I try politely to refuse. He is gesturing for me to come down to the front row, right where he is standing, right behind where the trophy is going to be presented to Germany captain Philipp Lahm in just a second. I try to decline again, but it comes as an order from our top boss, so I can't really refuse.

There's the generosity of the Qatari people for you.

I try to convince him that I shouldn't, that all the more senior members of the team should be there next to him. But he's not having any of it.

'Come down here, your team just won. Enjoy it.'

So that's how I end up with my Qatari colleagues in the live TV feed, and all the pictures of the German team lifting the trophy which I'll tell my great-grandchildren about one day. They'll laugh at me and tell me to stop hallucinating; that thing called television doesn't exist any more.

All of the German team members have picked up their medals now, and the coaching staff have passed by to collect theirs too. There is Oliver Bierhoff, my hero from the 1996 Euros winning team when Dad allowed me to stay up to watch the final on TV in Doha, and I wave at him. We met a year earlier at a football conference in Germany, where we somehow got to chatting about the mid-life crisis. Now everyone is all smiles, though. The famous golden trophy has been handed over and is lifted high, high, high into the Rio night. We are right there in the middle of it. There is golden confetti raining down over us all, and I grab a handful to keep as a souvenir. It's still in my suitcase to this day, the suitcase with 'Qatar' written in large letters on the front which my father gave me from his athletics competitions, in the little side compartment where I will always keep it. That night I go to celebrate with a German journalist and a whole lot of Germans on Rio's famous Copacabana walkway.

There are hundreds of Germans walking up and down the street, some waving flags, some shouting Germany chants, others looking deliriously happy.

'We Germans don't know how to celebrate, do we?' I say to the journalist with a laugh. 'Imagine if it had been the Brazilians who won, how they would be dancing and singing!'

But celebrate we do nevertheless, in our German way. That night we are on top of the world in Rio de Janeiro.

Two years later I returned once more to marvellous Rio, and to that same stadium. This time it was for the Olympic Games. Qatar's Olympic Committee had set up Bayt Qatar ('The Qatar House'), a hospitality and culture house, and we were showcasing the latest progress in our legacy programmes and stadiums. One of the many visitors we brought to our stand and to see the entire Qatar House was Coach Evaristo.

'Coach Evaristo, can I offer you a glimpse of Qatar in your hometown?' I asked him when I called, one day before the opening ceremony of the Olympic Games.

'Of course I will come,' he said, moved by the call and the gesture. 'Can I bring my family?'

And so Coach Evaristo came to visit us that day in early August 2016, and he brought his family with him too. It was difficult to show him our stadiums that day. People from Qatar were swarming around him, reminiscing about the team and the players he used to coach. Finally I got him into our stand, where the scale model of Al Rayyan Stadium was displayed.

'This place, when I came, did not have any stadium,' he said. 'I tried to convince them to build stadiums around all of Qatar, that it would benefit their football. This was the club where one of my best players, Mansour Muftah, played his football.'

He smiled at the memory. I remembered that it was also the club where Khattab Al Daffa had played all those years earlier. We set up the camera and I interviewed Evaristo in front of the stadium model.

'Rio is my home, and the place where I live,' he told me that day, 'but the second place which I call home is Qatar. I'd love to be there for the 2022 World Cup.'

For me it was exactly the other way around. Qatar was my home. And then there was Rio, beautiful Rio, which was also becoming something of a favourite city, even after just three visits. There was of course Spain too, where my daughter was born and where more good news awaited.

Evaristo stayed in Bayt Qatar for over three hours that day. I had to bid him farewell because our bus was leaving for the opening ceremony of the Olympic Games. It was to be yet another memorable visit to that citadel of modern football, and a spectacular ceremony awaited.

Brazil knows how to put on a party. It knows how to make you dance, move in your seats, jump up and sing out loud. That night Brazil did just that, in a festival of creativity, of sounds and sights and a sea of flags. Qatar's team marched in near the beginning, because the country is spelt with a 'C' in Portuguese, as it is in Spanish. I proudly waved the flag of the country of my birth, just as Dad had done at the opening ceremony of the Sydney 2000 Olympic Games sixteen years earlier.

The following day was my flight back to Spain, where my daughter was turning four years old that day. I jogged that morning along Copacabana beach, the frothing waves covering the scenic golden sands in a spectacular mist. As I jogged up to the beach volleyball venue near the Leme part of the iconic beach, I thought of the good news coming from Spain. To my left I could see the statue of Christ the Redeemer. Up ahead was the beautiful outline of Sugarloaf Mountain. Out to my right the sprawling ocean, wide and blue and beautiful. Sixteen hours later I was running into the arms of my daughter in Valencia airport on her birthday, filled with a happiness that only your children can give you.

The wonderful news that summer was that my wife and I would be having another baby girl. She would be born in Qatar, like me, in February the next year in the tiny town of Dukhan, where competitive football had first been played in the country. We too were writing our own history. Three generations of the Krug family to live in and call Doha their home. And the second generation to be born in Qatar. I can already imagine the look on people's faces when one day she says 'I was born in Qatar'.

And I believe that people will be inspired by what this small country with the big sporting dreams has become.

2017. KHALIFA INTERNATIONAL STADIUM
The man who can make it snow in the summer

'Legacy' is a key word in mega events, which Qatar has translated from the loftiness of a word on paper into a tangible reality on the ground. Since the summer of 2018, a full four years before kick-off, I have been working with Generation Amazing, the social and human legacy programme born during Qatar's bid in 2010, which aims to use football for development to empower and educate one million young people by the time the World Cup gets under way in 2022. By September 2018, our Secretary-General His Excellency Hassan Al Thawadi had proudly announced in New York that the programme had positively impacted the lives of over 250,000 beneficiaries, including building football pitches and safe play spaces in twenty-six communities across the Middle East and Asia.

The most lasting element of our work once the tournament concludes is that if all future mega events leave a legacy as significant and life-changing as that of Qatar, then it can be a game changer for the way major events are able help to shape social change. Here in Doha, the World Cup has helped to significantly accelerate progress on workers' welfare for a large segment of the population. If future editions of the tournament in each country can credibly address one social issue, whether that is gun violence, binge drinking, or any other issue affecting the society in question, then sport can truly claim to be a force for positive social change.

That is the vision we are working towards, and the reason why, seven years after starting to work for FIFA World Cup Qatar 2022™, the job still gives me goose bumps just as it did on the very first day.

The country I was born in has everyone talking about it these days. No one confuses it with a washing powder anymore. We may wish sometimes that certain people washed their mouths with a strong washing powder before tossing around some of the dirt that is thrown Qatar's way, but I do believe it will be a good thing in the end.

Does that surprise you? After all the controversy? They love saying that about Qatar, as you may have noticed. The 'controversial' World Cup hosts. The 'World Cup in the desert'. I smile when people say these things. I love the desert. And 'controversial' also means people are talking about you. If you go by the wisdom that any publicity is good publicity, or however that saying goes, then you do see how the country is achieving its goals.

So far the journey has been up and down, and up and up and down once more, with still three years to go until the World Cup at the time of writing this book, but there is something which has always taken me, and still does take me, by surprise. It is the natural, innate, stoic resilience, the desert-like tranquillity and self-belief of the Qataris. Their ability to dream bigger than a canvas of stars, but then to go about implementing their vision with a determination which some may mistake for arrogance. The first stadium to be completed for 2022 was a case in point in this regard.

In December 2016 I sat down to interview Nasser Al Khater about the moment that had just passed. Six years to go until 2022 – exactly halfway to the World Cup. It felt like a momentous occasion, but plenty more were just around the corner.

'Challenges have been there from the beginning,' Al Khater said that day. 'As for any World Cup organisers, there will always be challenges. If you talk about critics, there have been critics from the day we were bidding, and there were critics from the day we won. Qataris by nature are resilient and can endure. We've listened to our critics and we've answered our critics. I think it's time now for our critics to listen to us. I think that in 2022, when the world descends on Qatar to watch the World Cup here, our critics will be proven wrong.'

If this was his half-time team talk, what would he say to his players at the halfway mark to 2022, I asked?

'I think as a coach I'd be very proud of the team, and commend them on a job well done, the team being the entire nation. The focus was high in the first half, but let's not forget there's another 45 minutes where we need to maintain the momentum, and we need to be as resilient and endure as much as we have in the past. If we do that, we should rest assured that we'll get a positive result,' he said. Then he suggested that I should also interview our Secretary-General.

That interview took place upstairs in Hassan Al Thawadi's classy, elegant office on the 37th floor of Al Bidda Tower, after we'd waited as he finished another interview with the local TV station Al Kass in a nearby room.

'OK, Matthias, let's do this,' he said in his usual all-action way. You will find few people who have the drive, determination and intensity of Hassan Al Thawadi. He sat down and we began the interview. When I asked him about the advances that had been made in building Qatar's stadiums for 2022, he revealed something new. I still loved my exclusives.

'We will inaugurate the first stadium for the World Cup this coming May, for the final of the Amir Cup in Doha,' he revealed.

At the end of the interview I asked him how much pride he would feel stepping into Lusail Stadium for the final of the 2022 FIFA World Cup™ in Qatar.

'I cannot even begin to imagine it. I could not imagine the emotions I would feel, when we were bidding in 2010, if we won on 2 December. Even now I have not been able to process those emotions, so I cannot imagine my emotions in 2022. What I'll do is take it step by step, enjoy the ride, every moment and every success, and overcome every obstacle we face from now until 2022. Then when we get to the final in 2022, I'll look for you to ask the same question again.'

I thanked him for his time, and told him I would find him at Lusail Stadium in 2022 and ask him the same question.

The spring of 2017 was an emotional one for me personally, as my second daughter was born in Qatar, at the Cuban Hospital in Dukhan. It was one early morning at the end of February, and our room in the spacious new hospital surrounded by the vast desert felt like the most wonderful place on earth. It was as if life had started anew when I held our baby daughter in my arms that day. My father came to visit us in hospital, having driven along the new highway from Doha to Dukhan with our elder daughter and my mother-in-law Marisol. It was a special journey for my father, having often made the same drive across a pot-holed desert road many decades earlier in the old blue Toyota Land Cruiser with us four kids packed in the back. Now his son had grown up, and he came to visit and hold his little granddaughter (although the wonderfully effusive Cuban nurses said they had never seen a bigger baby) in his arms. He smiled a toothy smile from ear to ear that day, as the second generation of the Krug family was born in Qatar. At some stage they might like to give him a Qatari family name too. The Al Krugs of Muaither, or something like that.

A couple of life-changing weeks followed at home with my wife, first daughter and our newborn baby. The time away from the office gave me a new perspective on the incredible opportunity we have with this World Cup in Qatar. Upon returning to work, the biggest moment in the preparations to date awaited. As our Secretary-General had stated, our first stadium was to be completed that May, more than five and a half years before the start of the tournament. Had anyone in the history of hosting World Cup tournaments ever completed a stadium that far in advance? Probably not. Perhaps the

Germans, with their famous efficiency, in 2006. But here we were, preparing for the first stadium opening. It was a momentous stage, and a fitting occasion, with the most important football match of the year set to take place there. His Highness the Amir of Qatar would inaugurate the revamped Khalifa International Stadium, with the best teams in the country battling for a place in a match that had historically always sold out. Now, with the first stadium for 2022 set to open, interest in the game was incredibly high.

Nasser Al Khater led the organising committee for the match, and seemed to be permanently based in the stadium those last days before the opening. It wouldn't have surprised me to find he had a bed there somewhere where he took the few hours' rest he gave himself. He is a perfectionist, and in those days it told more than ever. Then there was the tireless Shaikha Al Thani, who was leading on the communications elements of the stadium opening, and who seemed to embody everything noble and resilient I have always detected in the Qataris over the years. Even at the most challenging times, she always kept her optimism and her smile in place.

There was something magical about those last few weeks before the 2017 Amir Cup final. The whole team in the newsroom worked around the clock to produce a series of fifteen stories, a social media hashtag which reached millions, and fourteen social media videos which helped to create excitement around the opening of the stadium. One of the stories was another in a long line of interviews I'd done with Xavi over the past few years. A few weeks earlier he had won his first trophy in Doha, the Qatar Cup, and now his team was just one match away from the Amir Cup final at Khalifa International Stadium.

We met again for the interview in The Torch hotel that warm day in May, on the 20th floor overlooking the stadium far below.

'It would be a dream to play in the first venue to be ready for 2022,' Xavi told me, looking as excited as a kid as his glance went admiringly over the newly renovated venue which had hosted some of Qatar's biggest sporting moments over the years. I thought back to my own first experience at the historic venue, sitting in the bleachers with my family for the final of the World Youth Championship. The likes of Neymar, Lionel Messi, Carles Puyol, Luis Suarez, Andres Iniesta, Cristiano Ronaldo, Raul and Zlatan Ibrahimovic had all played there, and I'd admired their skills over the years. But Xavi had never walked out onto that pitch. Not yet.

'I am excited to play the final in this stadium; I can feel the passion building up to this match. Qatar is a country which is doing things well. It is a long-term project until 2022, but the first stadium is already being delivered. You can see that football is in the air; they breathe it here and that is something marvellous. More than five years before the World Cup it is fantastic to see how the stadiums are being prepared for the tournament.'

Then he added, with a view to the future use of the stadium: 'What I try to transmit to the young people of this region is this passion that I have for football. This is a historic opportunity to play a World Cup at home and to do it well.'

Xavi and his Al Sadd team made it to the final that year, against the 'Lions' of Al Rayyan, and it was announced that Khalifa International Stadium would indeed be the venue for the match. We had our dream final. Over the last few days before the final I constantly visited the stadium and looked at the finishing touches and arrangements being made. On the pitch, I interviewed Yasser Al Mulla, the Qatari behind the perfect green grass laid down in a record-breaking thirteen and a half hours at the centre of the magnificent stadium around us. 'This very stadium is where Qatar won the Gulf Cup in 1992,' he said. 'And where they hosted the 1995 Youth World Cup and the Asian Games in 2006. I am honoured to have created the pitch for this wonderful stadium.'

Every aspect of the preparations was meticulously taken care of. Then there was Dr Saud Abdul Ghani. The Qatar University professor, who had shown me the innovative cooled helmets developed for workers in Doha a few months earlier, walked into the centre of the stadium wearing a helmet and with a thermometer in his hand. He was responsible for the cooling system installed at the venue, making it the largest open-air cooled stadium in the world.

'The air doesn't escape, you see, because cool air is heavier than hot air, and so it doesn't rise,' he explained, just a few days before 48,000 spectators would fill the stadium and his concept absolutely had to be working. 'It is done using district cooling, which makes the technology 40 per cent more sustainable than traditional cooling methods.'

I simply nodded and wrote it all down, having never been very good at science at school. But it sounded right, and the blasts of cool air from 500 valves specially designed in Qatar were astonishing. Would it work, though, with 48,000 people watching the biggest game of the country's football calendar? We were about to find out. Dr Saud never had any doubt.

'Of course it will work,' he said with a carefree laugh. 'If you want, I can make it snow here inside the stadium in summer. Look, you just have to turn the cooling up further, and we can get the temperature right down to...'

'Just please don't say that on camera,' I laughed. 'We don't want people to be freezing cold inside the stadium.'

The story we did on the world's biggest cooled stadium went around the world that day. A couple of days later the world's media arrived. Journalists had come from the UK, from France, Germany, Spain, India, from nearby Dubai and faraway China, all to see this new stadium being inaugurated.

The day before the opening of the stadium we gave the visiting media a tour of the newly finished venue, and they got the chance to interview Nasser Al Khater from a vantage point overlooking the entire stadium. A little later we brought Xavi along to have a look inside the stadium where he would be playing the next day.

'This is a big stadium,' Xavi told me, walking out onto the pitch. 'It smells of a big stadium, like the Camp Nou, a real venue for a World Cup.'

The following day, Qatar inaugurated the new Camp Nou of the Arab world. A massive crowd had made their way to the venue. Security was efficient and thorough. Walking up to the stadium, you could start to feel the cooled air from fifteen metres away. Inside the stadium a wall of white-clad spectators filled the stands. It was an awe-inspiring setting. I'd never seen anything like it in Qatar in all those years attending and reporting on major sporting occasions. Next to me in the media zone a journalist from China had unfortunately chosen to come dressed in only shorts and a t-shirt. He kept rubbing his hands together throughout the entire match, trying to generate a bit of heat. And no wonder. It was extremely cool inside the venue.

'Congratulations, it works, incredible how cool it is in here,' I said as I called Dr Saud from inside the stadium.

'Of course, it's working perfectly! We've measured 20 degrees on the pitch and 23 degrees in the spectator seating area.

I believed then that he could actually make it snow in Qatar in summer.

After a spectacular opening ceremony culminating in fireworks which outlined the numbers '2022' above the stadium, and the official ribbon-cutting by His Highness the Amir Sheikh Tamim bin Hamad Al Thani, as he declared the stadium ready to host FIFA World Cup Qatar 2022™ on behalf of 'every Arab', the country's national anthem sounded out from the marching band out on the pitch. It gave me goose bumps once more to hum along as the entire stadium joined in and the game got under way.

It could not have been the perfect day it turned out to be without some magic on the pitch. With the score tied at 1-1 just before the final whistle, the midfield magician Xavi took over in the 91st minute. With the lottery of a penalty shoot-out looming ever closer, he skilfully lobbed the ball over his own head with a deft back-heel. Then the Al Sadd captain nudged it on with his forehead before playing an inch-perfect pass through to his Algerian team-mate Jugurtha

Hamroun, who suddenly found himself through on goal. A stunning finish into the top corner of the net sent the crowd into a frenzy of celebration, or at least the part of it supporting the Foxes. I jumped up in celebration too. A few moments later Xavi and his team-mates received the winners' medals and trophy from the Amir of Qatar. I gave the Barcelona legend a big hug in the mixed zone afterwards.

'You did it,' I said. 'You did it.'

'Incredible... what a stadium, what a moment...'

It was a real World Cup atmosphere that day in Doha, with all of five and a half years remaining until kick-off in 2022.

As he left the stadium that day I caught a glimpse of our Secretary-General. As always, he was on the way somewhere important – the airport, I believe. But in best persistent reporter fashion I got in a few questions in the mixed zone. I asked him what that night meant to him.

'It is one of the proudest moments of my life,' he replied. 'It is proof of what we've always said. People thought the cooling technology was only a dream. The reality is it was already in Al Sadd Club, and today it is in Khalifa International Stadium. It is continuing, becoming something normal and deliverable, and the delivery is on the ground. It has showcased the capabilities and quality we have. Everybody worked very hard and delivered a stadium that measures up to the standards we promised for the World Cup. Operationally, the team has done a fantastic job, and this is just the start.'

As my colleague Ali Zein and I walked back to the bus which would shuttle the journalists back to their hotel, I said to him: 'Let's go inside and take a picture on the pitch.'

A few days earlier in the newsroom he'd been shouting in frustration that one of his stories hadn't gone out in time. I liked it that way. We all worked as hard as we could those days, and I preferred a newsroom with a few temporary bust-ups and shouting matches over one that was as quiet as a library. You needed passion to win. Now we laughed heartily together about his earlier outburst.

We walked inside and took a picture on the centre circle. I picked up a piece of the golden confetti littering the pitch and added it to my collection of random football memorabilia. Out there near the touchline were all those colleagues who had organised the stadium opening. Shaikha reached out and shook my hand. She beamed happily, and you could see what it meant to all those on the pitch to have delivered Qatar's first stadium for 2022. It was one down, seven to go. But opening this first one would always be a special moment for all of us present, because it was a stadium that was close to everyone's heart.

Just a few days later, though, people in Doha woke up to altogether different news. Qatar's three neighbours, Saudi Arabia, the UAE and Bahrain, plus Egypt, had decided to impose a blockade on it overnight. All airspace was closed, Qatari nationals were ordered to leave those countries, and a general ice age descended on political relations. After a brief period of heightened shopping activity in the supermarkets, and a few chiller cabinet shelves momentarily stripped bare of the milk that everyone knew came in by road from across the Saudi border, normality soon returned to life in Doha. Still, it was perhaps the most worrying situation I had seen in Qatar over all those years.

Other books should, and probably will, be written about the folly of it all, and about the US President who had come to the region a few weeks earlier and, by his Twitterplomacy, apparently encouraged the blockading nations in their actions. The traditional regional balance of power which made Qatar one of the safest places on earth, and allowed my family to live there in peaceful surroundings for over thirty-five years, was in danger of being completely overturned. In such circumstances, other young nations might have folded and bowed to what ultimately amounted to demands that Qatar surrender its hard-earned sovereignty.

Qatar, though, did not. It responded with wisdom and resilience. The country's foreign minister must have travelled three times around the globe over the coming days. And construction work on the World Cup sites continued unhindered, with materials sourced from other places. News made the rounds of Qatar flying in 4,000 cows to speed up the country's bid to become self-sufficient in milk. During those difficult days our Secretary-General was invited to speak at a conference of the global trade union BWI in Berlin. We had signed an agreement with BWI for joint inspections of World Cup sites, and the positive outcomes of this cooperation were clear for all to see in Germany.

On the eve of his speech, *Bild* newspaper in Germany said they'd received a leaked copy of the much-debated Garcia Report, which FIFA had commissioned to look into the bidding conduct of all nine bidders for 2018 and 2022. While the timing of the leak was clearly somewhat suspicious, the findings were not. The report found no reason to strip Qatar or Russia of their respective World Cups. And you can see from the hundreds of pages of Michael Garcia's report just how thoroughly the American conducted his work.

Back home in Doha, I had started a legacy-orientated initiative for the newsroom called 'Pathway to 2022', which aimed to bring the best young Qatari media professionals from universities in the country to our newsroom to gain experience and ultimately tell their own story of the first World Cup tournament in the Arab world. A few days into the blockade, a young candidate called Alreem came in, and my Spanish colleague Isabel and I interviewed her. She made an immediate impression on me with her attitude. Still in the midst of her university education, she seemed ready to move mountains.

'My brother,' she explained, 'has been stuck in the UAE. He couldn't fly back; he had to come through Oman. It was very bad. But they won't be able to stop us. I want to help my country. I want to write stories, to contribute my small part to making this tournament a great success.'

Within a week of joining she had already written her first story and stuck it proudly on our newsroom clippings wall, which was filled with our articles from all around the world. Every day she came to my desk with new ideas. For someone leading a newsroom, you can't ask for more than that.

The first of Qatar's 'boycott-busting' flying cows (as the *Gulf Times* dramatically called them) arrived a few days later. Rather fittingly, I thought, the first batch to arrive consisted of hundreds of German cows which had found a new home in the desert. More cows were to be flown in from Australia. That's where my sister Anna lives now, with her wonderful family of five. Dad visited her there recently for a few weeks, to get to know his latest little grandchild, a lovely baby girl named Heidi. While he was there, Anna took him out to a shooting range to try his hand at skeet shooting.

When he returned to Doha, after a marathon flight which was originally meant to stop over in Dubai but now had to be re-routed through Kuwait because of the ban on Qatari planes in UAE airspace, we had a chat about the 'Qatar crisis', as it had become known.

'What do you think?' I asked him. 'How serious is it?'

'It will be fine,' he said, with his trademark stoicism, picked up from almost four decades in this small Arabian Gulf country. 'And if anything happens, I will stand ready to defend my little plot of land. Why do you think I practised on the shooting range in Australia?'

I told him not to be silly and do nothing of the sort, but then I've always been nicknamed the 'Kofi Annan' of the family (after the former UN Secretary-General) for my famously diplomatic and peace-loving ways (except when it comes to securing the remote control for the TV during World Cup matches). I didn't know whether he was serious or not. But you can certainly imagine someone who has hopped through a minefield to escape an oppressive political ideology rejecting any compromise when it comes to defending his much-loved garden with its little patch of tomato plants.

In the end, I suppose that's what it is all about. Finding your little patch of this marvellous planet which you can proudly call your home. In my case it is a country which can make cows fly and snow fall in the desert. Will my father ever find another home? Recently he turned 65 in Doha, the place where he landed in 1982 as a 28-year-old full of dreams. In the many years since that great escape from East Germany he has gathered many lovely family memories with the skill of an expert fossil-hunter, and swapped his old brown leather jacket for a maroon sports jacket with five letters written across the back: Q-A-T-A-R.

JUNE 2018. MOSCOW
A World Cup love story

When I was a small boy growing up in Qatar, I listened on the radio in my father's old car as the news bulletin announced that West Germany had just become World Champions. That was the start of a long love story, back in the year 1990. As a youngster in Doha I leafed through the World Cup history book and became enchanted by the famous goals scored and the heroes who led their countries to the ultimate football glory.

Twenty-eight years later I found myself on a plane flying to Moscow to be at the World Cup again, for the third time in my life. Landing in Russia on 11 June, three days before the tournament was set to begin, I found the airport had only a few decorations or signs of football in the offing. It smelt slightly of petrol, or something like that, but not yet of football. We had landed in the heart of the football world and, along with colleagues from our Generation Amazing 'football for development' programme, I sought out a photo opportunity at the luggage belt with the Russia 2018 logo in the background. A towering Russian came up to us, patted us on the back and gave us a cheer. It was the first sign of World Cup fever building up, and of the brilliant Russian hospitality we would witness over the coming weeks. As we arrived at the legendary President hotel, which is under the administration of the President of Russia, the realisation finally set in: I was about to experience my third World Cup. At the back of the hotel the Moskva River flowed elegantly through Gorky

Park, and a massive statue commemorated Peter the Great. In the distance, a cluster of skyscrapers stood tall, reminding me of Doha.

The English language newspaper available in the hotel, the *Moscow Times*, had the headline: 'Game Time: But is Russia Ready?' It is the eternal question, given the nature of mankind to doubt everything which has not been done before, and one which also dogs us in Qatar.

We would all soon find out just how ready Russia was. That night we drove past the Luzhniki Stadium, which was set to host the opening game in just a matter of days. It looked majestic from the outside, but how would it be from within?

It felt incredible to be at the World Cup. This was the culmination of a difficult year at many levels, but here I was, about to see the world's greatest football celebration. Later, as we walked through the city at night, the plaza outside Red Square was alive with fans and chants from people from many countries, sporting their national team shirts. Argentina, Mexico, Peru... the world was arriving to celebrate football, and fans from South America were making their mark with their characteristic passion and colour. We walked through Moscow for almost two hours that night, and although the weather was chilly you could feel the passion emanating from the groups of fans everywhere. I stood in the midst of them for a while, enjoying the atmosphere. These people were as crazy for football as I was.

The following day you could feel the excitement everywhere around the city. There were just two days remaining until kick-off, and football fever was rising everywhere you went and looked. A group of eight workers from Qatar were arriving at the airport to experience their first-ever World Cup thanks to our Generation Amazing programme, and I wanted to be there to greet them. We waited for the group to emerge as football fans from all corners of the globe arrived. When they came out of the sliding arrivals door, excitement could easily be seen on even the tiredest faces. We greeted the group from Qatar, and took a photo together in front of the Russia 2018 sign near the coffee shop. That was the start of it all. And from then on it didn't stop. Happiness is difficult to grasp sometimes, but there it was. In the streets of beautiful Moscow. In the eyes of fans from all over the world. In the Russian people with their stoic, sincere friendliness, which at times you only got to after peeling away a few onionskin layers of gruffness. At other times you didn't need to do any peeling. It was just there. Always beautifully there, like the sparkling lights on the street at the very heart of the city leading to Red Square.

This street of lights, otherwise known as Nikolskaya Ulitsa, soon became a gathering point for fans from across the world. It turned into a melting pot of humanity, and I passed through it often and with great pleasure during those days. You only needed to go up and down it once to meet someone from virtually every country taking part in the World Cup. Fans chanted and drummed and danced and drank. In the evenings and at night it became so full that at times you could only get through very slowly, and stuck to someone else's back. Everyone wore a smile. It was a festive atmosphere. You saw shirts of all colours, and costumes of the craziest shapes and sizes. I seem to remember seeing a man with a horse's head being carried around by five colleagues. There were the traditional Mexican hats, inevitable at any World Cup. And everywhere you looked there were Russian fans making friends, welcoming people to their country, having a whale of a time.

At the start of the tournament the emblematic Red Square next to the Kremlin was closed for a few days, for a concert taking place there. So on the first day of our workshops with the eight workers from Qatar, I walked early in the morning through the 'street of lights' over to the hotel where Xavi was staying, to talk him, over breakfast, through the schedule for the day. And then, for good measure, a German World Cup-winning captain and another great midfielder, Lothar Matthaus, stopped by and said hello. He exchanged a few words with Xavi, one genius midfielder to another, and then I got in a request for a selfie. There I stood next to the player who had lifted the World Cup for Germany at the start of my football journey. In a split second the selfie was taken and he moved away.

We headed with Xavi to meet the group of workers who had made the unlikely journey from Qatar to experience their first-ever World Cup. The Barcelona legend is as humble and inspirational a player as you will find, and he was magic, as always, in the way he interacted with the group. There were two days of workshops building on the workers' leadership and communication skills, after which more than thirty journalists from around the world joined us for a football activation with Xavi and the eight worker ambassadors.

All eight had started as participants in our Generation Amazing 'football for development' programme. Then, over the space of two years, they had developed into coaches, passing on their experience to others in their communities. Now, the eight of them were here in Moscow, experiencing their first-ever World Cup. This is what the World Cup is truly about, more than victories or defeats, goals or sliding tackles – it is about meeting new people, giving opportunities to those who would otherwise not have them, understanding new cultures and traditions. Also there that day were disabled youth from the Best Buddies organisation in Russia, and when all of the journalists had packed their bags and headed off to cover another story, I went over and finally got to play some football with them myself. Although these Russian youngsters didn't speak my language or I theirs, we shared a moment united just by the common language of passing a football between us.

'When I was growing up in my village in Bangladesh,' Sirajul, one of the eight inspirational ambassadors, told me later that day as we headed to the opening ceremony and first game of Russia 2018, 'we did not have a television in my house. So we watched the World

Cup on our neighbour's screen. Now I have this opportunity to see a World Cup live, in person, and it is an incredible feeling. Not many people from Bangladesh have this opportunity.'

There were other unforgettable stories too. Hasan from Sri Lanka had to move villages as a small boy after a tsunami and then a terrorist attack struck his hometown in quick succession. He adapted to his new surroundings by taking up football, playing for his local team, Liverpool FC. When he finished school he took a job in Saudi Arabia, but didn't like it and returned to Sri Lanka. Then another opportunity beckoned, this time in Qatar. Within a few months he was feeling homesick, but it was football which helped him to integrate into his new surroundings, as Generation Amazing began offering football for development classes at Labour City. Within two years, Hasan had progressed from being a participant to becoming a coach imparting his knowledge to others. He was selected as one of the eight worker ambassadors to travel to Moscow, and now there he sat in the Luzhniki Stadium in Moscow, taking photos with Russian fans with that gigantic, powerful smile of his.

Next to me on the left sat Abdul Azeez Suleiman, who had dreamed of becoming a football player in Ghana and, when he didn't get an opportunity to play in his home country, took a job in Qatar. Having arrived in Doha, he started taking part in Generation Amazing football training and the annual Workers Cup, where he met and shook hands with FIFA President Gianni Infantino. After that handshake, he remembered, he was too nervous to play his best football in the game that followed. Below us now in the impressive Luzhniki Stadium the opening ceremony was starting. We waved our Qatari flags high into the Moscow sky, but amidst this celebration of football it was an intensely sad day for me and my family, as my grandfather Ulf sadly passed away after a long battle with illness. Born on 'the 3.3.33', he died eighty-five years later, on the opening day of the football tournament he always followed so loyally.

There was a wonderful moment in the opening ceremony where a pianist played classical music suspended above the Moskva River. The Russians found their voice that day in the stadium, and their players found their range, hitting five unanswered goals past their opponents from Saudi Arabia. It united an entire nation in celebration, with the whole stadium erupting in unbridled joy. In my memory stays a photo I took during one of the goal celebrations, where one young Russian fan celebrates wildly while another extends a hand of greeting to our worker ambassador from Ghana. If some of the wild pre-tournament headlines in certain tabloid newspapers were to be believed, the Russian fans were all racist hooligans. Nothing could have been further from the truth during this tournament. And I already know that Qatar will equally confound all expectations and defy its critics with the greatest tournament the world has seen.

That summer we had a large team of observers in Russia who were there to learn and take knowledge and experience back to Doha. Germany played their worst-ever tournament, crashing out in the first round, but even that couldn't dampen my excitement about what was a brilliantly organised Russian World Cup. With Nasser Al Khater and Bora Milutinovic we visited the Chinese television studios overlooking Red Square, and we saw numerous others with Xavi Hernandez and our other spokespersons. And I had the privilege of attending nine games at the tournament, taking my World Cup total to seventeen. Undoubtedly the highlight of those unforgettable Moscow summer days was working together and experiencing the enthusiasm and excitement of our inspirational young ambassadors, and seeing seemingly all of humanity coming together on the streets of the Russian capital. After the France-Denmark game which we attended with some of our Generation Amazing youth ambassadors, a man came up to us and seized the Qatari flag from the hand of one of the youngsters. He wouldn't stop waving it. It turned out he was from one of our neighbouring Gulf countries, and was showing his support for Qatar's World Cup in 2022. Winning, I understood again at that moment, was not important. Especially after a 0-0 draw. The most important thing was this coming together of people from all across the world because they all love the same game. The power this creates has the potential to change the world, and it is this power which Qatar is looking to channel into a good cause for 2022.

The World Cup in Russia drew slowly to a close, having defied all of its critics along the way. Everything from security to the hospitality with which people were welcomed to the Fan Fests was impeccable. A new understanding of Russia and Russian people was born. And so it will be with Qatar, too, in 2022. During the last days of the tournament there were numerous activations and even a Qatar house on the banks of the Moskva River, which welcomed visitors and gave them an idea of what to expect in 2022. On the final day of the tournament, His Highness the Amir Sheikh Tamim bin Hamad Al Thani officially took over hosting responsibilities 'in the name of all Arabs' from Russian President Vladimir Putin, in a ceremony held at the Kremlin. It was a symbolic, powerful and highly emotional moment for all of us who have worked on this project for so long: Qatar is now officially the next World Cup.

It gives me goosebumps when I think of what this country will be like on the opening day of the World Cup. The Metro will be running. The magnificently designed stadiums will be ready. The airport will be buzzing and the whole country will be decorated in World Cup colours. A multitude of friendly volunteers will be on hand. Perhaps most exciting of all, the traditional Arabian hospitality will be on show in full force to welcome the world.

Lusail Stadium will be vibrant and majestic, and walking up into the stadium you will be greeted by a wave of noise, that noise which only the World Cup can generate. Then a whole country will get behind the national team and believe that anything is possible, if only you plan for it well enough and believe in sporting miracles.

For as our Secretary-General, His Excellency Hassan Al Thawadi, said in a speech which he gave in fluent Spanish at the Casa Arabe in Madrid in late 2017, at which football legends like Real Madrid captain Fernando Hierro were present: 'We may indeed be dreamers. But like the best football players we have our feet placed firmly on the ground.'

EPILOGUE: FEBRUARY 2019. DOHA

The young Qatar team that brought home the Asian Cup

For a sporting miracle to be truly unforgettable, of the type that shuts down normal traffic and life for days and then remains in a country's football consciousness for generations afterwards, you should be able to credibly claim that no one saw it coming. Qatar's journey at the 2019 Asian Cup in the UAE was just such a fairytale story.

It made the football world sit up and take notice; it fired up a young generation of Qatari players to dream of being like the striker Almoez Ali, with his exuberant violin-playing goal celebration, or the boxing-inspired forward Akram Afif – and absolutely no one saw it coming.

Well, perhaps that is not entirely true. One player saw it coming, and did so – much as in his playing days – well ahead of everyone else. That player was Xavi Hernandez. The legendary Catalan midfielder correctly predicted seven of the eight Asian Cup quarter-finalists. He also correctly guessed the two finalists, as well as the winner of the tournament, on Qatari sports TV channel Al Kass days before the event started, and was soon hailed on social media as the new 'Paul the Octopus', after the animal oracle that won worldwide fame for accurately predicting scores at South Africa 2010.

Clearly, though, Xavi had put much more thought into his predictions than Paul.

On 9 January, the day Qatar opened their 2019 Asian Cup campaign against Lebanon, Xavi walked out onto the training field at Aspire Academy in Doha to shake hands with a visibly excited Joshua Kimmich. The shooting star of the German national team was meeting his longtime FC Barcelona idol for the first time in Doha on the sidelines of the Bayern Munich winter training camp.

Together they talked about their childhood idols to a group of wide-eyed schoolkids brought together by the Generation Amazing 'football for development' programme. Behind them stood Aspire Academy, which had developed the majority of the team that was representing Qatar in the Asian Cup that day.

'The other day I did a prediction game on Al Kass, and I put Qatar as champions,' Xavi told me with a smile, standing on the green carpet that is the pitch at Aspire. 'It will be difficult, but I think they could very well reach the quarter-finals, and once there the small details will decide. The first game is very important because it gives you an indication of the rest of the tournament.'

A few hours later, Qatar's tournament opener against Lebanon kicked off in Al Ain, and the Maroons scored an important initial victory. After a goalless first 45 minutes, the second half proved decisive. The first goal was a beautiful free kick just after the hour mark which defender Bassam Al Rawi curled in to give Qatar the lead, followed by a second goal which would take on additional significance as the tournament advanced. A nice combination took the ball rapidly towards the Lebanese penalty area, where Almoez Ali was on hand to tap the ball home into an open net.

It was to be the first of a record-breaking goal haul for the Qatari striker, who signalled his intention to step into the historic boots of legendary Al Ennabi attackers like Mubarak Mustafa and Mansour Muftah. More than anything, that second goal showcased Qatar's new football philosophy.

'Qatar has talent, a good coach, they are working very well. I think there will be surprises. I have followed Felix Sanchez and the training sessions. I think there is talent to do great things,' Xavi concluded that day as he waved goodbye to the schoolkids and handed Kimmich a Qatar shirt with the number 22 on the back.

Of course talent and a functioning football philosophy are not formed in a month or even a year. It can take well over a decade.

Felix Sanchez Bas is a football coach who easily and passionately transmits his ideas about football in any conversation. The friendly, bearded Catalan arrived in Doha in 2006, the same year that Aspire Academy started its hugely ambitious development of the future generation of football stars in the country.

The FC Barcelona youth academy La Masia continued to bring on top-quality talent in those years, having already produced the likes of Messi, Iniesta and Xavi, and so Qatar decided to bring the Catalan coach into the setup at Aspire, in addition to a number of other Spanish experts and later on the Spanish Director-General of the Academy, Ivan Bravo. The idea was simple, as most brilliant ideas are – in order for the Qatari side to play possession football with attacking flair, they brought on board the experts who had perfected that style of play.

More than great technique and a great many passes, though, the football philosophy at Aspire Academy became one of forming intelligent players who were able to make their own decisions on the pitch. Also, and equally important, the football leadership off the pitch took the wise decision to give the system time to work.

By 2014, that patience was beginning to reap rewards, as the first successes of the new Qatari football philosophy became visible. The young Qatar under-19 team led by coach Felix Sanchez were proclaimed Asian Champions in Myanmar that year, with the same group of players who would later propel the side to glory at the senior tournament five years later.

Perhaps the most remarkable thing about the next five years was that Felix Sanchez was given the trust and the time to lead the same group of players through a number of important age-group tournaments to gain further invaluable experience. In 2015 the young Qatari side travelled to New Zealand, where they played in the FIFA U-20 World Cup as Asian Champions. A phone interview I conducted at the time with Sanchez showed that the focus was very much on gathering experience in the present to produce champions for the future.

'These boys can be in a great football age in 2022, when they will be 25, 26, and there is a great desire among all those who work with the team for them to be competing in their home World Cup in 2022. It is a long journey, but it will be enriching for them to experience this U-20 World Cup, which is the closest you will get to the World Cup,' Sanchez told me as his team prepared to kick off their group matches against Colombia, Portugal and Senegal.

His team lost all three matches and went out in the first round, with Akram Afif scoring their only goal from the penalty spot, but the following year they came within a whisker of qualifying for the Rio 2016 Olympic Games football competition. By the time Sanchez was made Qatar's national senior team coach in 2017, he was clear about what approach would lead the team to success – giving these young home-grown talents experience and time to mature in the maroon shirts of Qatar.

In November 2018 the team – with an average age of just 24 – showed what they were capable of, in a surprise 1-0 away win against Switzerland in Lugano with Afif once again scoring, as he rounded on the goalkeeper for a shock victory that had the European media taking note. That result, coupled with a 2-2 draw with Iceland in Belgium a few days later, as well as a 4-3 win over Ecuador in Doha a month earlier, showed the Catalan coach that his team were making real strides and were ready to spring a surprise or two at the Asian Cup in January 2019. A football journey of well over a decade was about to produce the biggest ever miracle in maroon.

Qatar's first exclamation mark of the tournament came in their second group game, against North Korea in Al Ain. Aspire Academy graduate and former Eupen forward Almoez Ali scored an astonishing four goals in a single game. Newly crowned 2018 Asian Player of the Year Abdelkarim Hassan and defender Boualem Khoukhi also grabbed one apiece in a resounding 6-0 win, which secured qualification for the Round of 16. The stage was set, then, for an emotion-charged final group game against Saudi Arabia.

'Qatar had less pressure going into the game,' Dr Mahfoud Amara, author of 'Sport, Politics and Society in the Arab World' and Director of the Sport Science Programme at Qatar University, told me as he explained the special significance of what the media quickly dubbed the 'blockade derby'.

'For the team from Saudi Arabia, and later on that of the UAE, there was much more pressure, not only thinking in football terms. Every goal scored by Qatar destroyed the momentum of the other team.'

The political context of the game was quite understandably the focus of much of the global media attention in the build-up to the game. While both sides did their best to focus on the football, the eighteen-month blockade of Qatar by Saudi Arabia, the UAE, Bahrain and Egypt clearly set the tone for the match. On 17 January, as Qatar and Saudi Arabia took to the pitch in Abu Dhabi, the intensity of the game was an indicator of the importance of the occasion.

A draw would have been enough for Qatar to win the group and avoid meeting the highly-rated Japanese in the next round, but the young team in maroon did more than that and pulled off a memorable 2-0 win – with Almoez Ali netting a brace as he scored a minute into first-half stoppage time and then again ten minutes before the end. The skilful Qatar striker celebrated by playing an imaginary violin, something he had seen Arsenal strikers Pierre-Emerick Aubameyang and Alexandre Lacazette doing on social media, and had vowed to try out next time he scored.

'The two goals I scored against Saudi Arabia were very important for the team, especially since the first goal I scored came after we failed to score a penalty at the end of the first half. So it gave the team all the strength and confidence to keep up the pace in the game,' Almoez Ali explained to me after the championship.

'The second goal was proof that we deserved to win and to be on top of our group. I am very proud that I scored these two goals against the three-time winners of the tournament.'

Qatar was through to the knockout stages, and the Asian Cup was about to get serious. The favourites for the trophy at this stage were Japan and Iran, with South Korea and Australia among the other big names left in the running. For Qatar's second-round game against Iraq on 22 January, I visited my old friend, former China coach Bora Milutinovic, at his apartment overlooking the Doha skyline to watch the game together. Within two minutes of the match starting, Coach Bora had already predicted a result for me.

'Qatar will win the game,' he told me confidently, sitting on his sofa, notebook in hand to write down magic scribbles which likely only other coaches could decipher. 'They have much more quality than the other team.'

Here, then, was another candidate to succeed Paul the Octopus. And sure enough, another stunning free kick from defender Bassam Al Rawi shortly after the hour mark had me jumping in the air and Coach Bora smiling widely. It proved enough to take Qatar through to the quarter-finals, where they came up against the highly favoured South Koreans.

'Come back for the quarter-finals,' Coach Bora said. 'I think it has brought Qatar luck that we watched the game together.'

The next game offered Qatar the chance to make history, with their previous best having been two quarter-final appearances. Across Qatar, football fever – with all the associated superstitions and public viewing festivals – was now beginning to take hold. Meanwhile, in the UAE, where the tournament was taking place, the picture was the complete opposite: the young Qatari team, who had yet to concede a goal in the tournament, could not count on any

Qatari fans being there to support them, due to travel restrictions as a result of the blockade imposed on the country.

And so it was that an unusual combination of a great many fans of Qatar from Oman, a superfan from South Korea and two Australians came out to publicly support the Maroons in their unlikely quest for Asian silverware.

Brooke Reid is an unusual Qatar fan, with a bubbly personality and a lot of new followers on social media. She works in Qatar but comes from Australia, half a world away from Qatar, and was Head of Transport for the Asian Cup when it was held in Doha back in 2011. For the 2019 edition of the tournament, she transported herself to the UAE to watch the exciting Qatari team in the stadium, and then shot to fame through a viral video on social media. Nowadays she gets requests from Qatari women to visit them and is thanked with roses for supporting Qatar's football team when the country's own local fans were barred from attending.

'You could really feel that the people in Doha cared about this team, and a lot of expatriates like myself also got behind the Qatari side,' Brooke says, sitting in the West Bay area of the city a few weeks after the tournament. 'I think the blockade helped people here to feel more patriotic. Before the Iraq game, I said to myself: if they win this one, I will go to the UAE to support the Qatari team.'

And so she flew over to watch her adopted team. Wearing a Qatar shirt under her cardigan, Brooke entered the stadium for the quarter-final game against South Korea on 25 January. Meanwhile, on his sofa in the apartment overlooking the Doha skyline, Coach Bora already had an idea of who would win.

It was to be an evenly fought game, with both sides testing the opposition goalkeeper before a left-footed rocket from midfielder Abdulaziz Hatem streaked into the back of the net in the 78th minute. Qatar were through to the semi-finals, sparking wild celebrations among football fans in Doha. On Qatari television, repetitions of the winning goal ran on loop with a popular song providing the soundtrack for the celebrations.

'Come back for the semi-finals,' Coach Bora told me that day in Doha. 'It will bring us more luck.'

Back in Abu Dhabi, the unlikely Qatar fan from Australia got into a taxi to watch the next game – her home country taking on the hosts for a semi-final spot against her adopted team. The UAE edged the game against Australia 1-0, to set up a second 'blockade derby'.

Only four teams remained in the tournament, and on 28 January Japan dispatched Iran 3-0 to book their place in the final. The following day, Qatar took to the field against the hosts. On his sofa in Doha, the footballing equivalent of an earthquake detector sensed insecurities in the UAE goalkeeper very early on in the semi-final in front of a full house of local fans.

'Look at the goalkeeper, and the way he just played the ball out,' Coach Bora told me that day. After 22 minutes, Emirati goalkeeper Khalid Eisa let a long-range shot from the outstanding Boualem Khoukhi slip through his hands. Qatar had taken the lead.

'My friend Ruth came from Doha to join me for the semi-final,' superfan Brooke said. As a precaution she had refrained from wearing a maroon shirt, but carried two mini flags in her handbag.

'When Qatar scored the first goal, we jumped up and celebrated. It was an unreal experience. There was not a sound in the stadium, complete silence. Each time Qatar scored a goal, I jumped up, and tried to contain myself because people were looking at us. The shoes started flying early, even though the UAE players tried their best to stop the crowd.'

Shoes kept raining down on the Qatar players from the home side's hostile supporters. But the goals didn't stop coming either. A second goal arrived in the form of a brilliantly taken curling shot from Almoez Ali after 37 minutes, which Eisa this time had no chance of stopping.

'The goal I scored against the UAE meant a lot to me,' Almoez Ali told me of that fine finish. 'It was my eighth goal of the tournament, equalling the record of Ali Daei, and that goal powered the team forward because it allowed us to start the second half with a two-goal advantage against the hosts.'

In the second half Qatar's captain Hassan Al Haydous scored a third with a delightfully cool chip ten minutes before the end, followed by a fourth goal from Hamid Ismail in injury time. Qatar had reached the final in some style. The streets of Doha once more turned into a giant sea of waving flags and honking cars.

'After winning against the UAE in the semi-finals, I realised that we can do it and that the dream of winning the Asian Cup was getting closer to reality. That game was the turning point for me and for the team as well,' goal-machine Almoez Ali added.

By extension, an entire nation was now feeling the positive energy of reaching a continental football final for the first time at senior level.

'The Asian Cup triumph came at just the right time for Qatar; it boosted the confidence of a nation,' Dr Amara pointed out. 'It was the triumph of resilience, the triumph over adversity. Economically and politically Qatar had shown they were able to overcome the blockade, but now they also triumphed on the sporting field, and symbolically it came in the UAE. A whole nation could now see the benefits of investing so consistently in sports.'

Only a single game remained in the tournament, and it pitted record four-time champions Japan against first-time finalists Qatar. A complaint from the UAE before the final about the eligibility of two Qatar players was squarely rejected by the organisers of the tournament. Qatar was ready to take on Japan. Surely there could be only one outcome.

Bilal Mohammed Rajab knows a thing or two about playing in important finals for Qatar. Rajab is a tall defender whose first few white hairs peek elegantly out from under his traditional 'ghutra' headdress, and whose warm smile speaks of his passion for the team he represented for over eleven years at the highest level. It was the former Qatar captain's headed goal that had handed the hosts a much-celebrated 1-0 win over Iraq for the gold medal in football at the 2006 Doha Asian Games.

'I played for Qatar for eleven years in a total of 111 games, starting in 2004, and we won two Gulf Cups and the Asian Games gold medal. Everyone remembers the goal I scored in the Asian Games final against Iraq, but actually I was just the lucky one, because the ball hit my head from a corner and went in. I didn't know much about it,' he told me with an honest laugh over a coffee at a Josoor Institute educational workshop in Doha.

'It was very special to win the Asian Games in front of our home fans. We had won the Gulf Cup at home two years earlier, so our fans expected us to win. We were happy to be able to deliver for them.'

That had been the Qatari team's biggest achievement to date, to be followed by the Gulf Cup triumph in Saudi Arabia in 2014, during which Rajab captained the team and lifted the trophy after defeating the hosts 2-1 in the final. Now Team Qatar had the chance to lift another trophy. But once again they were the outsiders in the final against Japan.

One thing that was clearly on the side of the team playing their first-ever Asian Cup final, though, was momentum. Having not yet conceded a goal, and with sixteen goals scored, Qatar was undoubtedly the team of the tournament, and its emphatic win over the UAE was another statement of intent, much as Germany's 7-1 win over hosts Brazil in 2014 had paved the way for their World Cup triumph.

Would the young Qatari side feel the pressure against the favourites in the final?

The answer came 12 minutes after the national anthems had rung out across the stadium and the game began. After a patient build-up with a series of intricate passes across the pitch, Akram Afif got the ball on the left wing before cutting in to his right foot and floating a delightful chipped pass in towards Almoez Ali. Surrounded by four Japanese defenders and with his back to the goal, Ali had it all to do, but he only took three touches to do exactly what was needed.

The first touch was a left-footed control, the second placed the ball up in the air with his right foot, and the third magically conjured up a bicycle kick which whizzed past Shuichi Gonda in the Japanese goal. Cue madness at the public viewing festivals in Doha, and sheer disbelief from the Qatari television commentators. Gonda played his club football in Portugal, but he had just been beaten by a stunning goal which even Cristiano Ronaldo would have been proud to score.

'For my famous overhead kick against Japan, I controlled Akram Afif's cross and thought about what to do with the ball,' said Almoez Ali, explaining his thought process on the pitch.

'I thought: shall I pass it to someone who can see the target, since I couldn't? Then I decided to take that chance, and yes, I did it. I couldn't believe it was me who did this, it was really unbelievable. I saw the goal over and over, just to realise that it was real. I was overwhelmed and speechless.'

It was the record-breaking ninth goal of the tournament for Almoez Ali, surpassing the record of former Bayern Munich and Iran striker Ali Daei, who scored eight goals at the 1996 Asian Cup, and coming at a crucial time in the final.

'Almoez Ali grew up in Doha in my neighbourhood, Al Rayyan, and I knew his brother well,' said Rajab of the player who would win the tournament's best player and top scorer awards. 'Almoez started playing in the second division and was spotted by Aspire Academy, and spent time playing at Eupen in Belgium, which improved him a lot as a player.'

But it was not just the young striker – the entire Qatari team was inspired on the pitch. Just before the half-hour mark, Abdulaziz Hatem scored a second goal for Qatar with a curling left-footed effort which could well have come from the boot of a certain Argentinian superstar playing for FC Barcelona. It was clearly to be Qatar's day, as it had been Qatar's tournament. In the second half Japan pulled a goal back through Takumi Minamino in the 69th minute, the only goal conceded by Felix Sanchez's team in their seven games.

At this stage a young team could easily have started to doubt themselves, but Qatar's players showed the mental strength and ambition of real champions. Akram Afif, the first Qatari to play in La Liga, stepped up in the 83rd minute to take an extremely high-pressure penalty and slotted home with a coolness which belied his young years. Then he took off his shirt and boxed at thin air for a few seconds as his team-mates started to come to terms with the fact that they were about to be proclaimed champions in just ten minutes.

A few weeks later I met Fahad Al Thani, Qatar's first professional boxer, who invited Akram to his majlis after the tournament to gift him a pair of boxing gloves. 'His celebration was inspired by the same man who is my hero, Muhammad Ali,' Fahad told me. 'I think he watched some of his videos before the final.' When I spoke to Afif a couple of years earlier, he told me his ambition was to try and win the World Cup in 2022.

Thinking and dreaming big had now finally paid off for Qatar. Al Ennabi, the team in maroon, had floated like butterflies and stung like bees. Qatar was proclaimed the greatest team in Asian football and Hassan Al Haydous lifted the silver trophy, sparking massive celebrations across Qatar. The streets were filled for days with people dancing and celebrating the country's first-ever Asian Cup trophy. As we walked home from Coach Bora's house that evening my daughter got up on my shoulders and waved a Qatar football shirt at the people sitting on top of their cars in the middle of the street.

'The most important goal I scored in the tournament was no doubt the one in the final against Japan, because it was a decisive one in my footballing career, and it was a decisive goal for the team in the pursuit of winning the tournament for the first time in our history,' Almoez Ali concluded. After the tournament he received a gift of a signed shirt from Lionel Messi, who had clearly been impressed with the finishing he saw from the youngster.

'For me, winning the Asian Cup was a dream and now it became true. I couldn't be happier, and without a doubt this achievement will boost our morale before our next challenge for the Copa America in Brazil.'

For the next few days there were continuous celebrations and car processions across Doha, as the team was welcomed back home to a glittering airport reception by His Highness the Amir of Qatar, Sheikh Tamim bin Hamad Al Thani, and His Highness the Amir's Personal Representative, Sheikh Jassim bin Hamad Al Thani. The country's visionary approach to developing young football talent and forming a team of champions was celebrated by Qatari and global media alike.

For QFA President His Excellency Sheikh Hamad bin Khalifa bin Ahmed Al Thani, himself a former football player, the result showcased just how far the players had come: 'This is a historic day for Qatar football. The team delivered under pressure. I congratulate His Highness the Amir Sheikh Tamim bin Hamad Al Thani on this amazing victory for Qatar. The players deserve all the credit for their beautiful performance.'

So just how significant was Qatar's achievement in lifting the trophy?

'Winning the Asian Cup is the greatest football achievement for Qatar to date,' explained former Qatar captain Rajab. 'In addition, it is really important timing, because I can see fans and young people really interested in the national team now, before 2022. They are still a young team, and will inspire kids for a long time to come.'

The result also meant that Qatar would travel to the Copa America in Brazil in June 2019 as Asian Champions, as an invited team alongside beaten Asian Cup finalists Japan. 'Before, if we had a competition like Copa America we would think: that's difficult. But now, with the potential this team has, they are looking to develop even more. Everybody should feel proud; everybody worked towards this goal and finally we achieved it,' Rajab added.

Qatar's success in 2019 also added to a list of classic sporting miracles, according to Dr Amara: 'There have been many successful underdogs in the history of football. I think back to Germany losing to Algeria in the 1982 World Cup, or Denmark's dream run to the title in the 1992 European Championship after they were called in as a last-minute replacement having already been on holiday.

'Now we have this achievement from Qatar in winning the Asian Cup in 2019. It also ranks highly in terms of sporting achievements for Arab nations, and was celebrated in different countries across the region because it is something special as one of the smallest countries in terms of geography.'

Jordi Cruyff sits across from me one afternoon in early February on the 14th floor of Al Bidda Tower in Doha, sipping a glass of traditional Arab tea with a look of genuine surprise on his face.

He is in Qatar for a training camp with the Chinese club side he is currently managing, and we discuss the legacy of major sporting events and the diametrically opposed challenges facing football in the two countries. In the country where Cruyff is coaching now, the effort goes into developing a system to bring on world-class players from a mass of youngsters, while in the country he is visiting the Aspire Academy approach is all about perfecting a system which will make the players of a small population compete with the best in the world.

'No one expected Qatar to win the Asian Cup,' says the former Barcelona and Manchester United winger. 'It shows Qatar is on the right track. Now they need to continue in this way.'

High praise indeed, coming from the son of Johan Cruyff, the legendary Dutch midfielder associated both with the sweeping Total

Football played by Holland in the 1970s and with being a coaching and philosophical catalyst for FC Barcelona and Spain's rise to prominence through their breathtaking tiki-taka style of play.

Ivan Bravo sits on the red sofa outside his office with an aura of complete tranquillity the day I come to meet him at Aspire Academy, the state-of-the-art talent development centre which he leads and which is sprawling out in front of him. This is what it must be like to meet the Dalai Lama, I imagine, to have something approaching the level of inner peace which this former Real Madrid Director of Strategy exudes as we start speaking about his football journey in Qatar.

'It has been a long journey, and no one knew how it would end. When I came to Qatar in 2011, the idea was simple: to improve football in the country. To do that, we went to the essence: to improve the player and the style of play. I came with ambition, and we mapped out a journey which has led to this Asian Cup triumph. We still regularly remind ourselves of the journey we drew up for eight year-groups of Qatari football players – those born between 1992 and 2001 – and the different tournaments they would compete in through the years.'

With this document as their roadmap, the team at Aspire Academy set about their work, which included changing the playing and training habits of the players; getting key players experience playing in European teams; and regularly playing against top international youth teams a year or two older than their Qatari counterparts.

'The problem in football is that planning something on paper is good, but there are always challenges which come up along the way. I give the Qatari leadership and the QFA President a lot of credit, because they dreamed big, and had the patience to go on a journey and see it through. Over the years we have kept working hard, and when there were natural moments of doubt, we insisted and kept believing.'

Looking back, Bravo remembers former Real Madrid captain Raul Gonzalez training on attacking movements with Almoez Ali at the Asian Championships in Myanmar in 2014, and the passion and day-to-day commitment the legendary striker brought to the project, as well as the importance of having Felix Sanchez regularly advised by Xavi Hernandez, who he calls 'one of the five greatest thinkers in the history of the game'.

Seeing Ali transformed into Asia's best striker at the tournament confirmed to the Spaniard that Aspire Academy is continuing on the right path.

'When you see Almoez Ali scoring that goal in the final and the team lifting the trophy, you are happy for Qatar,' Bravo concludes with a smile, epitomising that aura of inner peace which has marked the entire conversation. 'To see the QFA President so happy, the reaction of the fans in Qatar, it is something fantastic, and everyone worked so hard to achieve it. This is a young team, they are 22 or 23 years old, so they have so much potential to develop further. The important thing mentally is that they have won something now, they know that feeling. When you look at comparable cases in world football, you see that no one has done something similar. If you look at the number of players we have here in Qatar, and see the size of Asia as a continent, you see that it is an achievement which is very difficult to repeat. Now we have to convince ourselves to continue on the journey, and to reach the World Cup here in Qatar in a position where we are able to compete against the best teams in the world.'

A few days later I chance upon the Aspire scout who spotted Almoez Ali playing for a second division side in Doha all those years ago. Juan Luis Delgado had seen the quality of the youngster immediately, he told me, but still he marvelled at his incredible capacity to turn even half a chance into a goal at the 2019 Asian Cup. When I asked about the bicycle kick in the final, he laughed and said: 'That was something else, that came from God. Like Maradona's "Hand of God" at the World Cup in 1986, this was Qatar's "bicycle kick of God".'

With a new football philosophy at least partly derived from the Cruyff legacy, Qatar continues on its unique sporting journey. There may well be some setbacks and challenges along the way, as there always are at the highest levels of any sport. This small country where I was born and which my family came to call home is resilient and determined enough to deal with those setbacks, as it has dealt with the many critics and mud-slingers.

You can also be sure, though, that there will be more miracles in maroon. The magic will come in making those future miracles coincide with the opening game of the FIFA World Cup™ at Lusail Stadium in Qatar, on 21 November 2022.

ACKNOWLEDGEMENTS

Many people have contributed in big and small ways to the writing and publication of this book, which means so much to me on many different levels. In the first instance, it is a book about my family, and I would like to thank you, my dear wife Luisa, and our wonderful daughters Kimi and Lisa, for your continuous support, love and valuable input into the creation of this book. I would like to dedicate this book with much love to my inspirational mom Antje and dad Joachim, and my incredible siblings Anna, Hans and Tomi, for always being there and their continuous support in the journey that is life.

This is also a book about the place I call home, the country where I was born and which I hold so close to my heart: Qatar. In writing the book I have had the privilege to speak to many inspirational Qataris and others making this life-changing 2022 FIFA World Cup™ come alive. It gives me goose-bumps when I think of Qatar welcoming global football fans in 2022. I would like to thank in particular Hassan and Nasser for always believing in me, in the vision behind this book, and in the powerful story which Qatar's young and transformational football history has to offer; my bosses including Mushtaq, Afraa and Moza from whom I have learnt much; and my colleagues and friends with whom it is a pleasure to work together.

There have been many players, institutions and individuals from across Qatar's sports industry, including the Supreme Committee for Delivery & Legacy, the Qatar Olympic Committee, the Qatar Football

Association, Aspire Academy and others, who have been most helpful. Special thanks go to Xavi, a football visionary and a friend; to Coach Bora for those chess games and watching the 2019 Asian Cup and many other games together; and to my fellow author Michael for the many conversations and insights which helped me visualise the transformation of this text from manuscript into a book. Thanks also to Anne Ruth and David for your insights through many conversations.

Finally, thanks to the fantastic people at HBKU Press for their belief in this book and hard work towards making it a reality, in particular to Rima, Ghenwa, Zeyad and the many others who brought it all to life. And to my grandfather Ulf, who was a big Germany fan and would have loved to read this book if he could, and to my grandmothers Gudrun and Dora. And to La Mimi, who learned to make lovely dresses so that she wouldn't have to cook, and learned to watch and speak about football, as my mother did, because of my love for the game.

This is a book about daring to dream, and working hard to turn your vision into a reality.